D0891852

Celtic Revival?

Celtic Revival?

The Rise, Fall, and Renewal of Global Ireland

Sean Kay

To Chris Hill
May the best of the luck of
the Irish always be with you!
With great appreciation for
your visit to Ohio.

Delaware, OH, October 2012

ROWMAN & LITTLEFIELD PUBLISHERS, INC.
Lanham • Boulder • New York • Toronto • Plymouth, UK

Published by Rowman & Littlefield Publishers, Inc.
A wholly owned subsidiary of The Rowman & Littlefield Publishing Group, Inc.
4501 Forbes Boulevard, Suite 200, Lanham, Maryland 20706
http://www.rowmanlittlefield.com

Estover Road, Plymouth PL6 7PY, United Kingdom

British Library Cataloguing in Publication Information Available

Library of Congress Cataloging-in-Publication Data
Kay, Sean, 1967-
  Celtic revival? : the rise, fall, and renewal of global Ireland / Sean Kay.
    p. cm.
  Includes index.
  ISBN 978-1-4422-1109-4 (cloth : alk. paper) — ISBN 978-1-4422-1111-7
(electronic)
  1. Ireland—History—21st century. 2. Ireland—Economic conditions—21st
century. 3. Ireland—Social conditions—21st century. 4. Ireland—Civilization—
21st century. 5. Northern Ireland—History—21st century. 6. Northern Ireland—
Economic conditions—21st century. 7. Northern Ireland—Social conditions—
21st century. 8. Northern Ireland—Civilization—21st century. I. Title.
  DA966.K39 2011
  941.50824—dc22

                                                                    2010053532

"Our object in building up the country economically must not be lost sight of. That object is not to be able to boast of enormous wealth or of a great volume of trade, for their own sake. It is not to see our country covered with smoking chimneys and factories. It is not to show a great national balance-sheet nor to point to a people producing wealth with the self-obliteration of a hive of bees. The real riches of the Irish nation will be the men and women of the Irish nation, the extent to which they are rich in body and mind and character."

—Michael Collins, August 1922

Contents

Preface and Acknowledgments

The immediate work that went into this book resulted from two years of intensive research that culminated in a several-month stay in Ireland while I was working as a visiting scholar at the Institute for British and Irish Studies at University College Dublin in the summer of 2010. In a sense, though, the present volume is an initial update of my own perspective on a country that has been a second home since 1987. My wife, Anna-Marie Madigan, grew up in Clonsilla, County Dublin, and emigrated to the United States in the summer of 1986. We met when I was playing music at a local bar in Kent, Ohio, where I was an undergraduate student at Kent State University. She is a Montessori school teacher and had a choice of going to New Mexico or Ohio. Needless to say, I am very glad she chose Ohio. Before I met Anna-Marie, Ireland did not register high on my view screen, but now it is in my blood. At our wedding party in Dublin in 1992, Anna-Marie gave a toast, at the end of which she said, "And I'd like to thank Sean because if he wasn't here, I wouldn't be here." Nearly twenty years later, it is I who owe the thanks, for the love she has provided, along with our three daughters, and for opening my eyes to the Irish people.

I am grateful to all those who sat down for interviews for this book and to the many people who worked to help me arrange them—in Ireland and also in Washington, DC, and New York City. I have done my best to retell the stories that these individuals related to me and to place them in the proper context. The people who have helped in this regard know who they are, and they know that I am deeply appreciative. I owe great gratitude to Ben Tonra and Jennifer Todd of the Institute for British and Irish Studies at University College Dublin, and to Matt Burney of the British Council. I would particularly like to thank several members of my family in Ireland who took the time to discuss a wide range of issues, sent information, and encouraged me to challenge my own assumptions: Mary and Des Mullan, Orlagh and Gerry Lyons, and Eugene Madigan and Elaine Durkin. I am also very appreciative to Des Mullan Sr., Mary Mullan, and Garrett Mullan. I also thank Aoife Mullan, who helped out in a number of ways using her perspective as one of Ireland's next generation of hope and who reminds me of the scholars and artists that Ireland has long celebrated. I relied heavily on a number of people up at the Summit Inn in Howth for the occasional Guinness break at the end of the week. I am sure one or two will remember my commenting out loud that my father-in-law would have thought I looked pretty funny—a Yank at the bar in the pub with his laptop, updating his Facebook page. I owe a special thanks to Dougal Cousins, a good friend, for keeping me on the ball regarding all things Irish and beyond. Our family in Ireland runs big, and all must be thanked in addition to those above: Emer and Jason, Declan and Cria, and our beloved brother Matthew. Matthew Madigan was in my wedding party, was my brother-in-law, and was my best of friends—we miss him daily. The list of young ones is long, but all played a role in inspiring this book; in addition to Aoife Mullan, there are Iseult and Finn Mullan; Matthew, Naoise, and Rhea O'Leary; Andrew and Alibhe Madigan; Anna and Gerry Lyons; and Millie McNulty.

At Rowman & Littlefield, I am always in debt to Susan McEachern, with whom I have now worked for nearly fifteen years. Susan and the team at Rowman & Littlefield set the highest of standards in the literary profession, and I am grateful to Carrie Broadwell-Tkach, Alden Perkins, and Jen Kelland. In Washington, DC, I am appreciative of Carol and Tom Wheeler, Nicole and Melvin McNamara, Anthony Lake, Philip Gordon, and Trina Vargo. Patric Cronin, Susan Eisenhower, Timothy Hoyt, Robert Pape, and Strobe Talbott all egged me on early to tackle the Irish question. A wide range of people have been colleagues and, more importantly, friends over the years, and for their encouragement as I embarked on this project, I am grateful to Pam Laucher, Jim Breece, Freeman Carmack, Joanne Meyer, Tim and Heather Prindle, Michael Tucci, Josh and Sam Spero, Chris and Jennifer Wolverton, Bart Martin, Richard Spall, Olivia Bull, Bridget Fahey, Craig Ramsay, Bill Louthan, Mike Esler, Joan McLean, Jim Franklin, Ashley Biser, Ji Young Choi, Mary Howard, Ted Cohen, James Peoples, Scott Calef, Chuck Stinemetz, David Robbins, and Rock Jones. I owe a special word of thanks to my brother in comedic arms, Dan Vogt.

My own family has interesting connections to Ireland—one of which I only learned about while finishing this book. Nearly one hundred years after the fact, I had stood in Derry, in July 2010, in the very same place that my great-grandfather, Clarence D. Laylin, had stood in May 1910. He had been transiting on business—and he made the same trek my family and I did—into Derry, then off to the Giant's Causeway. My mother provided me with a long and detailed letter he had sent to his mother on 11 May 1910 addressed from the North Counties Hotel, Londonderry. He wrote of their arrival by ship, "It was quite light, and as we left the liner and passed up the narrowing Lough Foyle on our trip to 'Derry, we could see the shore as plainly as if it were midday. We received very pleasant impressions of the Emerald Isle in this way." He described the old walls of Derry: "In the first place, 'Derry of old was a walled city, and the walls are still intact, forming a promenade around the central portion of the modern city, and being intersected here and there by streets but let in through arched gateways. . . . Then too, the cannon on the walls . . . told the story of the famous siege of 'Derry in the Jacobian war of 1688." He continued, "The quaint buildings both ancient and modern structures being in a strange architecture, the funny jaunting cars and two-wheeled carts, the narrow streets, and a dozen little evidences of the foreign all added to our interest." South of Derry, he "climbed another hill, surrounded by an old fort . . . said to have been built by the Druids, and to have been the place where the ancient Irish Kings were crowned." "The views," he wrote, "were magnificent . . . the glimpses of the Foyle as well as the Donegal mountains and the subjacent woodlands." Having looked on these views a century later, I can affirm that "magnificent" is indeed the word still.

Clarence Laylin had business out in the country, where he wrote that his host "presented me with a real . . . 'Shillelagh' which will be quite a souvenir of the trip." I now have that very same shillelagh stick, a gift from my mother, who found it among her mother's things. A generation later, Clarence's daughter, Anne Laylin Grimes, my grandmother, traveled to Ireland in 1992 for our wedding in Dublin. As Anna-Marie and I had been living in Brussels the preceding year, we decided to enjoy the family, and we took them along on the honeymoon—about a dozen Americans, family and friends, traveling all over Ireland. There she was, my eighty-year-old grandmother, singing folk songs in Doolin, singing folk songs at Dirty Nelly's, singing folk songs at Fox's Pub, and singing at our wedding—an interesting selection there of "The Old Gray Mare." Anne Grimes was a wonderful spirit—and a famous collector of folk tradition and music in Ohio—and she was the life of the party. My parents were there with us too—David and Jennifer Kay—and, thus, our own generations have for over one hundred years now enjoyed the Emerald Isle. I am deeply grateful to my parents for their support and love—Tá mo chroí istigh ionat.

Finally, I would like to thank my mother-in-law, Anna Madigan, and father in-law, Matt Madigan. For nearly twenty-five years now, they have been hosts, friends, and parents to me. I am a much better scholar, father, and person for knowing them. Matt and Anna Madigan are the essence of real Ireland. Always the gadfly, Matt Madigan remains to all who knew him the truest of romantic heroes. To Anna Madigan, may you always have walls for the winds, a roof for the rain, tea beside the fire, laughter to cheer you, those you love near you, and all your heart might desire. This book is dedicated, last but not least, to my wife, Anna-Marie, and our three children, Cria Kay, Siobhan Kay, and Alana Kay. I could never have taken on the monumental task of writing a book without the support of my family. Most importantly though, for all of our challenges, the truth is that for our children, for their cousins in Ireland, and for all the people of Ireland and the world beyond—the future is a bright one. It is from within this next generation that our best days lie ahead. May you always walk in sunshine, may you never want for more, may Irish angels rest their wings right beside your door.

Introduction

"There is no accounting for human behavior," my father-in-law, Matt Madigan, used to say. To me, he was the essence of what makes Ireland great—reflecting the character and the spirit of the Irish people. I know that were he here to advise me, and debate, the issues confronting his country today, he would be quick to point to the long arc of history that Ireland had traversed. When one does that, one sees that the Celtic Tiger—the period beginning in the early 1990s that reflected high, sustained economic growth—is best understood as a consolidation of long-standing trends already underway in Ireland. The period from about 2001 to 2008 was the aberration—but it was a deeply costly one for this small island nation. Today, the Irish are in a sour mood—not really interested in hearing about great spans of history. They are paying the price for the behavior of a fairly small number of people, who have yet to really be held accountable—bankers, politicians, and priests. This is the story of what happens to a nation when it loses its wealth, its faith in government, and its trust in religion. Ireland has undergone extraordinary changes that offer many lessons to the world. This book argues that, yes, Ireland is a nation in dire straits—but the foundations for a revival are already in place.

Ireland is a mystical island steeped in tradition and history. Once, in 1987, while driving us up a country road on the way to the Hill of Tara, a friend said, out of nowhere, "Look, it's a leprechaun!" I was surprised to follow his pointing finger and see a tiny man with a walking stick, a sack on his shoulder, and tweed coat and hat. I took my eye off him, and the next minute he was . . . gone! Okay, it was just a little fellow with a sack. But the moment was as real as the fairy tales that also form a living part of Ireland's mystery. These spirits come alive if you walk on a rainy day in the mists

1

of Glendalough or in the mountains of Kerry. They come alive walking on Grafton Street at Christmastime. They come alive in the pubs and the churches and the parlors of homes in the cities and the countryside. They come alive in the spirit of Michael Collins and the artistry of William Butler Yeats and so many others. In summer 2010, as I drove in the mountains of Connemara in the west of Ireland with our daughter Siobhan, we came across a church along the road and a big sign that said, "Stop and pray." But we did not have to. We had just passed over a mountaintop, and as we went over the pass and came through the fog, on the radio was playing the Bob Dylan song "Knockin' on Heaven's Door." At least at that moment, on that day, if there was heaven on earth, it was there in the mountains of Connemara.

This book places a two-year period, 2008 through 2010, in the broader scope of a fundamental transformation of Ireland—one that marks much more than the end of the Celtic Tiger. Whatever is said about the Irish and their place in the world today, one thing is certain: they live in interesting times. For many Irish, these times are deeply troubling; for others, they are challenging. In the long run, however, they are an opportunity. At the core of the transformation in Ireland has been a social revolution. Issues taboo for generations are now spoken of openly and frankly. A classic Irish trait of having certain things that "we just don't talk about" is, if not entirely gone, nearly so. This tradition of not discussing serious problems was very much at the root of Ireland's collapse—and the breaking of this tradition is the foundation on which the country's revival is being built. This book traces these changes by looking at the context: the economy, the politics, social challenges, the Catholic Church, multiculturalism, Northern Ireland, and globalization.

I hope this book will reach a number of audiences. First and foremost, I write it for the people of Ireland. Countless Irish people I encountered in doing this research had an expression stuck to their faces that read, "What the hell? How did this happen? What's next? Can it get worse?" To be in Ireland in the midst of historic change was fascinating for me as a writer and scholar. For most Irish, the story of the rise and fall of the Celtic Tiger is not new. The source of daily headlines in papers and on television, it cannot be escaped. But very little in contemporary Ireland allows for reflection on how these realities fit within a larger vision of change for the nation. This is understandable when families are burdened with the immediate pain of severe economic dislocation. Still, context is needed to place current trends in any kind of framework for the future. Many Irish people have never even been to Northern Ireland. Many people who live in Belfast have never traveled into the Ardoyne. Many Irish live in a still undiscovered land—too often jetting off to Spain for a holiday and not appreciating their own backyards. Finally, this book seeks to lay a new starting point for the younger generations of Ireland and globally—their future, and with it that of a nation and indeed the world, rests in their hands. This book seeks to place the news that burdens the Irish today in a context that will contribute toward understanding and facilitate progress.

A second key audience is the general public and students with an interest in Ireland, and its relationship to Europe, the United States, and the world. The very thin understanding of Ireland that people in the United States embrace every year on St. Patrick's Day has always surprised me. I have also found that many in the Irish American community are disconnected from their own homeland. Many Irish who leave Ireland have stopped following the daily news there, living their own lives and grappling with their own immediate concerns. Interesting to me, though, is the prevalence of false images. Ireland is anything but a conservative Catholic country. It is a modern, liberal republic that, on a range of issues, like gay rights, is far more progressive and advanced than even the most liberal parts of the United States. Ireland is an international leader in the quest for peace in Northern Ireland and beyond and the desire to advance the cause of human rights in a world that very easily forgets people who are left behind.

The reader will find that I have filled this book with three elements: facts, interviews, and personal asides. The personal asides provide my perspective and analysis—and mine alone. I hope that they are of value and, even if disputed, will add to the discussion that Ireland and the world needs. This book is intended for both the very well informed and the general reader with an interest in what in the heck is going on in the world. Those who live in and study Ireland regularly, I hope, will find bits they recognize as well as something new. I was very fortunate to find just how welcoming and open people from all levels of Irish society were in discussing the change going on in their country. This book captures a wide range of views—from former Taoiseach and current government ministers, from generals, priests, rock stars, and writers, from the rich, and from the homeless—of Ireland at a moment of profound transformation. But I also weave through a personal narrative, and so I hope the reader will take the data and the interviews and also note that my experiences are my own. There is a difficulty in writing about Ireland—or anywhere really—in that for every one perspective, one can find a hundred other points of view. It is also important to use some perspective given Ireland's size and population. For Americans, a rough guide to understanding the data in their context would be to multiply by one hundred. So, reading that Anglo Irish Bank will receive €34 billion, you might think, Well, heck, that's half the budget of the CIA. Multiply that thirty-four by one hundred, however, and you will get an idea of what that sum means in the American context: a lot of money—more money than you can imagine. Also, the Irish often speak in "colorful metaphors," and the reader should be warned that this book contains some of that language;

I assure the reader it is far tamer than some of the discourse on the streets of Dublin!

Ultimately, this is a book written out of deep love for Ireland, which I think of as a second home, and admiration for its people. It does come with some "tough love," which required an academic detachment I often found difficult to achieve, knowing how hard life became for many Irish with the collapse of their economy and the anger that many felt toward their situation. It would be difficult to understate how much I personally have learned and come to appreciate in new ways by undertaking this study. This book shows that, in the end, Ireland's future is a positive one, and the rest of the world can learn key lessons as Ireland moves forward.

1

Dublin in the Rare Old Times

**RING A RING A ROSIE, AS THE LIGHT DECLINES,
I REMEMBER DUBLIN CITY IN THE RARE OLD TIMES**

Few musical groups capture the spirit of Ireland like The Dubliners, and the song "Dublin in the Rare Old Times," sung by the great Ronnie Drew, can send a chill down the spine of anyone who has lived through the changes that Ireland has witnessed. A folk song with an eye toward the nostalgic days of yesteryear, the tune gains new meaning in the early twenty-first century. New generations of Irish are thinking of a different "rare old time"—the Celtic Tiger—and wondering what went wrong and what the future holds. This country has moved from isolation to become the most globalized economy in the world. It moved from the economic stagnation of the 1980s to become one of the wealthiest countries in Europe during the Celtic Tiger, then to face economic ruin as one of the largest debtor countries in the world by 2010. Had it promised what Ireland did in its initial bank guarantee in 2008, the United States would have provided the equivalent of over $30 trillion. In the space of several years, the Irish people lost faith in their economy, confidence in their government, and trust in their church. This book traces how such rapid and dynamic change has impacted Ireland and draws lessons for people around the world. Today, citizens everywhere are grappling with economic crisis; political transformation; social challenges like crime, health, and education; religious and cultural change; peace; and globalization. Ireland has something to say about these issues and can, perhaps, help us all toward progress in the twenty-first century.

A road sign to nowhere at the entrance to the now largely abandoned Shannon development zone, once a leading case for the globalization of the Celtic Tiger.

IRELAND AT THE GLOBAL CROSSROADS

Writing about Ireland is no easy task. Yes, this small island is home to just 4.5 million in the Republic of Ireland and another 1.8 million in Northern Ireland. One can drive across this country in a few hours—though on some days it can seem to take nearly as long to get from one end of Dublin to the other. One street can make a world of difference on this island, where symbols of past, present, and future dreams lie everywhere. It is a relatively straightforward place to describe—telling the story of independence, the building of political and economic institutions, integration with the European Union, the troubles of the North, or the special Irish-American relationship. To know the land and people, however, requires a recognition that this is a place with many layers of reality. There is a reason that Sigmund Freud is famously quoted (probably incorrectly, though) as saying of the Irish, "This is the one race of people for whom psychoanalysis is of no use whatsoever."

A software engineer I met with in Dublin while writing this book framed the issue with a joke: "How many Irish does it take to screw in a light bulb?" he asked. The answer is none because "the Irish fellow says, 'Oh, it's grand, I'll be happy enough just sitting here in the dark.'" The Irish have a unique ability to put on the blinders and move forward. One defense mechanism, deeply embedded in culture, has been to say, "We don't talk about that"—a statement applicable to nearly any topic. This tool was useful during the British occupation, a time when boasting or showing weaknesses invited danger. But putting on the blinders can also lead to a serious inability to grapple with change and thus incur very high costs. As early as 2005, it was clear that Ireland was highly vulnerable to the shifting winds of globalization and internal political and economic mismanagement. It would not take much to send the country into a deep economic tailspin. Yet, there were three general reactions: "Ah, come on, man, it'll be fine," "Ah sure, I know, but we might as well enjoy it while we can," and "We don't talk about that." Meanwhile, the government and bankers were keeping the economy afloat—and protecting their newfound millions—by playing a high-wire casino game of credit and mortgages to sustain growth from 2001 to 2008. In September 2008, the entire country hit an economic wall as the economy crashed. In a deeply troubling moment, former Taoiseach (prime minister) Bertie Ahern had said to an applauding audience in 2007, in reference to individuals who were talking down the economy—"cribbing and moaning," he called it—"I don't know why people who engage in that don't commit suicide."

Ireland—north and south, east and west—is a place of common identity and deep difference. One can travel there for decades and still not dig down to the essence of the place—if such a thing exists. There is also an understandable wariness of outsiders coming in and telling Ireland what it should do. At the same time, as one person I met said, "people are eager to talk to you—we need someone to give us a collective kick in the ass." I frequently ran into friends quizzically curious to know if I had figured out what the heck was going on. In reality, no one knows where things are headed in Ireland or the world. We are at a moment of transition that has people from Dublin to Detroit to Singapore to Sligo anxious about their futures, yet cautiously looking for the light and opportunity at the end of the tunnel.

At the end of a recent visit, just hours before flying back to the United States, I took a walk to the top of Howth Summit, just north of Dublin. Walking alone up the hill, I encountered a gorgeous horse looking at me over a fence. I stopped for a moment and took a step forward, but the horse turned away. Yet, it never took its eye off of me. It seemed to turn as far as it could without taking its eye away—always sizing me up. Funnily enough, as I took a step back, the horse looked straight on and . . . nodded in a welcoming and trusting way—or so it seemed. To me, that summed up much of my experience of doing intensive research in a country like Ireland—working with a beautiful people who are always sizing you up with a wary eye but, in the end, are welcoming and trusting.

Given the economic calamity facing the Irish people, they wanted to talk more than ever, about virtually anything and everything, when discussing this book. In fact, I have never spent so much time talking with people about the things we do not talk about! From Sinéad O'Connor to senior-ranking priests in the Dublin archdiocese, from former prime ministers to my friends at the local pub, from senior members of the Labour Party to politicians with Fianna Fáil and Fine Gael, from economists to social workers and union leaders, from entrepreneurs to software designers, from human rights activists in Derry to senior police officials in Belfast to members of the Independent Monitoring Commission working on disarming paramilitary forces, from the chief of staff of the Irish Defence Forces and the foreign minister to antiwar and proneutrality protesters—everyone wanted to talk. People of all walks of life pondered a significant, even philosophical question: What kind of Ireland do we want to be?

This book seeks to spark a conversation about Ireland in order to draw lessons at a global level—especially for my own country, the United States. I worked as a member of the informal team that, from 2007 to 2008, advised Barack Obama's presidential campaign on foreign policy, which included providing occasional analytical support on Irish issues. I recall a moment during a presidential debate in which the Republican candidate, Senator John McCain, said, "Right now, the United States of American business pays the second-highest business taxes in the world, 35 percent. Ireland pays 11 percent. . . . Now, if you're a business person, and you can locate any place in the world, then, obviously, if you go to the country where it's 11 percent tax versus 35 percent, you're going to be able to create jobs, increase your business, make more investment, etc." This quote reflects the nearly complete disconnect that politicians had from the realities in Ireland, the United States, or anywhere else. During a recent visit, one image stood out to me as symbolizing the stark reality of how this divergence played out in Ireland. While Dublin has always had street beggars, there were more than I could ever remember. One sunny afternoon, walking up Henry Street toward O'Connell Street, I saw a derelict man lying face down and motionless in a shop doorway. I quickly noticed that he was okay; yet, it dawned on me that, for all I knew, this man might have been laying there dead. I—along with tens of thousands of others—would have merrily walked by, paying no mind. Is that the kind of Ireland we want? Is that the kind of America we want? Is this the kind of world we want?

The McCain quote from the 2008 debate came at the very moment when the Irish economy was crashing into one of the deepest economic catastrophes in the history of the modern world. It was as if a category-five hurricane had converged as a perfect storm of global crisis and internal political and financial disaster. Fintan O'Toole, one of Ireland's leading commentators, points out in *Ship of Fools* the harsh reality of the Celtic Tiger. By

2009, the economy was expected to begin shrinking by 13 percent, making Ireland's the worst national economic performance among the world's advanced economies and "one of the worst ever recorded in peacetime in the developed world." Per capita debt was €37,000, 25 percent of office spaces in Dublin were vacant, and the Irish stock exchange had fallen by 68 percent. Average family income had been cut nearly in half between 2006 and 2010—not including the dramatic decline in housing values. O'Toole shows that, in a comparative perspective, ten years after the Celtic Tiger economy took off, Ireland's per capita gross domestic product (GDP) was just a bit higher than that of Mississippi and Arkansas—two of the United States' poorest states. By 2006, just before the economic crash, Ireland's gross national product (GNP) would have ranked the country equal to the sixth-poorest state in the United States. Between 2000 and 2006, Ireland was shedding nearly twenty thousand jobs per year, hidden by a bubble of construction and uncapitalized mortgages. By 2009, Ireland's per capita income about equaled that of the United States, with an average of $46,200. This was not bad for a country that had, just twenty-five years earlier, been on the edge of national poverty. Indeed, a central point emerges in this book that while times are really bad in Ireland, the starting point has better foundations than the country has ever before enjoyed. Still, the challenges are huge. Ireland, by 2010, had some of the highest prices in Europe, among the highest relative poverty in Europe at 20 percent, a sovereign debt crisis, a 32 percent budget deficit, and 14 percent unemployment. This is what Senator McCain thought was a good idea for the United States—let alone Ireland?

LIKE A MONET PAINTING FROM AFAR

This book does not seek to reconstruct the growth of the Celtic Tiger or to explain again why it collapsed. Excellent books have covered this topic already—particularly Shane Ross's *The Bankers: How the Banks Brought Ireland to Its Knees* (2010), Fintan O'Toole's *Ship of Fools: How Stupidity and Corruption Sank the Celtic Tiger* (2010), Matt Cooper's *Who Really Runs Ireland: The Story of the Elite That Led Ireland from Bust to Boom . . . and Back Again* (2010), and David Lynch's, *When the Luck of the Irish Ran Out* (2010). The current volume explores major changes that took place before, during, and after the Celtic Tiger that illustrate dramatic challenges and opportunities. It shows how, in a very short period, globalization reshaped Ireland, which serves as a microcosm of the twenty-first-century world. Ireland mirrors many of the fundamental abilities—or inabilities—of other societies to address contemporary challenges. The central argument is that, despite serious ongoing challenges, there is tremendous opportunity for Ireland, the United States, and the world to make progress in this new century. The real issue is not a matter of "Yes, we can!" as presidential candidate Barack Obama asserted during the 2008 American campaign. Rather, for Ireland, the United States, and the world, it is "Will we?"

Ireland has a perception problem. From the outside, it is viewed as a quaint place with lovely green hills, nice beer, good music, and welcoming people. All of this is true, of course, but reflects only one layer of the real Ireland. Generations of emigrants saw Ireland through a prism of nationalism and cultural identification—even if that meant passing the hat in Boston, Chicago, and New York pubs to raise money for an Irish Republican Army that had nothing to do with the heroes of 1916. When my wife, who was raised in Clonsilla in west Dublin, first came to the United States in 1986, the kind family she lived with politely took the time to show her how a television set worked. Perhaps they turned on *The Quiet Man* with John Wayne and Maureen O'Hara? Well intentioned as her hosts were, Ireland did in fact have television at the time—yes, just a few channels, but they worked! When I first started visiting Ireland in 1987, many American friends said to me that it must be hard going to such a violent and war-torn place—only to realize they were talking about the North, which had little to do with life in the Republic. Meanwhile, the American vision of leprechauns and St. Patrick's Day served as a nice, though flawed, image of the country. In fact, St. Patrick's Day as currently celebrated with parties and parades is largely an American invention. I often play Irish music in a pub in the United States on March 17, only to note that most of the American audience would not know "Carrickfergus," "Finnegan's Wake," or the "Fields of Athenry" if it hit them on the head. In the United States, the day is really an excuse for a national drinking binge. Ireland today has "stolen it back," as one senior government economist told me, turning it into a weeklong tourist attraction and party—Dublin's Mardi Gras. A priest in Ireland said to me that the day has effectively turned pagan. One thing is certain—no self-respecting Irish person would ever drink green beer.

Ireland is often perceived from the outside as a reactionary, conservative, Catholic country. Debates in New York City about whether the organizers of the annual St. Patrick's Day parade had a right to ban gays from marching reflected this view. Just twenty years ago, it was technically illegal to be gay in Ireland. You would not know that from watching the annual Gay Pride Parade that now runs through Dublin. Over five thousand marchers come from all walks of life—gays, straights, teachers, police, you name it. In July 2010, Ireland passed national civil-partnership legislation recognizing the legal rights of gay couples. The majority favoring this was so overwhelming that passage did not require a final parliamentary vote. I watched the debates inside the parliament chambers and also walked outside among the antigay protesters—all five of them. This Catholic country has more progressive human rights guarantees for gays and lesbians than the United States. Former finance minister and senior Labour Party politician Ruairi Quinn has said since the early 1990s that Ireland is a "post-Catholic" country. Yet, Quinn told me that the relationship between the church and society is, nonetheless, still "the elephant in the room."

In 2010, perception and reality converged on an Ireland mired in catastrophic financial crisis with few options for moving forward. Deeply in debt, with banks not lending, housing values collapsing, consumer prices through the roof, an already overtaxed population, and an undertaxed corporate world, the country faced 14 percent unemployment, deep austerity, and a sustained, painful transition that cut to the core of nearly every family. The Irish people had to be reminded of their potential as doubt pervaded the nation. For example, Niall O'Dowd, founder of the Irish American magazine *The Irish Voice*, is one of the United States' most important commentators on Irish perspectives. An Irish-born emigrant who came to the United States in the 1980s, Niall O'Dowd is a thoughtful observer of events in his native country. On 15 July 2010, he wrote in the *Irish Times*, "There seems to be a deep sepulchral gloom about in Ireland, especially in the media, where the worst traits of negativity are flourishing." He added, "There is no percentage in wallowing in the 'whatshuddabeens' of the recent past. Ireland needs to take a leaf from the American playbook, where dogged optimism, despite all the recent setbacks, remains a defining trait." O'Dowd focused on a new plan by the Irish government to build the country into a "silicon republic" by emphasizing major investment in research and development based on a theory that this initiative would generate global investment, and thus create jobs, because of Ireland's reputation for top-notch education.

O'Dowd's emphasis was the right one. At the same time, this transformation would require some very heavy lifting and long-term patience. As Richard Bruton, a leader in the Fine Gael political party told me, "We have been dining out on the claim of strength in our education system for twenty years now." In fact, Ireland's education system, while good, ranked around the middle of European countries; a 2006 Organization for Economic Cooperation and Development survey ranked Ireland fifteenth in quality of secondary education (Finland was first). Moreover, the pipelines that would build the infrastructure of a "silicon republic" or a "smart economy" were eroding due to a decline in government investment that predated the post–Celtic Tiger budget cuts. Irish secondary-level students, meanwhile, were turning away from hard sciences, math, and engineering—with the country facing serious deficiencies in math scores in particular. In many Irish secondary schools, teachers trained in math were nonetheless teaching areas of the subject they were not qualified in. According to multiple people engaged in the effort to build a smart economy, the government itself had no idea what the concept really meant and had eroded the core foundations necessary to build it. Even worse, a single-focus theory of economic progress risked tossing aside core qualities that made Ireland unique in the first place—music, culture, literature, and creativity.

Some economists initially hailed the Irish government for making "tough decisions" with major cuts in its budget—including pay cuts as high as 20 percent for some public-sector services in late 2009. This combined with the government's having to finance the Irish banks at an initial cost of over €40 billion. Major retailers, like Arnotts Department Store, were being taken over by banks, themselves financed by the people who shopped at Arnotts. The "gem" of Dublin—the new Docklands, a bright, shiny area of development on the east end of the River Liffey—was found in late 2009 to be €213 million in debt. As a senior member of the Dublin Docklands Development Authority told me after having "been over every single inch of the place," "What went on in there is like a John Grisham novel." Meanwhile, the downturn has taken a toll on society, and the bill for the debt has yet to come due. Take a walk on any given day down Thomas Street toward the old Liberties and the Guinness factory, and you can find social welfare offices where the lines stretch far down the road. Meanwhile, Ireland's best-educated and most talented young professionals are packing to leave home once more for foreign lands. By June 2010, there was a backlog of 64,519 Irish passport applications for overseas travel. Still, walking up and down Grafton Street among all the happy tourists, one would think nothing was wrong—except for the fact that tourism to Ireland declined by over 20 percent in 2009 and 2010.

As its economic situation worsened through 2009 and 2010, Ireland earned a place among Europe's "PIGS"—Portugal, Ireland, Greece, and Spain—all peripheral EU countries with serious debt crises that placed the entire eurozone at risk of failure. In July 2010, however, Taoiseach Brian Cowen went to Wall Street and declared, "Ireland is certainly moving into a new era because we have consolidated progress that we have undoubtedly made." That same week, he declared that Ireland had "turned the corner." I've met Brian Cowen—he is friendly and affable. I also understand the need to say positive things to keep an economy moving and a nation's psychology on track. The simple truth, however, is that by 2010 not only had Ireland gotten nowhere near the corner, but things were likely to get much worse before they got even marginally better. The long-term economic prospects cast a dark shadow on this small country now more vulnerable than ever to the ebbs and flows of external events beyond its control. The deep budget cuts had a deflationary effect as the Irish people stopped spending, the banks stopped lending, and hopes of new foreign direct investment or growth in the American economy were unlikely to bear fruit. By early 2011, Cowen's Fianna Fáil party was at a mere 14 percent in public-opinion polls, and

Cowen was the most unpopular politician in Ireland—the butt of many a tragic joke. Earlier in the year, he had barely survived a no-confidence vote, sustained only by a tiny margin of support among junior coalition Green Party members of parliament. In late 2010, the Greens pulled the plug and forced an early general election to come in 2011.

The external misunderstanding about Ireland's situation was made clear in a general reaction to an August 2010 decision by *Newsweek* magazine to name Brian Cowen one of the world's "top ten leaders" for taking tough decisions on the Irish budget. A *Wall Street Journal* headline on 20 August 2010 read, "Ireland Gasps after *Newsweek* Names PM One of Top 10 World Leaders." The *Journal* pointed out, "As finance minister and prime minster, Cowen has presided over the worst economic crisis in modern times. The fact that he is being credited for fixing the same problems that his party helped to cause is not lost on the public." The *Journal* quoted Joan Burton, the Labour Party finance spokesperson, as saying of Brian Cowen's recognition, "If you look back to the time of Marie Antoinette, she got high marks from other potentates and rulers who seemed to be far more impressed by her than were the population." The *Wall Street Journal* editorial concluded, "Can *Newsweek* see something we can't? Or does Ireland look like a Monet painting from afar—full of color and exuberance and order, but a mess the nearer you get?"

THOMAS FRIEDMAN: STILL NO APOLOGIES?

All of us with ties to Ireland share a personal and happy vision of "home." The tears on departure are always too much to bear. Many of us have also suffered pain as loved ones across the sea have faced challenges that we could not be there for. Ireland is an easy place to love—and when it comes to meeting serious challenges, sometimes it is just easier to look the other way or wish for better days to come. I am guilty of it myself. So, we have to cut ourselves some slack when assessing a place we love. It is not hard to appreciate the cultural tendency to look away from tough things. Uninformed judgments, like that of *Newsweek*, are harder to understand—for even if the magazine were correct, the person deserving accolades would not have been the Taoiseach but rather his finance minister, Brian Lenihan, who in the face of a very serious cancer diagnosis held fast on hard and sustained choices for the Irish economy. Yet, Lenihan too was not without problems: a December 2010 survey of economists by the *Financial Times* voted him Europe's worst finance minister. Writing on 6 December, the *Financial Times* said that Lenihan was "overwhelmed by the crisis in Ireland's banking system and the implosion of the country's economic growth." Brian Cowen, though a protégé of his predecessor, the disgraced Bertie Ahern, is perhaps more a victim of naiveté than a man with bad intent—although by the end of his term, he seemed to be clinging desperately to power, using every mechanism he could rather than factoring in the larger interests of the Irish people. As Joan Burton told me, "He never believed that all of his wealthy friends, flying around in their helicopters and with their big houses could ever literally lose *everything.*" To be fair, no one in Ireland really knows what is going on. Even among political leaders, businesspeople, and economists, few predicted what has happened, and even fewer have any real concept of how to move the country forward again, given the mountains of debt and beholden position the bailout put Irish banks in vis-à-vis the European Union and the International Monetary Fund in late 2010.

One person, however, truly owes Ireland a reassessment: Thomas Friedman. A columnist for the *New York Times*, Friedman is famous for his studies of globalization and his theories of liberal economic global convergence and sophisticated interactions across borders. His book *The World Is Flat: A Brief History of the Twenty-first Century* (2005) is read widely, and many teachers use it as a baseline for understanding the modern world. I know this well because, in summer 2007, my family took a car trip to Colorado. Our then high school freshman daughter had been assigned to read and discuss Friedman's book while on our travels. Between Ohio and Dodge City, Kansas, I learned all I needed to know about how flat the world is—literally, Kansas is really flat, and long too for that matter. Friedman is an important analyst and must be taken very seriously. Overall, he offers solid efforts to explain globalization. As regards Ireland in the context of globalization, however, Friedman is wrong.

Thomas Friedman acknowledges that globalization has its upsides and downsides. In his assessment of the trajectory of globalization, however, he writes, "I do get a little lump in my throat when I see countries like China, India, or Ireland adopting a basically proglobalization strategy, adapting it to their own political, social, and economic conditions, and reaping the benefits." Friedman understandably celebrates that globalization has helped many societies—including Ireland—move out of serious economic stagnation and decay. "When done right and in a sustained manner, globalization has a huge potential to lift large numbers of people out of poverty. And, when I see large numbers of people escaping poverty in places like India, China, or Ireland, well, yes, I get a little emotional. No apologies."

It could be argued that Ireland, in fact, did not do globalization right. Had the country been satisfied in 2001 or 2002 with a slower growth rate of around 3 percent annually, perhaps it would be much better off. The problem is that Ireland did exactly as Friedman suggested a country should do. He saw Ireland as "one of the best examples of a country that has made a huge leap forward by choosing development and reform retail of its governance, infrastructure, and education." Friedman praised the Celtic Tiger as recently as 2005, when some experts there knew Ireland had already gone haywire. Central to Friedman's point is his discussion with Michael Dell—founder of Dell Computers, who set up shop in Limerick and told him in an e-mail exchange, "What attracted us? A well-educated workforce—and good universities close by. Also, Ireland has an industrial and tax policy which is consistently very supportive of business, independent of which political party is in power. I believe this is because there are enough people who remember the very bad times to de-politicize economic development." According to Michael Dell, "The talent in Ireland has proven to be a wonderful resource for us." Friedman also celebrated Intel in Ireland, which he said saw many of the same benefits. He praised government goals to double the nation's PhDs and "set up various funds to get global companies, and brainy people of all kinds, to come to Ireland to do research." Friedman's theory about Ireland and globalization posited that the Republic was getting four basics right—infrastructure, education, governance, and the environment.

Thomas Friedman was so enamored with Dell—which does make great computers and has a terrific worldwide operation—that he even derived a theory in *The World Is Flat* that "no two countries that are both part of a major global supply chain like Dell's will ever fight a war against each other as long as they are both part of the same global supply chain." Friedman argues that this updates his theory, which he claims has held up well, that no two countries that both have McDonald's will ever go to war with each other. He asserted this claim despite the major war fought between the United States and Yugoslavia in 1999 or the subsequent one between Russia and Georgia in 2008—all countries with McDonald's. To be fair, Ireland is quite safe from invasion regardless of whether other countries have Dell. The point about Dell is important because Friedman used it to prove his assumptions about Ireland as a model for other countries to emulate. Dell was a key symbol as Ireland's largest exporter and essential to Friedman's praise of Ireland's "amazing story" of success.

Within five years of Friedman's writing *The World Is Flat*, Dell and Intel were laying off large portions of their workforces in Ireland. In 2007, after learning it was not liable for €74.6 million in development aid from the Irish government, Dell moved major operations from Limerick to Poland. Dell's move to Poland was ironic, as during the Celtic Tiger, tens of thousands of Poles had moved to Ireland for work. By 2010, about half of them had left—going back home to Poland. In January 2009, citing high labor costs, Dell announced it would lay off nineteen hundred of the three thousand people working in its manufacturing plant at Limerick. The *New York Times* quoted the mayor of Limerick, John Gilligan, as saying, "I am very, very bitter about this"; he warned that in time Polish wages would converge with the rest of Europe's, and so the Poles should be wary that "Dell will probably head for Ukraine in six to eight year's time."

Dell's location in Limerick had actually already belied much of Friedman's central thesis about Ireland. At the height of the Celtic Tiger, Limerick had unemployment rates five times the national average, educational under-development, and multiple pockets of serious depravation dominated by violent crime. On 6 December 2010, RTÉ aired an expose of Limerick that showed children destroying property for fun, organized crime and gangs, suicides, and areas of the town that looked like war zones. Mayor Gilligan told the *New York Times* that in his estimation, "We were overreliant on Dell. We shouldn't have put all our eggs in one basket." Meanwhile, just three weeks after announcing that they would not have redundancies, Intel announced that it would lay off three hundred people at its Kildare plant as part of a six-thousand-person global workforce reduction. When these jobs go, so do those that service these employees. This was, as Fine Gael labor spokesman Damien English told the *Irish Independent* on 18 February 2009, a "devastating blow . . . to families, and to the country as a whole." Meanwhile, the *Irish Times* reported closures or cuts among the follow-ing companies in Ireland during an eighteen-month period from January 2009 through April 2010: Dell, Waterford Crystal, Ulster Bank, Superquinn (grocery store), Dublin Bus, Kostal (electronics manufacturer), SR Technics (aircraft-maintenance company), DHL Deliveries, Intel, GlaxoSmithKline, and Bank of Scotland, among others.

In July 2010, I visited an area in Shannon, not too distant from Shannon Airport, that had fit Thomas Friedman's arguments perfectly. It had been a perfect location for global business investment taking advantage of an eager and well-educated workforce just a stone's throw from a global transporta-tion hub. Today it approximates a ghost town. Walking around a shopping mall on what should have been a busy Saturday, I noted that store after store after store was either empty, going out of business, or for sale. Some had simply been abandoned. A once bustling Johnny Rockets diner had become a shell for a low-end fish-and-chips shop, which sat empty. Right next to a sign advertising the location for GE Infrastructure Sensing stood a massive "to let" notice. Driving into Shannon's development zone, I was welcomed by signs that read "Shannon Development: Building a Better Future"—juxtaposed against massive, empty office buildings. Nothing was written on the classic Irish road sign next to the Shannon development wel-come sign: it was blank—a road sign to nowhere. In nearby Ennis, pub after pub had closed. During a two-hour walk around the city center, I counted ten shut-down and dilapidated pubs. Those were the ten that I could see. By 2010, on average, one pub in Ireland was closing per day. Venturing back over to Dublin and walking in the neighborhoods of classic Georgian houses with their brilliant doorways, one would see sign after sign after sign announcing "to let."

Writing in the *New York Times* on 1 July 2005, Friedman argued that the core choice for the future of Europe was to "follow the leapin' leprechaun." Friedman argued one of the best things Ireland had done was to "make it easier to fire people, without having to pay years of severance. Sounds brutal, I know. But the easier it is to fire people, the more willing companies are to hire people." Friedman—in a wildly inaccurate statement—wrote, "And by the way, because of all the tax revenue and employment the global companies are generating in Ireland, Dublin has been able to increase spending on health care, schools and infrastructure." In reality, the government at the time was not only *not* generating revenue but beginning to accumulate massive debt. Meanwhile, poor infrastructure, inflated prices, and high wages would contribute to the exodus of many companies from Ireland. In July 2010, Moody's Investor Services downgraded Ireland's debt ranking and changed its outlook on the country from "stable" to "negative." This evaluation was based on the Irish government's gradual but significant loss of financial strength, as reflected by its "deteriorating debt affordability," according to Moody's officials quoted in the *New York Times*. In its assessment, Moody's also took into account Ireland's increased liabilities due to having no money in its banks. According to American business network CNBC (in a September 2009 study), by 2009 Ireland had the highest external debt in the world as a percentage of its GNP at 1,312 percent. By 2010, its gross external debt was estimated to be $867 billion.

Friedman argued in 2005 that the Irish path was far superior to that of Germany, which was holding onto jobs and major industrial production. Yet, while Ireland was, by 2010, facing economic disaster, the *New York Times* headline for 13 August read, "German Growth Lifts Europe's G.D.P. in 2nd Quarter." An article published on 28 August 2010 in the *Irish Independent* asked, "Why do we ape Boston instead of Berlin?" While many in Ireland have for some time argued that the country has more in common with the United States than many of its European partners, the author wondered why "we do not look eastwards from time to time for ideas on how to run our country, especially as the Germans are making a much better stab at things these days than either the Irish or the Americans." In Germany in 2010, unemployment was low, and the economy was expanding, while the country was also implementing austerity programs. Meanwhile, the Irish government compounded its problems by "buying advice from the Morgan Stanleys of this world rather than German and French banks and management consultants. . . . These American-trained economists are influenced by a spendthrift culture that believes in consumption and credit." Germany, the piece concluded, "is, in short, an exciting place to be right now. . . . A country that embraces change and hard work and is enjoying some success as a result."

An assertion central to Thomas Friedman's case for Ireland was that the country had gotten its governance right—based on a working agreement over the economy between the government, trade unions, farmers, and leading corporations. This social partnership allowed for a moderation of wages and prices and for a spirited effort to gain foreign direct investment. The social compact was likely Bertie Ahern's only successful contribution as Taoiseach. Still, seemingly sensing Friedman's cheerleading toward Ireland and its leadership at the time, Ahern boasted to Friedman in 2005 of having "met the premier of China five times in the last two years." Jumping forward five years, the social compact was effectively dead. In an unprecedented political transformation, after nearly one hundred years of two-party dominance by Fianna Fáil and Fine Gael, the Labour Party, headed by a charismatic and effective Éamon Gilmore, emerged for a time in spring 2010 as the most popular party in Ireland. In a March 2010 Dáil (parliament) debate, Gilmore brazenly called out the Taoiseach, Brian Cowen, as having committed "economic treason" against the country when he served as Ahern's finance minister. Not only was the social compact dead, but Bertie Ahern—who had told those who raised concerns about the economy to commit suicide—was long gone from government. He resigned in disgrace as Taoiseach and leader of Fianna Fáil in May 2008 following a string of accusations of corruption, financial fraud, and lying. Of Ahern's legacy, Michael O'Leary, the head of Ryanair (one of Ireland's most successful enterprises), said on the *Ray D'Arcy Show* on Today FM on 12 November 2008, "Bertie squandered the wealth of a generation, and I think in time it will be proven he was a useless wastrel."

THE TIMES THEY ARE A CHANGIN'

Few people in Ireland might have known it, but in the spring of 2010, probably the most recognizable face of Ireland in the United States was singer Sinéad O'Connor. A horrid string of scandals—indeed crimes—involving child abuse in the Catholic Church were being uncovered in the United States. Simultaneously, the pope had sent a letter of apology to Irish Mass goers for a betrayal of trust in the church stemming from Ireland's child-abuse crisis. On both accounts, Sinéad O'Connor was suddenly seen in a new light. For twenty years, one of Ireland's greatest musical talents had been ridiculed and ostracized—especially in the United States. Many Catholics dismissed her as the radical who had ripped up a photo of Pope John Paul II on *Saturday Night Live* in 1992. In her *Saturday Night Live* rendition of Bob Marley's song "War," she painfully substituted the words "child abuse" for "racism" in a key verse. It was a not too subtle hint that she was singing about Ireland with "war in the East, war in the West, war up North, war down South." "Children, children . . . fight!—we find it necessary," she sang. She finished the song by holding up and shredding a picture of the pope. She then declared, "Fight the real enemy," in front of tens of millions of viewers on live American television. This incident ended much of her career in the United States and landed her in the top ten on VH1's list of the one hundred "most shocking" moments in rock and roll.

Nearly twenty years later, the surfacing of story after story about child-abuse crimes in the Catholic Church shed new light not only on Sinéad O'Connor but on Ireland's entire relationship to Rome. O'Connor emerged as a primary spokesperson on this issue in the United States, appearing on *Larry King Live* and *The Rachel Maddow Show* and penning an op-ed piece in the *Washington Post* on the pope's letter of apology to Ireland. A letter to the *Washington Post* on 31 March 2010 by an Irish person living in the United States reflected that Sinéad O'Connor had come full circle: "It was a sickening shock when the church scandals of which I was naively unaware came to light. Ms. O'Connor was aware of them a long time ago. Now I can understand her earlier actions, which I had found offensive. I honor her for speaking out."

Jumping forward from 1992 and *Saturday Night Live* to 2010 and Ireland's *Late Late Show*, Sinéad O'Connor was warmly welcomed to the stage by popular host Ryan Tubridy, "Ireland's Jay Leno." He announced that she would sing Bob Dylan's "The Times They Are a Changin'"—of which he said, "What an appropriate song." This time, the audience understood clearly when she began the tune by saying, "Okay . . . so, I'm going to dedicate this to the pope." Sinéad O'Connor gave this classic protest anthem new life with one of the most evocative performances in the history of Irish television. Few moments have so well captured the mood of a country as when she sang forcefully, "There's a battle outside and it's raging!" The last verse of Dylan's tune struck deepest as she changed the word "mothers" to "bishops": "Come bishops and fathers, throughout the land. . . . And don't criticize what you can't understand . . . for the times they are a changin'."

The changes in the Irish Catholic church form one part of the deeper transformation with far-reaching consequences—and opportunity for Ireland's future. Up to the 1980s, outsiders were largely confined to tourists and Spanish summer students there to learn English. Today, Ireland is a multicultural and global society. I recall the first time I noticed these accelerating changes after flying all night to Dublin from Columbus, Ohio, in 2001. I was invited to visit a gym—out near the brand-new Blanchardstown Centre. I do not recall what the place was called, but it might as well have been a California Fitness Center. Hazy with jetlag, I wondered whether I had left the United States or not—Ireland was being Americanized. Fortunately, there was a pub close by—just up the road from the brand-new Mc-Donald's drive-through—which helped. Yet again, all is not what it seems in Ireland. Walking that afternoon into the American-style Blanchardstown Centre mall, I noticed standing among the crowd of shoppers a tall, splendid, striking Arab man dressed in his traditional attire. I had never seen anyone like him in Ireland before. Today, walking down Lower Abbey Street and in other areas of Dublin, you will see Polish shops, an Africa Center, Chinese, Indians, and Pakistanis. Strolling across O'Connell Street, you are more likely to see protesters advocating for religious reform in China or standing behind information tables on Islam than espousing a particularly Irish cause. If you order a taxi, your driver is as likely to be from Africa as from Athlone. This legacy of the Celtic Tiger—the permanently changed demographic map of Ireland—provides a key to future economic progress. In the summer of 2010, I saw a terrific sight at the Burren in Clare: two young Muslims dressed traditionally, playing tourist at one of Ireland's classic dolmens. Yet, this path to progress is by no means guaranteed. Ireland is a welcoming country and has handled its transition to multiculturalism better than other European nations. But racism also runs deep in a country that has, for most of its history, been mostly white, mostly Catholic, and mostly an island. Today, some of the most dynamic and innovative leadership in Ireland is taking place at the grass roots, seeking to create a thriving multicultural society.

Equally significant is the transformation occurring in a new generation of young people. For those between the ages of twenty-five and forty in 2010, the Celtic Tiger shaped their life experience. Young professionals could choose where they would work, what they would do, and for how much. Credit was cheap, and money flowed freely. Because this cohort had never experienced previous downtimes, its members have fallen hard while representing the highest percentage of unemployed. Among the "no" votes in the last EU referendum held in 2009, the highest proportion came from this younger generation. Many of these young people today have lost faith in institutions of government. They hear economists boast about how, because of the European Union, Irish companies have a labor market of 200 million people to work within—which does nothing for a young, unemployed Irish professional. Worse, many of these young are also Ireland's best and brightest talents, who are once again left with little choice but to emigrate. As one young woman bitterly said on a radio call-in show I heard in the summer of 2010 in Dublin, "I'm leaving this country in January, and I am *not* coming back!" Ireland risks losing an entire generation, the core of the country's future, as these individuals have lost faith in the economy, politics, the church—in tomorrow. Then again, another person, around aged fifty, said to me, "I emigrated twice in my life. I'll be fucked if I'm going to do it again."

Patriotism in Ireland is often seen as belonging to a bygone era. In the parliament, a member spoke emotionally about his patriotic love of Ireland

and was laughed at. A political activist said to me, on contemplating emigration, "There is nothing left to fight here." This is ironic because, as Elaine Byrne, a professor at Trinity College and a columnist for the *Irish Times* pointed out to me, "Think about the ages of people like Pádraig Pearse, Michael Collins, Éamon de Valera when they led Ireland to its independence. They were in their twenties and early thirties." Or, as Sinéad O'Connor told me, think about the revolutionaries in the Ireland of one hundred years ago: not only were they young, but "they were the artists, the writers, the poets." What will become of Ireland's young and creative class today? As O'Connor says of her own efforts, "I wanted to be sure that when I meet my maker that it can't be said that the artists didn't care."

Ireland has demonstrated bravery and leadership in setting an example for the world in negotiating peace in Northern Ireland. The peace process has taken hold at the high end of politics and business. During St. Patrick's Day festivities in Washington, DC, in March 2010, I witnessed up close friendly interaction between Northern Ireland's First Minister Peter Robinson of the Democratic Unionist Party and Second Minister Martin McGuinness of Sinn Féin. At a breakfast briefing held at the American Chamber of Commerce, Robinson teased McGuinness for being late because he had to eat two breakfasts. Both joked of the idea of McGuinness arriving wearing a bright orange tie (symbolizing Protestant identity) and Robinson wearing a bright green one (symbolizing Catholic identity). In his formal remarks, McGuinness made clear that any who wished to go back to the old days in the North would have to come through him first. As a high-ranking Northern Ireland Policing Board member said to me with deep emotion, reflecting on where Northern Ireland is now, "I am so . . . proud of how far we have all come." This person, who had just been up nearly all night observing antipolice riots by Catholic youth in the Ardoyne area of Belfast, said we have all "forgiven and forgotten—some very awful things . . . things we can't bear to look at again."

The political forces are united on the need for economic progress for the North, and the people in Northern Ireland are well positioned to prosper. On the streets of the Ardoyne (a strongly nationalist Catholic area) and in other parts of Belfast, however, the peace process has also left a vacuum of order and serious instability—especially among both Catholic and Protestant youth. Where paramilitary street justice used to enforce local rules, organized crime, especially drug dealing with its associated violence, has filled a security vacuum. In Derry, one would have to commit a serious crime to get busted after 11 p.m., as it simply is not safe for police to come to certain parts of town. In July 2010, Catholics in the Ardoyne in Belfast rioted against the police—instigated by a small band of Republican dissidents, these rioters sent a message not to Protestants but mainly to former IRA and police officials that they no longer controlled the streets. Really disconcerting in watching these street riots, however, was the age of those on the front lines throwing bricks and petrol bombs. Closed-circuit television images spread quickly in the press of children as young as eight years old turning to violence. In pockets of Northern Ireland, entire generations of young Catholics and Protestants are being lost, and little is being done about it. The ambitious aspire to become the local thug who runs the street. While it is not the case for most families in the Ardoyne, for a growing number of youth, a lack of role models, positive examples, or a sense of a future increasingly pervades these post–peace process Belfast streets.

Despite these challenges, it is important to account for the positive impact of change in Ireland and the world. As a professor at a major university in Dublin told me, we are collectively "purging ourselves of our sins" from the Celtic Tiger. The Celtic Tiger was transformational beyond the economy, and much of that legacy is fundamentally positive. A senior police representative in Dublin summarized this well in our interview, making the point that "we are no longer de Valera's Ireland . . . no more crossroads dancing. . . . We have washed away the past and modernized in one big swoop." The euphoria of the Celtic Tiger took a human toll with people "working too much overtime, people prioritizing money over relationships and values," so that "aspirations and hopes were too high," and the focus on a "cult of money" led to "competition and burnout." People now have little choice but to focus more on the nonmaterial things that matter. Family, friends, and health take priority for the long haul in all countries and now perhaps more so than ever in Ireland. As to the Celtic Tiger, says this police official, "we can now have a rebirth. . . . We are a different country now than we were going in." As Stephen Brennan, head of strategic planning at the Digital Depot/Digital Hub, a high-tech consortium located in the old Liberties in Dublin, said to me, "Now is the time for radically different things."

WHAT KIND OF IRELAND DO WE WANT TO BE?

What kind of Ireland? That central question recurred in the research for this book. This is the story of a society in limbo, eagerly grasping for something but unsure what. The chapters that follow draw on a wide range of interviews and extended visits dating from 1987 and spanning the last several decades as part of my effort to examine the implications of change. Much of the focus is on the period from 2008 to 2010, one of the most radically transformative times in Irish and global history. However, the book seeks to place that time in a broader context of challenges and progress. The pages that follow tell a story of crisis, transformation, and opportunity. It is the story of an island at the crossroads of globalization. It is also far more than a story about Ireland. The story that is Ireland's has for centuries reflected much of the experience of the world: colonialism, religious strife, mass migration, civil war, economic dislocation and isolation as well as expansion, and an embrace of a creative and dynamic culture shared at home and abroad. This is not just a story of and for Ireland; rather it is for all of us who are struggling to identify a place and purpose in the early twenty-first century. As the reader will see, there is reason for optimism in the long run because, despite the challenges, the opportunity for positive progress in Ireland and the world is very real indeed.

An electronics superstore in Ennis, closed down and for sale (summer 2010).

2

A Tiger's Broken Dreams

TREAD SOFTLY, BECAUSE YOU TREAD ON MY DREAMS

When William Butler Yeats wrote those words in his poem "He Wishes for the Cloths of Heaven," he encapsulated a sense of what was possible in the comforts of the good life. Yet, he also grounded this in the reality that as much as one would like to provide another with the "cloths of Heaven" in the end, "I, being poor, have only my dreams," which willingly would be "spread under your feet." Published in 1899 and inspired by an unrequited love, this poem's essence captures both the aspiration and reality that is Ireland. From famine to rebellion to civil war to massive emigration, Ireland has experienced very rough patches. The image of its longtime leader, Éamon de Valera, dominated much of Ireland's postindependence period of nationhood. De Valera had a vision of Ireland as independent, rural, and self-sufficient. By the 1990s, this Ireland was but a ghost—replaced by the Celtic Tiger—a period of dramatic economic growth previously unknown in this land. Suddenly, for generations of Irish, wealth was no longer a dream. Ireland was, after tiny Luxembourg, the wealthiest country in Europe by 2000. Yet, by 2010, this prosperity had come crashing down, and Ireland teetered on the edge of national insolvency.

DE VALERA'S GHOST: IRELAND IN THE 1980s

From Ireland's independence, the vision of its first leader, Éamon de Valera, dominated the nation's economy. De Valera identified his worldview with the very nature of Ireland. A speech titled "The Ireland That We Dreamed

25

Of," which he gave to the nation on St. Patrick's Day in 1943, famously captured this dream. (Though this speech is often referred to as the "maidens dancing at the crossroads" speech, he never actually used that phrase.) De Valera said, "The ideal Ireland that we would have, the Ireland that we dreamed of, would be the home of a people who valued material wealth only as a basis for right living, of a people who, satisfied with frugal comfort, devoted their leisure to the things of the spirit—a land whose countryside would be bright with cozy homesteads, whose fields and villages would be joyous with the sounds of industry, with the romping of sturdy children, the contest of athletic youths and the laughter of happy maidens, whose firesides would be forums for the wisdom of serene old age." To de Valera, Ireland should aspire to be "home, in short, of the people living the life that God desires that men should live."

Éamon de Valera died in 1975 having served in dominant leadership roles between 1917 and 1973. While he had a clear goal of Ireland as isolated and self-sufficient, he readily acknowledged that economics was not his expertise. Ireland still relied heavily on Great Britain for trade; thus, de Valera tended to view economics through the prism of Ireland's long struggle for independence. Had Michael Collins—de Valera's ally and, eventually, foe at the time of independence and civil war—lived, Ireland might have achieved earlier success in the global economy. Collins had gained training in accounting, finance, and management while working as a young man in London. He managed the finances of the nascent Irish government and penned pamphlets laying out a clear economic philosophy. Historian Tim Pat Coogan notes in *Michael Collins: The Man Who Made Ireland* (2002) that Collins believed foreign trade had to be stimulated by "making facilities for the transport and marketing of Irish goods abroad and foreign goods in Ireland." Collins believed that investors must be encouraged to put Irish capital in Irish businesses and that, when it hinders, taxation "must be adjusted." He advocated for devising and implementing land reform and agribusiness by studying other countries' models, including those of Denmark, Holland, and Germany. He pushed for economic development in all possible areas, including forestry, minerals mining, port expansion, and hydroelectric power. Had Michael Collins not been assassinated at age thirty-two in 1922, who knows what levels of economic development Ireland might have attained and when.

Speculation aside, despite important changes begun in the 1960s, the country remained "de Valera's Ireland" through the 1980s. The most significant symbolism of this came in the close relationship between Éamon de Valera's Fianna Fáil political party, business, and rural society—sustained via steep protectionist economic measures. Coogan points out in another book, *Ireland in the 20th Century* (2006), that in de Valera's first year as Ireland's leader, domestic taxes were placed on a total of forty-three categories

of imports. Meanwhile, welfare was handed out, especially to people willing to learn Gaelic, which created a strong political base highly resistant to
change. By the 1980s, the economy was defined by a 60 percent individual
tax rate, massive migration, deep debt, an overvalued currency, and up to
20 percent inflation. Ireland was living way beyond its means—a point
made in 1980 by Fianna Fáil Taoiseach Charles Haughey, who asserted,
"We have been living at a rate which is simply not justified by the amount
of goods and services we are producing." Yet, as Coogan notes, Haughey
personally owed Allied Irish Banks about IR£1.4 million. Haughey, it turns
out, epitomized a major attribute of the Irish economic system: deeply
embedded collusion between Fianna Fáil governments and wealthy private
interests. Various tribunals would subsequently find Haughey to have be-
haved unethically and "devalued democracy" in Ireland. Nonetheless, his
legacy was significant, both for his seeming stature while in government
and for his mentoring of those who eventually ruined modern Ireland—
particularly the disgraced former Taoiseach Bertie Ahern, who, speaking at
Haughey's funeral in 2006, referred to him as "boss."

I began extended travel to Ireland in 1987 and saw up close the realities
of the time. Life then was not as bad as it is now often portrayed. The time,
however, symbolized a ledge that Ireland would have to turn a corner on.
Emigration, in particular, was no longer sustainable as Ireland's best and
brightest were fleeing the country in droves. In 1987, forty thousand people
emigrated from Ireland. Unemployment totaled 250,178 and eventually
reached a high of 17.3 percent. Coogan quotes two young lads from Kerry
who summarized the reality of emigration as a relief for Irish politicians
because "they'll go away and maybe get jobs, and either send back their
money some day with money made. . . . But they won't be costing the
state anything—if they stayed at home, they'd be a terrible drain." To get
a perspective on this, I asked Ben Tonra (now a professor of international
relations at University College Dublin) what it was like for him as a young
adult in the mid-1980s in Ireland. Tonra pointed out that of the fifty-six
people who graduated from his school course in 1986, six remained in
Ireland within eighteen months. After completing a master's degree, Tonra
finally got one interview for a banking job, which did not pan out. "I left
for the U.S. six weeks later," he said.

My own impressions of 1980s Ireland came through the eyes of a nine-
teen-year-old on his second trip to Europe—castles and Guinness were very
high priorities. I took great pleasure in seeing U2 on the *Joshua Tree* tour
in Cork, with The Dubliners as the opening act. I had seen U2 live in the
United States on their earliest tours, but nothing could beat hearing Bono
sing in "Bullet the Blue Sky" that "Outside its America . . . but inside—its
Cork!" and seeing the ocean of people in the Cork football stadium respond accordingly with deep pride. One of the first places I saw on that

initial arrival to Ireland was the Ballymun Flats—seven very tall and visible towers in northwest Dublin, each named after a revolutionary leader like Pádraig Pearse and James Connolly (killed in 1916 by British forces after being captured in the Easter Rising). These were basically vertical public-housing slums, conceived in the 1960s as a sign of modern progress. By the 1980s, these seven towers were dens of crime, prostitution, and poverty; farm animals were even sometimes seen coming in and out. Entire subcultures and communities existed floor by floor as neighborhoods in the sky. They have since been torn down, but in the 1980s, one could not miss these monstrous symbols of Ireland's lasting inability to make real progress while trying to hide deep underlying problems. On *Joshua Tree*, U2 produced a song called "Running to Stand Still," which illustrated the pain that many in Ireland faced but kept tragically hidden. The song tells of a young woman in Ballymun who seeks change but cannot find a clear way out. Bono sings, "Sweet the sin, bitter the taste in my mouth, I see seven towers but I only see—one way out." The lyrics continue, "You've got to cry without weeping, talk without speaking—scream, without raising your voice." In the end, the young girl takes to the needle and heroin—the "poison, from the poison stream"—leading to pained screams of "Hallelujah!" in Bono's live renditions.

To place this period in perspective, I spent an afternoon talking with Dr. Garret FitzGerald, who led Ireland through much of the 1980s as Taoiseach from the Fine Gael party. FitzGerald is widely regarded nationally as a thoughtful elder statesman of Ireland, having witnessed and participated in much of the country's history. I was particularly impressed with his views on the impact of history on current thinking when he wrote in his book *Ireland in the World* (2005), "The truth is that all history is in some measure contingent—it is at least partly a product of a series of accidental events which of course occur within a broad framework of evolutionary change occasioned by such underlying factors as the flux of ideas about society and the state, technological change, and the interplay of economic forces." As head of Fine Gael, FitzGerald led coalition governments in Ireland from June 1981 through March 1982 and then from December 1982 to March 1987.

Spending an afternoon with Garret FitzGerald, born in 1926, is like taking a walk through history, while being subsequently coached on the lessons for today and prospects for tomorrow. He has an incredible eye for detail, and after two hours of nonstop conversation, I felt we should halt—lest I tire! Just then, though, we got to talking about a place in the United States, prompting him to proudly pull out his massive world atlas, which we then hovered over, discussing American geography and politics for even longer. Garret FitzGerald is one of the most thoughtful and socially conscious senior political leaders I have had the honor of meeting. His eye for history and how it shapes the current and future environment is unique. As he writes in *Ireland in the World*, "There is a case for occasional reflecting on what might have been, for this can help dispel the false sense that what actually happened was inevitable." When I asked him how the past has shaped today's situation in Ireland, his first point was classically Irish in sentiment and truth: "Small things have carry-on effects."

Garret FitzGerald deserves tremendous credit for laying the groundwork for the Celtic Tiger, which took off under the auspices of a Fine Gael–led coalition government in the 1990s. However, when asked for perspective on the contemporary situation in Ireland, he quickly pointed not to his party or experience but rather to a Fianna Fáil politician, Seán Lemass, who toiled under and facilitated the isolationist economic policies of de Valera for decades. When he became Taoiseach in 1959, Lemass introduced policy reforms he had been contemplating for several years. FitzGerald highlighted Lemass's focus on lowering corporate tax rates, modernizing education and making it more accessible, and transforming the Irish Development Agency (IDA, initially created in 1949 as the Irish Development Authority) as a means of advancing industrial and manufacturing reform and promoting Irish business interests "to sell and do the selling," as FitzGerald put it.

Ireland was deeply engaged in, and benefiting from, globalization long before the rest of the world plugged in. The country began a process in the 1960s of opening up to attracting pharmaceutical, computer, and medical manufacturing. FitzGerald's central point is that the Celtic Tiger "did not emerge overnight and that it is important to view [it] in a larger historical sense of progress." Historian R. F. Forster supports this argument in *Luck and the Irish: A Brief History of Change from 1970* (2007). Forster shows that in 1970, 25 percent of the two hundred thousand industrial jobs in Ireland were the result of foreign direct investment. He notes that by 1980, Ireland was already well populated by foreign direct investment, including Fujitsu, Analogue, Burlington, and Wang. By 1983, over 17 percent of the country's total manufacturing workforce was employed by American companies. Ireland was, in 1980, as Forster writes, "now established as the primary European base for U.S. microelectronics firms." While foreign direct investment expanded during the Celtic Tiger, the growth in American investment was only an additional 7 percent above that of the early 1980s. This emphasis—in electronics, pharmaceuticals, health care, and software—was, FitzGerald pointed out, all in place in the 1980s. The degree of change in the 1980s was reflected well, as Forster shows, in technological expansion. In 1949, Ireland had forty-three thousand telephone exchange lines. Only in 1978 did Ireland launch a program to get its phone system up to accepted European standards. This was important as business leaders had cited poor telecommunications as a major reason Ireland was losing investment potential.

The goal was to achieve a doubling of subscriber lines by 1985. By 1997, the Irish phone network was managing one billion calls annually.

As Ireland's foreign minister in the 1970s, FitzGerald was a central actor in moving Ireland into the European Community—now the European Union. To him, integration with Europe was crucial to Ireland's achieving a greater number of economic options than its existing trade dependence on Great Britain provided. This engagement with Europe was another "carry-on effect" that gave Ireland confidence in normalizing its relationship with Great Britain. Furthermore, it led to new export markets for Ireland and a diversification of the Irish economy beyond a traditional agricultural emphasis. By the time FitzGerald was Taoiseach in the 1980s, the European Community was providing structural funds for economic development that amounted to an annual average of 4 percent of the Irish economy. At the height of the Celtic Tiger, FitzGerald said, up to 7 percent of the Irish economy remained EU generated. Garret FitzGerald also highlighted major changes in education policy beginning in the 1960s under the Seán Lemass government as an additional carry-on effect. By engaging in a dramatic expansion of the second-level educational system and state-backed growth of third-level (university) education, the country provided new means of moving from a predominantly rural economy to a more modern society. Ireland transformed from one of the poorest-educated European countries in the early 1960s into one of the best educated by the 1980s.

As Garret FitzGerald said in our interview, "These changes were both permanent and incomplete." During the 1980s, it proved difficult to arrive at a social and political agreement on how to address deep structural deficiencies in the Irish economy. Long a second fiddle to Fianna Fáil in politics, the Fine Gael coalition governments that FitzGerald headed were divided between a desire to get structural debt in balance and opposition from his coalition Labour partner, who was under pressure from public-sector unions not to make cuts. Despite these difficulties, FitzGerald provided "early warning" of what was coming by way of Fianna Fáil. Showing prescience about Charles Haughey, FitzGerald stated in 1979 (about Haughey's nomination as Taoiseach by Fianna Fáil),

> He comes with a flawed pedigree. . . . His motives can be judged ultimately only by God, but we cannot ignore the fact that he differs from all his predecessors in that those motives have been and are widely impugned, most notably, but by no means exclusively, by people within his own party, people close to him who have observed his actions for many years and who have made their human, interim judgment on him. They and others . . . have attributed to him an overweening ambition which they do not see as a simple emanation of a desire to serve but rather as a wish to dominate, even to own the State.

On the very same day that FitzGerald made that statement, a wealthy property developer named John Byrne placed a sum of IR£150,000 into an account for Charles Haughey. In 2006, the Moriarty Tribunal (which took evidence on corruption during Haughey's time in politics) concluded that between 1979 and 1996, Haughey had taken IR£11.57 million in inappropriate payments from business friends.

As Taoiseach, Garret FitzGerald advanced energetic young ministers like John Bruton and Alan Dukes, who worked with Labour Party coalition leaders and were eventually able to consolidate the historical trends leading Ireland into the Celtic Tiger. The central point of the lesson provided by FitzGerald is that Ireland's progress in the 1990s had complex and long-term foundations in trade and tax reform, budget cuts and decreased regulation, education reform, integration with Europe, structural funds, and political compromise between government and major unions. Moreover, Ireland benefited from the economic growth generated by the vibrant American economy at the time and the rapid emergence of globalization. By the early 1990s, Ireland was ready for a common approach—ready to ride the Tiger.

PUNCHING ABOVE OUR WEIGHT

What began as a steady rise in economic growth and personal income soon grew into a deeply held sense of personal freedom that the Irish people had never before experienced. Suddenly, material goods were very important. Money and social status became free-flowing and upwardly mobile. By the turn of the century, it was, simply put, a great time to be Irish. For a young generation that had never experienced bad times, a wealthy and comfortable Ireland was the new norm—and the expected future. Thus, the desperate condition Ireland found itself in by 2008 came as a horrific shock to a country that had never previously experienced boom and bust. The question of why the Celtic Tiger crashed is important. Just as significant, however, is the question of what this process did to the shared condition of a country's population—and thus what the legacy is for the future. What happens inside a country that one minute is a roaring tiger at the top of the world as a model of successful market forces and globalization, then the next minute is mired in economic catastrophe—lumped in among the "PIGS" of modern Europe?

The Celtic Tiger period of dramatic economic growth was as important for an emerging sense of optimism and pride as it was for people's pocketbooks. Two of the people to emphasize this point to me the most were one of Ireland's leading engineers, Dr. Stephen Brennan, and one of Ireland's leading venture capitalists, Brian Caulfield. Both Brennan and Caulfield exemplify the creative skills and capacity unleashed in Ireland during the Celtic Tiger. Both pointed to larger trends in Irish society that occurred with a newfound sense of confidence that had been missing among the Irish people. The analogy that both turned to was sports. A first hint of things to come arrived in 1987, when cyclist Stephen Roche won the Tour de France and other major international races. For Brennan, though, it was Ireland's showing in various World Cup soccer performances—especially the defeat of returning champion Italy in the first round in 1994. Ireland was "euphoric and beginning to feel a national sense of pride and purpose behind what it could achieve." Caulfield agreed with this assessment but added the significance of the 1988 European soccer championships, which included Ireland's defeating England 1–0—a victory reminiscent of Ireland's 1949 defeat of England on its home territory. Caulfield noted that with the 1988 defeat of England, by the next morning people in Dublin were selling T-shirts with the statement of historic victory, the date, and the score. Caulfield also noted that a "sense of what was achievable" helped to break a symbolic attitude of "heroic failure" for Ireland—in sport and beyond. I saw this myself while traveling in Ireland during the 1992 Summer Olympics. The whole country ground to a halt to watch Michael Carruth win the gold medal in welterweight boxing in Barcelona. As an American (in typical arrogant fashion), I found quaint all the attention for the one gold medal. I had lost track of how many the United States had won. I did not appreciate at the time the intensity of pride that this kind of accomplishment brought the Irish people. As I sat in a pub in Kilmore Quay on the sea in Wexford and watched the victorious Irish boxer on television, I looked down the bar. As rough an old fisherman as one could find sat alone, crying quiet tears of pride.

That Ireland's passion for sport would mirror the country's sense of itself is no surprise. Since its inception in 1884, the Gaelic Athletic Association (GAA) has served as a core organizing agency for uniting Irish culture and tradition in sports, dance, and language at home and abroad. The GAA was important during the youths of rebel leaders like Michael Collins. Indeed, the British government made unsuccessful efforts to ban the GAA after the 1916 Easter Rising. In November 1920, British auxiliary forces opened fire on GAA fans in Croke Park, killing fourteen Irish civilians. For the Irish, sport was as much a matter of local, regional, and national pride as it was about playing a game. Ireland's sport success in the 1990s would, however, also demonstrate an Ireland that was, in boxing parlance, "punching above its weight." Ireland's Michelle Smith won three gold medals and one bronze in swimming at the Atlanta Olympics in 1996. However, her performance was so out of keeping with her record to date that other swimmers quickly accused her of doping—illegal drug use intended to enhance performance. After various investigations of her and her coach, Smith was banned in 1998 from competitive swimming for four years, ending her swimming career. While Michelle Smith always denied the allegations, her achievements have been permanently tarred. This scandal symbolizes some of what came out of Ireland's Celtic Tiger experience. The country would achieve extraordinary heights but find that experience tainted by excess, greed, and cheating.

The 1990s and first decade of the 2000s embodied an extraordinary sense of optimism and potential for Ireland. During the height of the Celtic Tiger, the Irish had understandable reason to be exuberant. By 1990, Ireland's economy was moving into growth—on average, about 4 percent a year. The requirements of membership in the European Union beginning in 1992 locked in Ireland's well-timed economic reforms, making the country increasingly attractive for outside investment. Ireland's participation in the European Monetary System required it to align its annual inflation rates with other EU countries and to reduce budget deficits. While Ireland's individual tax rates remained relatively high, they were low when compared to other European countries. This remained especially true regarding the corporate tax rate that settled in at a very low 12.5 percent. By 1994, Ireland was in the right place at the right time. A low corporate tax rate, a highly educated, English-speaking population at a good geographic crossroads between Europe and North America, and membership in the European Union and eventually the Eurozone—all combined to create the Celtic Tiger.

These converging dynamics led Thomas Friedman and others to praise Ireland as a model for globalization, and early evidence justified this initial conclusion. Statistical reporting by the International Monetary Fund shows that by 2000, Ireland's gross domestic product (GDP) per capita was about $25,000, which exceeded that in Britain or Germany. Between 1996 and 2000, Ireland's GDP increased at an average rate of 9.66 percent per year. Unemployment dropped from its highs in the 1980s to about 4 percent on average. Between 1990 and 2005, the Irish workforce grew from 1.1 million to over 2 million—including at least 200,000 immigrants. Ireland began a major program of importing labor—even from Britain. Many Irish who had previously emigrated began returning home. Meanwhile, the Irish government negotiated a "social partnership" with major labor unions and political parties to sustain the basics of the economic growth agenda. Finally, the success of the Northern Ireland peace process and the associated Irish Republican Army and Unionist paramilitary cease-fires helped to consolidate an image that the island was a peaceful and stable climate. The Republic of Ireland, Northern Ireland, and Great Britain were moving their shared destinies into a new era. The Irish were getting rich, they were spending, and they were enjoying the good life.

By 2004, Ireland was at the very top of European measurements in wealth, quality of life, and seemingly every other standard of national well-being. In 2004, for the third year in a row, *Foreign Policy* magazine ranked Ireland as the "most globalized country in the world," noting that the country had managed to maintain foreign direct investment even with the global economic downturn that began in 2001. Ireland was continuing to grow in the information technology and pharmaceutical sectors in particular. Intel announced it would spend $2 billion in Ireland to manufacture new semiconductor components. Ireland would prove so attractive for foreign direct investment that its pharmaceutical investments would reach the point where all of Viagra and most Lipitor were manufactured in Ireland. By 2004, Ireland's pharmaceutical companies employed about twenty-four thousand people (with more holding jobs in proximate service industries) and produced over $36 billion in products per year. Meanwhile, 60 percent of the Coca-Cola produced for non-U.S. markets was being made in County Mayo. These are just a few among many other successful examples of foreign investment and export manufacturing.

The appeal of the Celtic Tiger as a model would reach, as *BBC News* put it on 21 March 2007, an "almost mythical status." The BBC noted that politicians, business leaders, academics, and union heads were all visiting Ireland to see how they might duplicate the Celtic Tiger experience. American circles heralded Ireland as an economic miracle. The Celtic Tiger, it was claimed, proved that the key to economic growth lay in less government regulation of the economy and lower taxes. Indeed, other nations should copy the Irish model. This fit well with the political and economic ideology that dominated the United States at the time. In 2006, the conservative Heritage Foundation published a prominent study by Sean Dorgan, CEO of IDA Ireland, which made the case for Ireland as a model to emulate. Dorgan asserted, "Ireland has become one of Europe's most remarkable success stories, evolving from one of the poorest countries in Western Europe to one of the most successful." This stemmed from "sensible policies" that focused on a "belief in economic openness to global markets, low tax rates, and investment in education." Dorgan stressed, in particular, that "Ireland now has by far the lowest tax burden relative to GDP of all Western European countries and is below the OECD [Organization for Economic Cooperation and Development] average." Furthermore, Ireland had developed an effective strategy of "using its tax system innovatively to attract and develop international businesses." He correctly pointed out that nine of the world's top ten pharmaceutical companies and twelve of the world's top fifteen medical products had developed substantial operations in Ireland with global service provision. Dorgan quoted Michael Dell as saying, "I don't think it's coincidence that Ireland and Dell share the same character and connection. Every success we've achieved around the world has been due to the old Irish recipe of big dreams, hard work, and strong relationships."

Also in 2006, Christopher Redman, writing in *Money* magazine, put the issue even more succinctly, arguing, "Ireland has become a shining example of what new wealth can do." Redman, however, also pointed out the limits of overthinking the portability of the Celtic Tiger, noting that corporate taxes in 1960s Ireland were zero. Foreign direct investment in 2006 only accounted for 10 percent of the increase in new jobs. Redman also pointed out that, in 2006, Ireland was experiencing a "property bubble sucking up almost half of the country's capital investment." Fintan O'Toole provides a further dose of reality in *Ship of Fools*, noting that, despite the claims of American conservatives about the value of Ireland's tax system, also essential to the Celtic Tiger were decisions by an activist government "to invest heavily in the expansion of state-funded third-level education." The "other intervention was the construction of a highly sophisticated system of social partnership in which the state, employers, trade unions, and other social actors agreed frameworks, not just for wages, but for national policy on a range of issues."

To get a sense of how the Celtic Tiger grew its stripes, I met with John Bruton, minister of finance for the Fine Gael–led coalition government in the 1980s. He then served as Taoiseach from 1994 to 1997, when the Celtic Tiger was reaching its most sustained progress. John Bruton's Fine Gael gained seats in the 1997 general election, but its coalition Labour Party took heavy losses. This led to the collapse of his "rainbow coalition" between Fine Gael and Labour and to Fianna Fáil's return to government. Bruton went on to become a highly successful EU envoy to the United States. We met in his hometown of Dunboyne for tea at a wonderful pub called Slevin's. It was interesting to see the classic Irish political moment when he walked into Slevin's and was immediately welcomed enthusiastically by the regulars, all of whom he knew individually. Bruton suggested that "the Celtic Tiger wasn't made because someone dreamed it up." He said that Ireland had "long been open to foreign direct investment, had low tax rates, and had an assertive IDA"—all dating back to decisions taken by people who had long since left political life. He especially credited Gerard Sweetman, who, as a Fine Gael minister of finance, in 1956 had laid the groundwork for Seán Lemass's moves to attract foreign investment in Ireland and to promote an export-driven economy. Bruton called the primary emphasis on Seán Lemass a "Fianna Fáil mythology" as it was "Sweetman who had done a lot of the real work." Bruton said that pragmatism and practicality had really created the Celtic Tiger: "Irish planners looked at the help-wanted ads overseas and looked where the interests were." Bruton told me, "I believe the IDA succeeded partly because they followed the U.S. sectors where employment was increasing and tried to get some of that to Ireland." An idea of "why not look for that help in Ireland" emerged. Not only was the Celtic Tiger not "dreamed up," but it also "stumbled and evolved" over time, he said. Of particular importance in this context was the unique character that Irish businesses themselves would bring to Ireland's changed perception in the world.

As Stephen Brennan (who now heads strategy and marketing for the Digital Depot, a cooperative of small and medium-sized software and computer companies based underneath the old Guinness windmill in the Liberties of Dublin) points out, Ireland was a major participant in a global "industrial revolution in software" for computers. This revolution would be central to the "new" nature of Ireland's place in the world and a sense of entrepreneurial spirit that emerged. By 2005, Ireland would be the world's number one exporter of software. Brennan, himself a PhD in physics, was a clear product of the advances in higher education in Ireland and reflected the fast-moving, highly innovative, and creative spirit at the core of the Celtic Tiger. Brennan, however, consistently emphasized to me the uniqueness of Irish talent in attracting major international investment that drove the Celtic Tiger in the 1990s. In particular, he said that its innovators had a unique "capacity of Irish to sell and market—with or without help from the Irish government." When Irish first started going overseas in the 1990s and traversing the networks of globalization, there would always be "a common reference point regarding the Irish." Whether in Asia or the United States, "there was always an image of the Irish in place—perhaps often stereotypical." What really got investors' attention, though, was the "surprising capacity of Irish to effectively make sales, and market to the world's largest companies." Just as importantly, Brian Caulfield noted that as an engineer in the 1980s, he found Ireland to be a "pretty desperate place." When he went abroad (to work for Siemens in the Netherlands), he and his Irish friends had a sense of "we can do this too." This kind of "self-confidence had been lacking," and the lack was replaced by a sense that "I'm as good," and "we can do this."

GREED CAME KNOCKING AT THE DOOR

In our meeting, Garret FitzGerald pointed out that the Celtic Tiger was moving along "reasonably well," though at a slower pace up to 2001. If, in 2001, Ireland had (now led by Fianna Fáil) been inclined to support a slower pace of economic growth, the Ireland of 2010 might not have been, as FitzGerald said succinctly, "a mess." That said, even during the height of the Celtic Tiger, Ireland faced serious underlying structural problems. While average per capita income was high, it was becoming increasingly difficult for Irish people to maintain their aspirations to wealth without incurring considerable personal debt. This became particularly true in the housing market, but also in terms of credit purchases, which banks were only too happy to allow. For large segments at the bottom of the economic ladder, poverty grew, as did long-term unemployment for those without skills who were thus left behind by the new economy. As the friends of Fianna Fáil government leaders got rich in the banking and construction sectors, there was little interest in imposing regulations or taking economic measures to achieve slower growth. The foundations on which the Celtic Tiger had grown successfully in the 1990s were replaced by an emphasis on a loan and credit scheme that made Las Vegas casinos look like churches. Mortgage rates fell as low as 4 percent, and often zero-point loans were made with very little investigation into the people getting them. Rather than rent property, people bought—a lot. Much of that property was also being built outside cities in more rural areas—requiring more cars and other amenities. By 2000, house prices were, according to the *Times* (UK), "outpacing incomes and rents by more than five to one. Household debt as a percentage of GDP had jumped from 60 percent to almost 200 percent."

Across Irish society, people's value was seen increasingly in material terms, that is, how much money they had, how many properties they owned, and where they vacationed and how often. Even without being able to afford it, everyone had to have the next big thing. One could go into any household, rich or poor, and often find a high-resolution flat-screen TV probably worth about €2,000—this kind of thing was the new measure of status. I recall sitting in a pub in 2001 and watching Irish people sitting across a table texting each other, not talking. Ireland had become a highly productive and hard-working society—and was eager to enjoy that success. But it had also turned into a rat race with unchecked borrowing and unchecked spending in what became (as one person said to me) a "cult of money." The *Times* quoted a high-profile Irish lawyer named Gerald Kean as saying, "The Irish are welcoming people. Greed came knocking at our door. We welcomed it in, fed it, and let it stay. Then it started eating us up."

While many stories can be used to illustrate this—many told well by Fintan O'Toole and Shane Ross involving disgraced former head of Anglo Irish Bank Seán FitzPatrick—my own personal choice is a lawyer named Michael Lynn, who set up a massive property empire built on sand. According to the *Irish Voice*, by 2007, he was in personal debt of over €80 million to various banks and lending agencies. Lynn used multiple mortgages, willingly given by banks, to shore up existing mortgages—none of which were secured by real capital. His own house in Howth near Dublin (next door to the creators of *Riverdance*) cost €5.5 million in 2006 but was financed by three mortgages worth a combined €15 million. Rather than pay his debts or risk prosecution for fraud, Lynn fled the country—he is rumored to be somewhere in Brazil.

Efforts to refill the coffers ultimately had an adverse effect as some of Ireland's top artistic talent opted to leave the country rather than pay taxes. Ireland had long embraced arts and culture for its intrinsic value and as an economic gain. This was historically secured by allowing a tax exemption, giving artists a leg up when growing their careers. Realizing that this allowed some of Ireland's richest people to claim the artist exemption, the government agreed in 2007, after considerable debate, to an annual cap of €250,000 in tax-free income. As a result, U2, a group deeply identified with

Ireland and that arguably owes the people a debt of gratitude for decades of support, left the country with its publishing wing. By relocating to the Netherlands, U2 could avoid the 42 percent tax the band otherwise would have paid at home. While this cap would affect other well-known artists, including directors Jim Sheridan and Neil Jordan and performers like Enya and Van Morrison, most of Ireland's lost artist revenue stems from U2's decision to abandon its country in 2006.

U2 argued that much of the band's publishing income was earned outside Ireland, that any good business would seek the best tax deal, and that their members still paid personal taxes in Ireland. Still, the *Sunday Times* reported in July 2010 that top-earning artists working to escape the tax were costing the country €30 million a year in revenue—with U2 accounting for most of that sum. U2's image on this score took a further hit when bassist Adam Clayton filed a lawsuit against his bank for allowing his personal assistant to withdraw over €4 million without permission from his personal accounts over a five-year period. Clayton argued in court that the Bank of Ireland should be held responsible for this because, he was quoted as saying in court, he "couldn't be bothered" to keep an eye on his own millions, the *Irish Times* reported on 6 July 2010. U2's well-honed image as campaigners against global poverty appeared to be missing a beat when it came to a sense of what the group's own country was going through. Bloomberg reporting on U2's decision to relocate in 2006 began, "Bono, the rock star and campaigner against Third World debt, is asking the Irish government to contribute more to Africa. At the same time he is reducing tax payments which could help fund that aid." Ironically, when U2 moved, poverty in Ireland was ranking among the highest in the developed world. By 2010, Ireland was reeling in economic catastrophe at a time when Adam Clayton "couldn't be bothered" to check his bank receipts. As for Bono, he fell uncharacteristically quiet, but one public statement in November 2007 gave away the limits of his concern when he said (attending a meeting of a government task force on famine in the underdeveloped world), "This country's prosperity (he chuckles) came out of tax innovation. So, it would be sort of, um, churlish, then to criticize U2 for doing what we were encouraged to do and what brought all these companies to Ireland in the first place." Bono went out of his way to praise Ireland's new leading "artist," Bertie Ahern (who's economic philosophy justified U2's abandonment of its people), at an event in 2008 on the anniversary of the Northern Ireland peace process. Bono said, "It's rare for a politician to be a great listener. . . . I think Bertie Ahern is a great listener." In early 2010, the Irish Revenue Commission approved an application from Ahern, a primary architect of Ireland's collapse, for an artist exemption for his autobiography. This was granted even though the rules for the exemption state clearly that it should not include biographies and autobiographies.

DUCK AND COVER

I recall sitting over a pint with a colleague at Oxford University in summer 2005 and discussing my worry about the Irish economy being too hot. I felt serious concern that people in Ireland seemed not to see the danger lurking. My prescient colleague said it would really take "only a relatively minor event" to send the Irish economy into a tailspin—"especially over property." A handful of observers in Ireland did see the problems inherent in Ireland's increasingly lame Tiger—and they specifically identified the primary problems as mainly internal among banks. One such mystic was David McWilliams, an economist who had once worked for Ireland's Central Bank. He early identified fundamental flaws in Ireland's property boom and argued that a new generation of Irish would have to pay for the excesses of the previous generation. McWilliams eventually became quite successful at turning his lectures into a one-person play at the Peacock Theater in Dublin in 2010.

In a 2009 presentation at Google headquarters in Dublin, David McWilliams pointed to two of the most serious flaws confronting Ireland: its low self-esteem and cultural avoidance of talking about serious problems. McWilliams suggested that Ireland did not now have the "self-esteem to go to our European partners and say, 'We are in real trouble.'" Meanwhile, "we are waiting for the cavalry to come over the hill," he said. "What has happened in Ireland is that the way we are going to deal with our past mistakes is—to make more of them." McWilliams told his audience of top innovators at Google that "in Ireland, we have a tradition here" of three phases when somebody comes up with a new or challenging idea. The first phase is "open ridicule. . . . You are undermined, besmirched, laughed at, and really held up to be a complete idiot." The second phase is "violent opposition to both you and the idea." The third phase is "universal acceptance"—after being ridiculed, and then violently opposed, in the third phase its "the taxi drivers . . . 'oh well, we all knew the property was going to fall.'" In a thick Dublin accent, McWilliams characterizes the third phase as being told, "Oh, Jay-zus, absolutely . . . you know, you thought you were on your own man—but I knew it—and so did all the maids down at the [inn]."

Another early-warning signal came from University College Dublin economics professor Morgan Kelly, who accurately predicted the collapse of the housing market and deep recession in 2006. Kelly used modeling to show that Ireland was on the verge of a 40 to 60 percent economic decline over a period of nearly a decade. He was harshly criticized at the time as "Dr. Doom" and accused of creating self-fulfilling prophecies for Ireland. McWilliams and Kelly were attacked because they directly challenged the classic Irish trait of putting on the blinders and pulling the veil down over those issues that "we just don't talk about." Only when their predictions became painfully true did the ridicule stop (though, of course, in 2007 Taoiseach Bertie Ahern had publically suggested that people like McWilliams and Kelly should commit suicide). By 2009, Kelly's warnings became increasingly dire about the long-term consequences of Celtic Tiger excesses. He wrote in the *Irish Times* on 29 December 2009, "By 2015 we will have seen what happens when jobs disappear forever. . . . Ireland is at the start of an enormous, unplanned social experiment on how rising unemployment affects crime, domestic violence, drug abuse, suicide and a litany of other social pathologies."

By 2001, Garret FitzGerald told me, Ireland had "lost its competitiveness." By 2006, Morgan Kelly was asserting, "We have spent the last five years learning to believe that exports and competitiveness do not matter, and that we can get rich by selling houses to each other. We are likely to spend a painful few years as we unlearn that lesson." In the fall of 2008, Ireland ran into a perfect storm of the global economic crisis fueled by financial mismanagement in the United States and a near total collapse of the Irish banking system. There was an initial sense that Ireland was a victim of the severe economic crisis rippling through the global economy. While there was an impact, Ireland was less vulnerable at this stage to a decline in foreign direct investment because in 2001 it had shifted its growth priority to lending, property, and construction. Independent studies have since confirmed that Ireland's problems were unique and mostly home-grown—generated by bad policy, weak regulation, and unethical behavior by bankers and politicians. As the *New York Times* noted on 18 March 2010, Irish banks had, by 2008, built up 2.5 times the country's GDP in loans and investments that "pushed the frontier in terms of reckless lending." The *Irish Times* editorial of 10 June 2010 summarized the results of independent expert analysis of the Celtic Tiger crash, asserting that these reports "conclude that our problems were largely home-grown and distinct from the international credit crunch. The Government's contribution came through a shift to cyclically-sensitive taxes, a narrowing of the tax base and growing uncompetitiveness, even as State spending rose sharply. The outcome amounted to a slow-motion train crash as the property bubble burst; the banks became insolvent and Government entered a period of deep denial."

Seemingly overnight the personal toll on the Irish people grew daily. In January 2010, the *Irish Times* noted that retail sales in Ireland had fallen by 8.2 percent in fall 2009 compared to the same period of 2008. In February 2010, RTÉ reported that in some occupations unemployment had reached around 30 percent, with people in the construction industry hardest hit. As many as 50 percent of Ireland's architects were unemployed, and some construction workers said they would work for free if it meant getting possible future contracts. Stories of lawyers and engineers driving taxis abounded. In February 2010, the *Irish Independent* reported that three businesses a day had gone bust in Ireland during the previous month, and 200 percent more companies had gone into receivership in January alone. Of these, 33 percent were in the construction industry. By April 2010, the *Irish Times* reported that the number of Irish companies in liquidation had risen by 34 percent in the first quarter of 2010 compared to the previous year, and retail insolvencies had increased by 171 percent. In March 2010, the *Irish Independent* reported that more than twenty-eight thousand homeowners were at least three months behind in mortgage payments and that €5.3 billion was owed in total mortgages in arrears for more than 90 or 180 days. Earlier in the year, the *Irish Independent* reported that as many as three hundred thousand homes were sitting empty. By April 2010, the *Irish Independent* reported that up to 170,000 homeowners were in negative equity. They owed more on their houses—and in many cases much more—than the houses were now worth.

The economic rise and fall would leave other scars on society besides empty houses and unemployed Irish. Despair ran high for many. As David Mellon of the Irish Property Council told the *Sunday Independent* in March 2010, "We are talking about people who invested in property, people who earned their livelihood from it in many forms; builders, plasterers, plumbers, developers and large and small investors. . . . They are now facing financial disaster, bankruptcy and destitution. . . . There are teachers, police, lawyers all caught in the crossfire. They are in a suffocating despair." The *Sunday Independent* reported that at least twenty-nine suicides could be directly linked to the housing crisis in Ireland. In 2008, Ireland saw a 24 percent rise in the annual rate of suicide. Long a difficult issue for Irish to confront, suicide was a leading cause of death among Irish under age thirty (especially among men) even during the Celtic Tiger, and it increased with the collapse of the economy.

Although, by comparative standards, Ireland is a very safe place, the country witnessed a substantial rise in violent crime both during and after the Celtic Tiger. Organized criminal gangs had become a serious issue in major cities—especially Dublin and Limerick. Between 1998 and 2008, Ireland saw a 32 percent increase in homicides with firearms. The number of gun killings in Ireland is five times higher than in England. At the core of much of this violence was a major spike in illegal drug activity in the country, in terms of both trafficking through Ireland and personal consumption. A police official told me that cocaine had become the "drug of choice" in Ireland and was "ravaging society." According to a report aired on the RTÉ program *Prime Time* in December 2007, an investigation they conducted revealed traces of cocaine in 90 percent of toilets tested in clubs, pubs, and workplaces. The situation regarding crime was certain to get worse as the economy continued its downward spiral. Budget cuts—particularly in police operations, including a cut of 50 percent in the operating budget for addressing organized crime in early 2011—would pose a significant problem.

Some parts of the Irish population left behind by the Celtic Tiger actually did not take the big hits that came with its collapse. Places like Finglas in west Dublin were working-class areas before, during, and after the Celtic Tiger. I went to a pub in Finglas one Saturday night in summer 2010 and quickly noticed an authenticity that reminded me of Ireland in the 1980s. People were making the most of the evening—especially enjoying the live music, which was outstanding. As is often the case, strangers here are sized up especially quickly—and I did not help my case. I had come from Howth, by the sea, and walked in wearing my T-shirt, shorts, and sandals. I was quickly "noticed" as an outsider and got the stares of the room. Thankfully, I knew a member of the band that was playing, and he saved me, pointing out that I was an "American tourist who had gotten lost and ended up in Finglas!" With that, one of the toughest-looking fellows in the pub came over and said, "Ah, well sure, that explains everything. How are ye?" We then had a great night of music, dance, and fun.

Finglas seemed to reflect much of the Ireland I had come to know in the 1980s. As we had walked into the pub early that evening, however, the bar staff were cleaning up glass off the floor. A funeral gathering held there that afternoon had turned into a massive brawl. This was not something I remembered from the 1980s. Heading home, our taxi driver told us a story of how earlier in the year he had witnessed a fellow, who had just been released from jail, killed up the road—shot to death in the head right in front of our driver. Finglas would see its share of murders and gangland killings, but in reality all of Ireland witnessed a dramatic rise in violent crime. In the 1980s you might hear of one or two killings a year, and it would be national news when it happened. Now, it was a weekly—sometimes daily—headline. By summer 2010, stabbings and shootings were occurring in broad daylight even in Dublin's city center—leading to large public showings of police forces. In the country, home invasions and murders of pensioners were not unusual. In August 2010, a twelve-year-old girl was shot to death in west Dublin by an eighteen-year-old boy.

I asked Father Ciarán O'Carroll, a senior priest in the Dublin archdiocese, for a sense of perspective on the growing violence in the culture. He said that at the "street level, we have lost focus on big moral questions." Father O'Carroll became deeply animated, clearly upset, when he pointed out that not far from his parish on St. Stephen's Green, "a guy had been stabbed recently up the road—in broad daylight! He died there on the street!" Father O'Carroll pointed out that "while there was a thousand people there, for twenty minutes there was no police or help." I was especially interested to speak with Father O'Carroll, a thoughtful and forward-looking priest, after reading a public talk he gave in 2007 in which he said, "Our country has witnessed an unprecedented increase in wealth over the past decade. Increased prosperity has brought many blessings. Sadly peace is not one of them. We have witnessed this past year a frightening and shocking increase in murders and gangland killings in our city and country. The number of such gang related murders reached over twenty this past year. Such violence, as our president noted in a recent interview, is 'a hideous and ugly development.'" "There is no true peace," Father O'Carroll asserted, "in a city where a twenty-two-year-old woman is shot dead at a party in north Dublin as happened last March—when a twenty-four-year-old was murdered here in June apparently 'by mistake,' where a Latvian immigrant is shot dead at the door of her home in Swords while her children sleep upstairs, where an apprentice plumber is killed by gunmen out to murder a suspected drug dealer."

WE ARE SEEING AN ECONOMIC
STABILIZATION, AND GROWTH AS WELL

These words about "economic stabilization" and "growth" came in early September 2010 from Finance Minister Brian Lenihan, who had walked Ireland through deep budget cuts and a major bailout of its insolvent banks—leading in November 2010 to a request for an EU and International Monetary Fund rescue plan worth €85 billion. At this point, however, not only Ireland was paying attention—so was the world. Ireland had earned international praise for tough budget cuts thought to differentiate the country from Greece (which had required a massive EU bailout in early 2010 as its economy collapsed). Irish economist Morgan Kelly warned, however, on 22 May 2010 in an editorial in the *Irish Times* that Ireland's situation was actually worse than Greece's because "unlike Greece, our woes do not stem from government debt, but instead from the government's open-ended guarantee to cover the losses of the banking system out of its citizens' wallets." Kelly pointed out, "Between developers, businesses, and personal loans, Irish banks are on track to lose near 50 billion [euro] if we are optimistic (and more likely closer to 70 billion), which translates into a bill for the taxpayer of over 30 percent of GDP."

Kelly reminded readers that in Ireland the tax scheme to attract foreign direct investment meant that the tax base for the government had to be measured in terms of gross national product (GNP) and not gross domestic product. "While for most countries the two measures are the same," he wrote, "in Ireland GDP is a quarter larger than GNP. This means our optimistic debt to GDP forecast of 115 percent translates into a debt to GNP ratio of 140 percent, worse than where Greece is now." Kelly projected that the likeliest endgame was that Ireland would have to make a deal with the European Central Bank to buy out its debt entirely and provide emergency funds to Irish banks "in return for our agreeing a schedule of reparations of

5–6 percent of national income over the next few decades." Repaying these reparations, Kelly projected, would "take singeing cuts in spending and social welfare, and unprecedented tax rises. A central part of our 'rescue' package is certain to be the requirement that we raise our corporate taxes to European levels, sabotaging any prospect of recovery as multinationals are driven out."

Summer 2010 in Ireland was lovely. June was one of the warmest and sunniest in memory. On the surface, the country was moving along—despite the continued warnings of David McWilliams, Morgan "Doom" Kelly, and others. Unfortunately, however, despite Brian Lenihan's protestations that the situation was stable, international observers were taking closer note of the goings on in Ireland. The international worry was initially that Ireland might have serious but contained problems. Then the concern became that Ireland could spark a contagion in Europe that would have a major impact on the global economy. On 31 August 2010, the *New York Times* ran a feature story on the Irish crisis beginning with a question: "Can one bank bring down a country?" The *New York Times* drew attention to the struggles of Anglo Irish Bank, which was receiving a bailout from the Irish government that equaled about 22 percent of the GDP of the entire nation. The *New York Times* quoted Peter Mathews, an independent banking and real estate consultant in Dublin, as describing what happened in Anglo Irish Bank in a raised voice of frustration: "It was mad—a credit cocaine run." He pointed to an industrial site in the Dublin Docklands that developers had paid €412 million for in 2006 and was now worth an estimated €20 million—if it could be sold at all.

In late August 2010, Standard & Poor's lowered Ireland's credit rating and announced its outlook was "negative" for the country, asserting that banking liabilities would make its 2012 debt-to-GDP ratio 113 percent. Within several weeks, international lending agencies had reacted as the relative costs for Ireland to borrow grew substantially. In September, the interest rate on Irish government ten-year bonds reached 6.7 percent, while credit-default swaps on Irish banks rose dramatically. The Irish government had hard capital assets, especially in some multinational holdings, that it could sell off to provide temporary reassurance to markets. But the depth of Ireland's crisis clearly now entailed much more than the "ebbs and flows" of the market, as Taoiseach Brian Cowen told the *Irish Times* on 7 September 2010. Meanwhile, Brian Lenihan's admonition that the Irish economy was stable seemed at this point to be more wishful thinking than serious economic analysis.

In spring of 2009, some American economists had already begun to look with concern at Ireland. Nobel Prize–winning economist Paul Krugman wrote in the *New York Times* on 19 April 2009 that the worst thing that could happen to the American economy was that "America could turn

Irish." Krugman noted that Ireland's problems were, to a large extent, the consequences of the kinds of deregulation and governmental indifference to markets that had also brought the United States to its economic crisis. The Irish crisis was quite similar to the unregulated mortgage experience of bankers in the United States. Krugman wrote, "One part of the Irish economy that became especially free was the banking sector, which used its freedom to finance a monstrous housing bubble. Ireland became in effect a cool, snake-free version of coastal Florida." Ireland's guaranteeing bank solvency was, Krugman pointed out, likely to put the Irish people "on the hook for potential losses of more than twice the country's GDP, equivalent to $30 trillion for the United States." He suggested nearly a year and half before the problem became apparent to everyone, "The combination of deficits and exposure to bank losses raised doubts about Ireland's long-term solvency, reflected in a rising risk premium on Irish debt and warnings about possible downgrades from ratings agencies."

Also writing in the *New York Times* on 2 September 2010, Peter Boone and Simon Johnson warned about the growing risk of contagion from Ireland's perilous position. Peter Boone is an associate of the Center for Economic Performance at the London School of Economics, and Simon Johnson is an economist at the Massachusetts Institute of Technology and formerly the chief economist at the International Monetary Fund. They pointed out that by late summer 2010, "roughly one-third of the loans on the balance sheets of major banks are nonperforming or 'under surveillance'; that's an astonishing 100 percent of gross national product, in terms of potentially bad debts." They concluded that Ireland would have a debt worth €26 billion, "or one-fifth of Ireland's national income, coming due in the month of September alone." Meanwhile, they showed that the government budget deficit was also at 15 percent of GNP, which was falling. Especially problematic for Ireland was that roughly 25 percent of its GDP was coming from multinational corporations that had set up headquarters in Ireland as tax havens but contributed little back to the economy as "ghost corporations." As a result, while some foreign direct investment helped Ireland's GDP grow in early 2010, in reality, when measured in terms of GNP, the economy actually shrank. Boone and Johnson warned, "Ireland, simply put, appears insolvent under plausible scenarios with current policies." Even worse, these economists projected the growing burden would be deeply painful for average Irish people. They concluded, "We estimate each Irish family of four will be liable for 200,000 euros in public debt by 2015. There are only 73,000 children born into the country each year, and these children will be paying off debts for decades to come—as well as needing to accept much greater austerity than has already been implemented. There is no doubt that social welfare systems, health care, and education spending will decline sharply."

Further illustrating increased international focus on Ireland in late summer 2010, Neil Shah of the *Wall Street Journal* wrote on 8 September 2010, "Ireland is rapidly losing the confidence of traders in the market for derivatives called credit-default swaps. . . . The cost of insuring Ireland's government debt against the risk of default, using these swaps, jumped to a record Wednesday, suggesting investors are more worried than ever about Ireland defaulting." Shah noted that on the day he wrote, it was costing $401,000 per year to insure $10 million in Irish debt for five years. The day before, it had been $382,000. Shah showed that the risk of contagion was high as "concerns about the health of Europe's banking system have unleashed a wave of risk aversion that is engulfing other countries on Europe's fringe too." As the American economy remained in low gear, there was little hope for further growth in Ireland due to increasing economic growth elsewhere. Worse, future growth would likely, for a generation, go to paying off Ireland's debt. If this was not enough to put anyone who cared off their lunch, the World Economic Forum released its *Global Competitiveness Report 2010/2011* in mid-September 2010. The report ranked Ireland twenty-ninth for global competitiveness—not an entirely bad ranking, actually. However, this decline from the previous year was attributed to "a weakening macroeconomic environment as well as continuing concerns related to financial markets." The measure of "macroeconomic stability" dropped from seventh in 2008 to forty-fifth in 2009 to ninety-fifth in the 2010 report. Most disconcerting was that Ireland ranked dead last—number 139 of 139 ranked in the world—in the category of "soundness of banks."

GRAFTON STREET IN NOVEMBER, WE TRIPPED LIGHTLY ALONG THE LEDGE

These lyrics from the haunting song "Raglan Road" evoke an imagery of Ireland, on Grafton Street in Dublin, that still can be found. However, Ireland had, by November 2010, at least one foot over the ledge of economic ruination. Grafton Street still bustles with tourists and locals enjoying themselves—but not many who are spending money. The Celtic Tiger generated retail rental costs on Grafton Street on par with Fifth Avenue in New York or with Paris and London's poshest shopping areas. One of the most staid storefronts, West of Grafton Street (a jeweler that once made watches for Queen Victoria) closed in early 2010. The *Irish Independent*, on 31 January 2010, quoted a jeweler who had worked there for forty-six years as saying, "We are a dinosaur. Grafton Street just doesn't attract our type of clientele anymore. Our customers were the discreetly wealthy and they are gone now." The story quoted the owner of Korky's shoe store, whose rent was €445,000 a year for a nine-hundred-square-foot shop. He said, "It should be our Bond Street, our Fifth Avenue, but look at it. Convenience Stores with jokey post cards on stands outside the shop, empty premises, and a proliferation of mobile phone shops. The pavement should be ripped up and they should start again. It just looks so grubby." Korky's was losing €5,000 a week. *Irish Times* columnist Fintan O'Toole wrote on 31 August 2010, "We know that, roughly from 2002 to 2008, we were in a long dream. We were in this weirdly hyper-real place, saturated with Day-Glo colors and animated by feverish distortions. In the way of dreams, contradictions simply coexisted. Everything speeded up to a frantic and frenetic blur. But at the same time, things seemed to float around in a dazed weightlessness." O'Toole ended his column with an admonition: "The cost of pretending that we have the money to throw into this black hole will be the destruction of all sense of decency in our society. We've already lost this war—let's stop throwing our last troops at the machine guns for the sake of an increasingly deluded sense of national pride. This time, let's actually wake up."

The statue in Merrion Square of Michael Collins, who led Ireland to its independence and was killed by assassins in 1922 during the Irish Civil War—in which the two historically dominant political parties had their origins. In 2011, this primacy was challenged by the emergence of a strong Labour Party. In the 2011 election a new government of a Fine Gael and Labour coalition came to power.

3

Waiting in the Long Grass

IF THERE IS GOING TO BE CHAOS,
AT LEAST LET IT BE ORGANIZED

This quote about organized chaos, which I attribute to my late father-in-law, Matt Madigan, has always served me well in a range of situations—especially loading cars full of children. Matt Madigan had his fingers on the pulse of Ireland as a detective in the Dublin police force and later a consulting detective working on corporate fraud investigation. Matt and I burned many a candle through the night, talking all things Ireland and beyond. He had a passion for life and a fascination for the world that was quintessentially Irish. His idea of "organized chaos" always struck me as a logical way to think about politics. This chapter explains how the collapse of the Celtic Tiger transformed Irish politics. The government, led by Fianna Fáil, would struggle with crisis management. The previously small Labour Party would emerge as the most popular party in Ireland for a time in mid-2010. Both Labour and Fine Gael would lie "waiting in the long grass" to see what might emerge and who might lead Ireland for the future. Meanwhile, the traditionally very small Sinn Féin party was, by 2011, polling almost equal to Fianna Fáil. Moreover, an innovative movement of independent thinkers began to gravitate around a loosely affiliated New Ireland movement, inspired in part by the economist David McWilliams. The harsh realities were, however, that while the Taoiseach, Brian Cowen, was forced to call a general election in early 2011, by 2010 the economic crisis in Ireland had grown so deep, it might not even matter who led as Ireland's fate was no longer in its own hands. After the country agreed to an EU and International Monetary Fund bailout, there were very few remaining policy levers that any Irish government could pull.

ECONOMIC TREASON

In March 2010, one of the most dramatic events in a parliamentary debate since those which preceded the Irish civil war occurred. Labour Party leader Éamon Gilmore accused Taoiseach Brian Cowen of "economic treason" against the country. Discussing the decision taken by Cowen's Fianna Fáil government to guarantee the assets in Irish banks in fall 2008, Gilmore said, "I believe, Taoiseach, that that decision was made to save the skins of a number of individuals—some of whom are connected to Fianna Fáil. . . . If my belief is correct, and I have not been convinced to the contrary, then that decision was an act of economic treason." A shell-shocked and emotional Cowen responded, "I will not be accused, frankly, of seeking to cause treason to my country. I find that beyond the pale. And, I'd never come into this house and accuse another Irishman of what you accuse me." When the leader of Fine Gael, Enda Kenny, jumped into the action, he noted that, as Taoiseach, Cowen had attended a private dinner with some of the key bankers who had so badly damaged Ireland while he was also serving as minister of finance. "Did you ask questions that a good minister for finance should ask in respect of what was a situation clearly beginning to spiral out of control?" queried Kenny. Cowen retorted, "I don't accept the contentions made by Mr. Kenny and I treat them with contempt." Kenny did not miss a beat: "That's precisely the problem, you also treat the citizens of this country with contempt." In early 2011, news broke that Finance Minister Brian Cowen had indeed had meetings with the leadership of Anglo Irish Bank and a central banking official after playing golf. Gilmore repeated his assertion, saying on 12 January, "If your Government knew that Anglo Irish Bank was insolvent and you asked the Irish people, the Irish taxpayers, to bail it out and to pay the cost we are now paying for it, that was, and is, economic treason. I stand over that."

Given Ireland's bloody past of civil war, an assertion of treason certainly caught people's attention. In the Irish Constitution, treason only includes levying war against the state. Nonetheless, the political impact of the charge was serious. As one Labour Party activist from south Dublin stressed to me, "You know what happens in Ireland to people who commit treason?" In the old days—as in before the 1990s—treason could bring the death penalty. The Constitution was amended in 1992 to limit punishment to life in prison with no parole before forty years. Still, Éamon Gilmore's comment captured the mood of the country and sent a shock wave through Irish politics. While Fianna Fáil would seemingly have little hope in the next general election in 2011, conventional wisdom suggested that the other major party, Fine Gael, would be the beneficiary. Yet, a June 2010 survey conducted by the *Irish Times* showed that the most popular political party in Ireland was Labour. In the poll, Labour held 33 percent of public support compared to Fine Gael's 28 percent. Fianna Fáil registered just 17 percent support. While subsequent polls would show Fine Gael holding its own against Labour, this initial showing of popularity was a historical first for Ireland's Labour Party. Éamon Gilmore's personal popularity stood at 46 percent compared to 24 percent for Enda Kenny and 18 percent for Brian Cowen. Though not necessarily a harbinger of the future, this snapshot reflected a sea change in the Irish political landscape. A survey published by the *Irish Independent* in February 2010 had already indicated growing national frustration. It showed that 79 percent of the Irish public was either "not at all satisfied" or "not very satisfied" with the way the government was handling the country's crisis. Only 12 percent approved. An overwhelming 91 percent favored criminal prosecutions against individuals in the banking sector who might be found to have skirted the law.

The new Labour position in Ireland revealed a growing sense that the dominant two-party system of government no longer worked. The two major parties, Fianna Fáil and Fine Gael, had their main lines of cleavage not over ideology but rather over the civil war politics of the 1920s. Fianna Fáil (which means "Soldiers of Destiny") has been Ireland's largest and most popular party. It came out of the Irish civil war with a strong business and rural backing combined with Irish nationalism. Established in 1926 and dominated for decades by Éamon de Valera, the party was also identified with the civil war sentiment that Ireland should be united and not have negotiated its own Republican identity absent the counties of Northern Ireland. De Valera's deep political impact is told in Clare legend. When de Valera reportedly came campaigning, he asked a local man for his vote. Not recognizing the Fianna Fáil leader, the man told de Valera something akin to, "No, I vote for no one but Dev." Fine Gael (which means "Tribe of the Irish") had its origins in the political leadership that backed the treaty negotiated by Michael Collins and others with Britain. These major cleavages divided the two parties for generations. Fianna Fáil emerged as somewhat "center left" and Fine Gael somewhat "center right," but each had its more conservative and liberal elements. Fianna Fáil leaders alienated some economic conservatives who bolted (in opposition to Charles Haughey as leader of Fianna Fáil) in 1985 to create the Progressive Democrats and in support of socially liberal and economically free market policies. The Progressive Democrats disbanded in 2009 after some minimal success in electoral politics. Meanwhile, Fine Gael would also go through periods of transition with a tilt toward European social democratic views under Garret FitzGerald's leadership and a fiscally conservative approach under John Bruton.

What made the Irish political system unique is that the country did not, in fact, have major ideological differences. Typically, the political parties converged on key issues ranging from social welfare to the reforms that underpinned the Celtic Tiger. As issues like divorce, gay rights, or peace in Northern Ireland gained public support, the parties incorporated these into their worldviews. Nonetheless, Fianna Fáil would become the party most closely associated with economic catastrophe. Fianna Fáil was especially identified as having close relationships to rogue bankers and as failing to pursue bank regulation. Still, Finance Minister Brian Lenihan pointed out in a debate over "no confidence" in the Cowen government in June 2010, Fine Gael leaders had banker friends too. In February 2011, Fine Gael won the election to form a new government, and Fianna Fáil was routed.

THE CELTIC CHERNOBYL

I knew that I had reached a point of personal confidence in discussing Irish politics while watching an RTÉ retrospective on Éamon de Valera in a pub. Someone said, "De Valera—there's the father of our nation." I turned quickly and inquisitively—some might say boldly—and said, "But wait, I thought Michael Collins was the father of the nation." It was obvious I was messing around, and everyone quickly enough nodded and said, "Yes, indeed, Mick it was—the Big Fella." Even Éamon de Valera famously said in 1966, "It's my considered opinion that in the fullness of time history will record the greatness of Collins and it will be recorded at my expense." In August 2010, nearly one hundred years after the 1916 Easter Rising, a leading Irish politician said, "The spirit of Collins is the spirit of the nation." That politician was Brian Lenihan. In August 2010, the annual commemoration of the death of Michael Collins held in West Cork made history by inviting Lenihan to speak. He was the first ever Fianna Fáil official to orate at this event traditionally associated with Fine Gael. Lenihan said, "If today's commemoration can be seen as a further public act of historical reconciliation, at one of Irish history's sacred places, then I will be proud to have played my part." He went on, appealing for national unity in the face of crisis, saying, "In meeting challenges and seizing opportunities, the Irish people have shown their courage, determination and creativity—just as Michael Collins and his comrades and colleagues did in the campaign for independence and in the establishment of our State." Michael Collins was, Lenihan said, "an astute politician; a man of extraordinary organizational and administrative ability; a pragmatist who believed he could over time bring Ireland total independence; a driven, ambitious man who was born to be a leader."

Especially noteworthy was Lenihan's description of Collins as "a man of energy and action." These words could accurately be applied back to Brian Lenihan. The son of a prominent Irish politician by the same name, Lenihan had emerged from the crash of the Celtic Tiger a "man of energy and action" in the face of deep economic and personal crises. He had served as minister for children from 2002 to 2007 and thus did not have his fingers dirty with banks when he inherited the finance portfolio in 2008. Hence, he received early latitude in public opinion while generating policies to steer Ireland through rough economic seas. Adding further to this challenge was Lenihan's diagnosis in late 2009 with serious pancreatic cancer. At times, Lenihan would look haggard, weak, even gravely ill in his public appearances. Yet, he remained steadfast in his commitment to stay on the job and to engage in some of the most difficult choices a minister of finance could make. Lenihan's illness also served as a tragic symbol of the challenge facing society in that (as a senior politician I interviewed stated off the record) "the one person who has the courage to take tough measures for the country is very ill, and really should not be in the job."

Brian Lenihan reassured the country and kept up his routine—never complaining about the difficult toll that both the job and his illness had to be taking. One of the first, highly dramatic actions taken in response to the 2008 economic crisis was a decision orchestrated by Lenihan to guarantee unilaterally all of the assets in Irish banks. As the global economy crashed and Irish liquidity disappeared overnight, Fianna Fáil leaders feared a massive run on the banks. A quick way to get capital into the banks was for Ireland to guarantee all assets in its banks worth a total in liabilities of €485 billion. Since, at the time, the total gross domestic product (GDP) of the Irish economy was €207.4 billion, this move assumed a radical level of risk. If these debts came due, who would pay? Ireland's move was unilateral, yet seemingly based on a theory that if they guaranteed the money in banks, external capital would flow in, thereby financing the promise to guarantee the money. Implicit in this theory was an apparent assumption that, if push came to shove, Europe would bail out the insolvent country.

This bank guarantee decision was followed by a medium-term plan to provide stabilization investments to capitalize Ireland's failed banks. Fianna Fáil approved a plan to create the National Asset Management Agency (NAMA). The Irish government planned to use its capital to provide coverage for bad assets, loans, land, property, and so forth, while banks would restructure. The overall goals, according to NAMA, were to "provide the banks with a clean bill of health," "strengthen their balance sheets," "reduce uncertainty over bad debts," and "ensure the flow of credit to individuals and businesses." The goal was a massive government- (i.e., taxpayer-) backed infusion of money into the private banking sector to stabilize the economic situation. Two major problems emerged. First, no one really knew just how bad it was in the banks. Second, the most insolvent, Anglo Irish Bank, was in no position to pay this money back—ever. To the amazement of most Irish people, Anglo Irish Bank is not even really a bank in the traditional sense—it had no ATMs or deposits; it was just a shell of mortgage and credit holdings. Nonetheless, the International Monetary Fund praised NAMA as an important step providing near-term economic stabilization. By fall 2010, when the NAMA plan was supposed to end, it was still unclear how much the bank bailout was going to cost the Irish taxpayer. Irish banks continued to lose money through that summer. An estimate in the *Irish Times* from 2 April 2010 put the likely projected total cost as high as €82.875 billion. The *Irish Independent* reported that same month that Goodbody Stockbrokers estimated that this would be the third most expensive bank bailout in all of history. Only South Korea and Japan had faced bigger banking failures in the history of banking collapse.

By September 2010, with the total cost of Anglo Irish Bank alone likely to be at least €35 billion, Brian Lenihan opted to split the bank into good and bad assets. The "bad" part, a "recovery bank," would either be sold or closed and would eventually be phased out. The other half, a "funding bank," would be owned by the Irish government. This was seen as a better option than the alternatives: fully funding an insolvent bank or closing it altogether. By 8 September 2010, however, the *New York Times* reported that Ireland was left with enough capital funds to maintain solvency only through the second quarter of 2011. The *New York Times* article quoted Daniel Gros of the Center for European Policy Studies in Brussels as saying that if Ireland's banks "can't refinance themselves, then numbers get very big very quickly." Gros noted that loans to the Irish banks from the European Central Bank were now about 40 percent of Ireland's GDP. He added, "I think things are going to get worse. . . . And, over time, the E.C.B. will have to refinance a very large part of the Irish banking system."

Two years later the decision to guarantee the banks was looking increasingly dubious. On 18 July 2010, the *Sunday Independent* ran a detailed story based on formal documentation regarding decision making at the time of the bailouts in fall 2008. The paper's summary showed that the decision to guarantee the banks was "made under great pressure, based on limited information, which turned out to be wrong." At the time of the decision, the estimated losses to cover in Anglo Irish Bank were said to be just €8.5 billion—at least three to four times less the actual final amount. At one key meeting in September 2008, a regulator told several senior ministers, including Brian Lenihan, there was an apparent consensus that there was "no evidence to suggest Anglo is insolvent on an ongoing basis." Merrill Lynch, brought in as a consultant to the government (for a total of four days of investigation and advice on 24 to 28 September 2008), advised that Ireland faced "the worst credit crisis ever." Merrill Lynch specifically advised the government that a blanket guarantee of the banks "was the worst thing that could be done—accelerating trouble for all other institutions." Instead, the *Irish Times* reported on 17 July 2010 that Merrill Lynch advised that Ireland should offer up a €20 billion emergency lending fund. Merrill

Lynch specifically warned against a blanket guarantee, which it forecasted could rise in excess of €500 billion. This would "almost certainly negatively impact the State's sovereign credit rating and raise issues as to its credibility." Furthermore, the report quoted Merrill Lynch as saying, "the wider market will be aware that Ireland could not afford to cover the full amount if required." To be fair, Merrill Lynch did indicate there was "no right or wrong" answer—only that it would be worse to do nothing and let a bank fail. Ireland paid Merrill Lynch over €7 million for subsequent advice over a ten-month period to follow—and a total of €34 million to outside consultants on the banking crisis. Amazingly, Merrill Lynch was a major actor in the housing market collapse in the United States and was eventually bought out, ravaged by scandal and collapse, by Bank of America.

Another pillar of the Fianna Fáil policy was to introduce substantial budget austerity via massive cuts in public spending. In autumn of 2008, the Special Group on Public Service Numbers and Expenditure Programmes was established, soon known as the An Bord Snip Nua—the cutting board, in effect. This group was charged to suggest major spending reductions across the public sector. The group, headed by economist Colm McCarthy, made recommendations in July 2009 that would cover €5.3 billion in government budget savings, to include 17,300 public service job cuts and a 5 percent cut in social welfare spending. This would also include cutting child benefit payments to families and scaling back educational programs. The education cuts were notable as they would include major staff and pay cuts, university-level staff cuts, cuts in funding to English-language support programs for immigrants, cuts in research-and-development programs, cuts in grants to private schools, merging small primary schools, cuts to school transportation, cuts to retraining programs, and overall staff cuts by 6,390. The number of police stations would be reduced by 50 percent nationwide. Health benefits, such as for dental, optical, and hearing devices, would also be reduced. Overall, health-care programs would also be reduced in size by 10 percent per year over three years. Individual payments for prescription drugs would increase, as would individual hospital charges. Costs for private facilities in hospitals would be increased by 20 percent. Every element of public-sector activity would be affected—from justice, police, immigration support, defense, and foreign affairs to support for arts, sports, and tourism.

These recommendations provided political cover for the government as it moved forward with brutal cuts. It also allowed opposition political parties to "wait in the long grass" while Fianna Fáil took deep political hits for the painful and sustained budget cuts. There was a basic reality, as former Taoiseach John Bruton said to me when we met in summer 2010. Bruton argued that in "every area—a nurse, teacher—we can be more productive. . . . We have to be able to do more with less to release resources."

He also noted the reality that, while cuts that reduce the budget "baseline for the long-term are worth making—those which take demand out of the economy are not." "What I am saying," said Bruton, "is that I prefer expenditure policy changes that reduce the expenditure baseline permanently and for the long-term, to changes that save cash in the short-term, but leave long-term liabilities unaffected." There was a particular concern in his assessment that Ireland risked taking "short-term costs without long-term impact." This would be especially true, he said, regarding pension growth relative to GDP over the next twenty years. As the *Irish Times* reported on 22 September 2010, the insurer Aviva estimates that each Irish person would have to save an additional €9,100 a year to meet existing expectations for retirement standard of living. Overall, Aviva forecasts a total gap in Ireland of €20 billion per year in the difference between expectations for retirement and what is actually being saved. Bruton, now out of politics, had the unique perspective of not speaking for his party, Fine Gael, but sharing only his own personal views. He identified the basic political choice that was so difficult: either to ask people to accept, across the board, equal cuts or to make the much "harder choice to make selective cuts in major areas of inefficiency." Furthermore, there was a serious dilemma in that the growing mood of the country was to pursue "guilty men for the collapse of the construction boom" in a way that would "discourage risk taking at a time when we need to be able to take risks." Popular desire for punishment in the "stockade would get the country nowhere." Nonetheless, the public sentiment was strong. As a union activist told me, "What we really need is to see those bankers tied up, in the stockade, right in front of Trinity College where we can pelt them with rotten fruit and vegetables."

There would be no pain-free path forward. Accordingly, in December 2009, the Fianna Fáil government announced a final budget plan that totaled €60 billion, cutting about €4 billion from the existing budget. This would be achieved by cutting public-sector salaries by between 5 and 15 percent and levying across-the-board spending cuts on health care, education, welfare, and social benefits. The *New York Times* quoted Brian Lenihan on 16 December 2009 as saying, "Further corrections will be needed in the coming years, but none as big as today's." By summer 2010, however, the Fianna Fáil government indicated that an additional €3 billion would have to be cut in the next year's budget. By fall that number was rising past €4 billion. Given the economic condition confronting Ireland by the end of 2010, this was only the beginning of the deep austerity that Ireland would confront, as the government was now considering a four-year, €15 billion package of cuts. The depth of the initially recommended cuts from An Bord Snip Nua and the December 2009 budget shocked public-sector employees and their related unions—especially police, nurses, and teachers. In April 2010, the government was thus able to frame negotiations held at Croke Park with major unions using an "either cut pay and benefits or lose jobs" approach. Meanwhile, unemployment skyrocketed, and the wage cuts and service-fee increases led to substantial deflationary pressures in Ireland—people stopped spending, and banks stopped lending. The situation grew starker as the darkness of winter descended in December 2010, as the Irish government formally announced its four-year plan to cut an additional €15 billion from the budget. Ireland entered 2011 on the cusp of possibly the steepest drop in national standard of living in modern history. As the fallout from NAMA and the cuts played out, the *Irish Independent* quoted economist Peter Bacon (who had been key to developing the NAMA concept) as giving the Anglo Irish Bank a new nickname—the "Celtic Chernobyl."

FIANNA FALLING

Fianna Fáil continued a dramatic decline through 2010 and into 2011 as it became apparent that the policy approach of guaranteeing insolvent banks that they had launched in Ireland was a monumental disaster. As one union official described the situation to me, "We wouldn't mind taking these hits if we had a sense that it was leading somewhere—but it just isn't. Our futures are being funneled into a black hole of banks." In June 2010, Fianna Fáil barely survived a no-confidence vote with its very small coalition partner, the Green Party, saving the government from having to call a new election. Being saved by a handful of Green Party TDs (in Ireland, a member of parliament is called a TD, for "Teachta Dalá") had the immediate effect of payback. Irish politicians spent the depth of the economic crisis in mid-2010 debating Green Party legislation to ban stag hunting using dogs. The irony of the politics would be difficult for Fianna Fáil, which had for decades positioned itself as the party of rural Ireland. Yet, now, as Deaglán de Bréadún wrote in the *Irish Times* on 14 September 2010, "The Fianna Fáil party is like a prisoner on death row who is facing the prospect of execution between now and the middle of 2012 but still hopes against hope that somehow or other this sentence will be commuted and maybe even a pardon granted."

The bulk of Fianna Fáil's problem hinged on its deep association with the collapse of the Irish banks and the policies that followed. However, some of it also had to do with a general appearance of incompetence. Nowhere was this light shown more—frequently unfairly—than on Mary Coughlan, the Tánaiste (deputy prime minister) and minister for education and skills in the Brian Cowen–led government. Coughlan had, during her years in government, produced and supported important policy initiatives. She also dealt successfully with challenges average people face, including having a deaf child and a husband who, as a police officer, lost a leg in an automobile accident. She has managed well the balance between being a professional woman and having a family.

Still, Mary Coughlan became more known as a gaffe-prone leader and attained the nickname "Calamity Coughlan." She once said, "IDA would be marketing Ireland as the innovation island—like Einstein explaining his theory of evolution." Needless to say, all things being relative, evolution belonged to Charles Darwin. She also said of Ireland, "We would like to revert back to the reputation we had, and continue to have"—blending time and space and relativity. I ran into my own interesting exchange with Coughlan in spring 2010 when I wrote to her in her capacity as minister to discuss the role of education and global competitiveness in Ireland. She kindly responded to me personally—but as to my question on the role of education, the minister of education and skills told me she thought that was a better question for the minister for foreign affairs. She kindly directed me to the website of the Irish Foreign Ministry to follow up. I certainly found it interesting that the minister for education and skills was responding to a question about the role of education in Ireland by suggesting I talk to the minister for foreign affairs. I joked to myself that perhaps the plan was to outsource education?

Writing in the *Sunday Times* on 21 February 2010, journalist and radio host Matt Cooper savaged the rise of Coughlan to positions of responsibility relative to the economy (at the time she was serving as minister for trade, enterprise, and employment, as well as Tánaiste). Cooper wrote, "She has neither the intellect nor the temperament for her two important roles and, were it not for the fact that she is a woman, I doubt she would have been given these jobs." He compared Coughlan to Sarah Palin in the United States, who, while sounding folksy and appealing, was out of her depth when it came to the substance of serious policy decisions. The gaffs could be easily forgotten. The problem was that Coughlan was, by 2010, a key leader who had to sell both at home and abroad what Ireland was trying to do to salvage its economy.

In a particularly damaging interview with the BBC given on 15 February 2010, she was harshly challenged by the host. Mary Coughlan seemed unable to launch a basic defense of Ireland's economic policies. Coughlan responded in platitudes, to the host's assertion that her government wore a "badge of shame." She seemed unwilling or unable to acknowledge the depth or nature of Ireland's crisis. She demonstrated no substantive understanding of the problem in the banking sector and the associated sovereign debt. She stated that "the structural economic problem we had was mainly on the basis of construction." Coughlan refused to address the issue of former head of Anglo Irish Bank Seán FitzPatrick's taking a more than €500,000 a year pension and the anger that was deepening among the Irish people.

She argued that the economy fell apart because all around Ireland there had been too much "exuberance." She would not address the challenge that corruption and wrongdoing were also at the core of the collapse. Coughlan was asked at the end of the interview about net emigration—the fact that Ireland's youth were again leaving the country in search of work. She said that the issue was arising because some people who had come to Ireland from eastern Europe had gone home. "Equally," she said, "we have a lot of people—young people—who have decided that they will go to other parts of the world to gain experience and I think the type of emigration—the type of people that have left have gone on the basis that some of them finally want to enjoy themselves—that's what young people are entitled to do." She added that it was "not a bad thing" that some of Ireland's best and brightest talents—PhDs—people with "greater talent, acumen, academically" have found work in other parts of the world.

Some of Mary Coughlan's troubles were generated by specific actions she took that led directly to the loss of high-skilled and high-paying jobs. In February 2010, the head of Ryanair, Michael O'Leary, lambasted Coughlan for the loss of five hundred engineering jobs that he had planned to create at Dublin Airport. A charismatic and extraordinarily successful Irish businessman, O'Leary created Ryanair as a no-frills, low-cost airline—Europe's largest. He too could be dismissed for some fairly wild ideas—for example, charging for use of toilets or having standing-room-only sections on flights. O'Leary also is a public denier of climate change, calling it "a load of bullshit." In one particularly bold move, he suggested in September 2010 that airlines should be allowed to remove a second pilot from the cockpit and instead train an air host or hostess to take over in an emergency. O'Leary went a bit too far for some with this idea, as it seemed to risk safety for profit. A senior Ryanair pilot and trainer based in Marseilles, Capt. Morgan Fischer, took the risk of publically criticizing his boss. In a letter sent to the *Financial Times* on 14 September 2010, Fischer wrote, "I would propose that Ryanair replace the chief executive with a probationary cabin crew member currently earning about 13,200 euro net a year." He added, "Ryanair would benefit by saving millions of euros in salary, benefits and stock options."

The point is that while it is easy for many to make light of Mary Coughlan, plenty of other important Irish leaders have had their own shining moments in the sun of calamity. Nevertheless, in a serious public-policy moment, in February 2010, Michael O'Leary released copies of his correspondence with Mary Coughlan over his proposals to push his rival Aer Lingus out of an empty hanger. He hoped that Ryanair could build its own aircraft-maintenance business there. This would have created an estimated five hundred top-skilled, well-paying jobs at Dublin Airport. O'Leary's only request was that Coughlan act as an intermediary with the Dublin Airport

Authority to negotiate the lease of the hanger, as he had previously had bad experiences with them. Coughlan refused to do this and apparently did not respond to regular inquiries from O'Leary. When she reluctantly did meet with him, the end result was a disaster. The previous year, over one thousand airport workers had been laid off. With this "nonintervention" by Mary Coughlan, they remained unemployed. Ryanair went ahead and built a new €10 million maintenance facility at Glasgow's Prestwick Airport with plans to open a second facility in a separate EU airport—not, however, in Ireland.

Alas, Fianna Fáil had a greater impediment in its leader, Brian Cowen. As indicated, I have personal regard for him. I met him briefly in Washington, DC, in March 2010. We chatted about Howth, and he jokingly advised keeping the developers out. Brian Cowen is friendly, earnest, and down-to-earth. His Achilles' heel strikes me as his having spent a lot of time running around after corrupt leaders and bankers before inheriting the position of Taoiseach. While his government's policies might not have done much to save Ireland from its economic catastrophe, it would be unfair to say that he did not work hard to do what could be done. On the other hand, it is also fair to say that as Ireland's crisis grew, his leadership skills were—at best—uninspired. Working hard and effectively leading a nation are, of course, two different things. By 2010, Brian Cowen had seemingly become more of a cartoon character than a leader. He had been depicted as the "nude Taoiseach" in paintings—unkempt and overweight, on the toilet and otherwise posing—hung by guerrilla artists in two national galleries in Dublin. Regrettably, many average Irish took to calling the Taoiseach "Biffo," meaning "Big Ignorant Fat Fucker from Offaly."

One of the most persistent criticisms of the Taoiseach was, as a senior civil servant said to me, "He isn't the greatest of communicators." This would often leave him widely exposed to ridicule. Thus, when Cowen appeared in an early-morning interview on RTÉ on 14 September 2010 and sounded "tired," critics pounced that he was either very hungover or actually drunk. A number of witnesses from a Fianna Fáil dinner the night before confirmed that he had, in fact, been out quite late but was only sipping on a few pints and enjoying a relaxing time. Still, a Fine Gael TD, Simon Coveney, "Tweeted" immediately on hearing the interview, "God, what an uninspiring interview by Taoiseach this morning. He sounded halfway between drunk and hungover and totally disinterested." Fianna Fáil colleagues acknowledged that Brian Cowen had sounded "hoarse" but no worse for the wear. The Taoiseach called the accusations that he was drunk or hungover "uncalled for" and said that politics had sunk to a "new low" in the country.

Brian Cowen had as much a right as anyone to enjoy a night out in his private time. However, it can also be said that he exercised bad judgment in agreeing to an early-morning interview afterwards. Martina Devlin, a commentator for the *Irish Independent*, put it well on 16 September 2010 when identifying the impact of the damage done by Cowen. "Thanks to him, we are a laughing stock internationally. He has resurrected the stereotype of the plastered Paddy at a time when we can least afford the humiliation, because we are under the microscope as never before." She added, "Internationally, we need to look stable; instead, our Taoiseach has made us look flaky. We need to look responsible; instead, our Taoiseach has made us look careless. We need to look dependable; instead, our Taoiseach has made us look wayward." The *Wall Street Journal* reported with some irony on 16 September that Cowen had particular problems articulating the following: "We've stabilized our situation. Our budgetary plans are on target."

The "drunken Taoiseach incident" prompted radio parodies and other fodder for comedians worldwide. On Dublin's 98FM, a parody of Steve Earle's classic recording of "Galway Girl" was sung with the lyric, "So we went out West for an old think tank—all day, all day, all day. . . . But to be honest wich ya lads, we just drank—all day, all day, all day. And I ask you friend—what's a Taoiseach to do—if he can't have a pint or 22? We stayed up all night until well after two—what does it matter 'cause the country's screwed." Foreign Minister Micheál Martin commented with understatement, "This is not good, the way it's playing out. . . . We clearly have to learn lessons from the entire event and how to move on." Missing in the humor over the Taoiseach was a key point made by the RTÉ host to Brian Cowen in the interview. The host summarized the situation confronting a young woman in Galway. She said, "I've no future as a result of what they've done. I've just graduated; I have no job prospects; I'm just wandering around the streets of Galway." This was Ireland's true hangover.

Recognizing the depth of the political difficulties that Fianna Fáil's problems presented to its electoral future, some leaders in early 2011, including Foreign Minister Micheál Martin, forced a leadership challenge to Brian Cowen. On 18 January, a secret ballot on a confidence motion reaffirmed Cowen's leadership as the party prepared for a general election. Martin asserted that the party's future was at stake and that its members had to ask, "Who can lead an effective, organized, and vibrant election campaign and then thereafter rebuild the party?" He added, "Our forefathers built this party. It has made a distinguished contribution to the country. It was involved in many significant milestones in education, European policy, the peace process and so forth. We owe it to ourselves, to the people who came before us and after us, to ensure that there is a vibrant Fianna Fáil party." Party members faced the reality that Martin was almost certainly right about their forthcoming electoral fortunes and their need to rebuild. On the other hand, they had stood together in bringing Ireland to where it was, and rejecting their approach now would validate criticisms of the party in government. Martin lost that round, but came out of the challenge with a new level of national respect for having pushed the issue and sought to get its members thinking anew about the party. Much more scathed, actually, was Brian Lenihan, who on the day of the secret ballot told a radio interviewer that he had not urged members to challenge Cowen for the leadership, a position directly rejected by members who said he had done precisely that. Most troubling for Fianna Fáil and its future, though, was a question that a television interviewer posed to Micheál Martin after he lost the leadership vote: "Does your party have a death wish?" In an extraordinary series of events, on Saturday, 22 January 2011, Brian Cowen announced in a press conference that he was standing down as leader of Fianna Fáil, though he would remain as Taoiseach through the election. The next day, the Green Party announced it was withdrawing from its coalition with Fianna Fáil, effectively ending its role in government and finally forcing an early election. On the day after Cowen announced his resignation as party leader, the *Sunday Independent* reported that Fianna Fáil had fallen to 8 percent in public approval. Soon thereafter, Micheál Martin emerged as the new party leader heading into elections—and Brian Cowen announced he would not stand, leaving politics for good. A new, uncharted era of Irish politics now awaited.

BUT ARE YOU HAPPY?

The former Speaker of the U.S. House of Representatives, Tip O'Neill, famously surmised that "all politics are local." In Ireland, as Garret FitzGerald said to me, "all politics are tribal." He added, Ireland has a "very odd system, tribal in nature, favoring localism." This can make it very difficult for the country to look past the very near term in planning. To FitzGerald, the "electoral system is a disaster." Senior Labour Party TD Ruairi Quinn put it to me that there is "no joined up thinking" in today's Ireland and that the country is "not working in holistic ways." Fianna Fáil would be gone from government after 2011. However, the real question on Irish people's minds was less who would lead but would it make a difference? Below the surface, the anxiety was intense and, at times, surreal. Riding into Dublin each morning on the commuter train, I often thought that everyone was moving around, but as if on a treadmill or a merry-go-round—moving, but going nowhere. Walk into a pub on a late afternoon and look around, and life seems grand. But watch the news bulletin come on the TV above the bar and see stories about the economy, and watch a room go silent—everyone is tuned in.

In this context the ascendency of Ruairi Quinn's Labour Party was a significant change to emerge in Irish politics with the collapse of the Celtic Tiger.

Quinn noted the deepening public sentiment that "we can't go back to business as usual"—which in Irish terms has meant a revolving door between Fianna Fáil and Fine Gael. Ruairi Quinn epitomizes the difficulty of developing effective long-term planning for the whole society as he has tried in creative and consistent ways. A well-regarded finance minister in John Bruton's coalition government, which rode the early wave of the Celtic Tiger, Quinn is colorful, charismatic, and very thoughtful while pulling no punches. Quinn's instincts follow his own professional background as an architect and town planner. He is the author of a memorable autobiography titled *Straight Left: A Journey in Politics* (2005). At the 2007 Labour Party conference, Ruairi Quinn stated, "After thirty years of Fianna Fáil's destructive and shortsighted economic approach . . . in 1997, it was Labour who balanced the budget. The first balanced budget in three decades was not the work of parties who feel it is their right to preach fiscal responsibility to us. In fact, it was ours—Labour can do better." Indeed, "during all the time that I was minister of finance, inflation was 2 percent or less. It has been consistently 4 percent and more under the two successive Fianna Fáil finance ministers." "A change is needed," said Quinn, "a change at every level of national government. We need to focus on solutions for people, not solutions for elections. We need to focus on the long-term prospects . . . not what will get us into August and into the tent at the Galway races." Ruairi Quinn was chosen in 2010 to serve as director of Labour's national effort to win seats in the next parliamentary elections. Labour's unmet goal was to win sixty-five seats and assume control of government in the 2011 general election. Though short, Labour's role in Irish politics was secured.

Quinn draws on his skills as an architect and the need for effective planning in both the near and long term. He also thinks big. When we met in Dublin in July 2010, Quinn and I spent a great deal of time talking about—of all things—China. "I'm not frightened by the rise of China," said Quinn. "I see them as future partners whom we will work with on our own terms." Quinn is outspoken on religion, having labeled Ireland as a "post-Catholic country" in the early 1990s. The key challenge facing Ireland is that the historically church-based emphasis on ethical issues "was not replaced." In fact, he said, "God was replaced with money during the Celtic Tiger years." Ireland has "no new ethical foundations." Quinn is also as Dublin as can be, referring to the Irish countryside not as "rural" but rather as "provincial Ireland." Quinn had his finger on the pulse of Ireland when asked why people were not out in the streets in protest. He noted the very real "shared consensus" in Ireland on the risks and realities of civil war and the desire for "unique social partnerships," having seen what real division can bring. Quinn also noted that the anger in Ireland was very real among the people. He said that "part of the anger is self-anger," driven by a "sense of regret of what could have been rather than what was." Quinn also spoke from real personal experience when he concluded the Irish health-care system has become an "unmanageable monster." "I am a graduate of cancer treatment and I can still remember, five years on, that extraordinary sense of total inner panic and fear that came right through me when my doctor said to me that one of the six samples tests which took place in Tallaght was cancerous," Quinn told the *Irish Times* on 4 June 2010. Not only did he beat the disease, but he cycled his bike to work in the Dáil throughout.

It was interesting to hold an extended conversation about Ireland in 2010 with Ruairi Quinn. He had, while serving as minister for enterprise and employment in 1994, delivered a speech titled "A Strategy for Ireland—2010." In that speech, Quinn laid out a vision of how the world would look in that year. He emphasized the need for Ireland to capitalize on its diaspora, which as a "global tribe" made the Irish family "more influential in global terms than any other European nation." He also observed that "100 years ago, coming from the slums and hovels that housed the working class, a group of men dreamt of creating a society of equal rights, of shared values, of public health, and free education, and decent living standards." Ruairi Quinn also advocated that Ireland return to some of the core foundations at the origins of the state one hundred years before. While the Labour Party had never formed a coalition government, its cause was one widely admired in Irish history. Having seen Irish people exploited by British landowners and trod upon in times of famine and emigration, people like James Connolly and Jim Larkin had set the tone one hundred years earlier for a century of egalitarian ideals and working-class sympathies. Nonetheless, despite aspirations laid out in 1994 by Quinn, the real opportunity for Labour would not emerge until 2011. Labour's sense of newfound prospects after the fall of the Celtic Tiger might well be contained in the quote of Larkin, which is at the base of his statue on O'Connell Street in Dublin: "The great appear great because we are on our knees: Let us rise."

Over the years, many Irish voters have dismissed Labour because of fears of what it might do with a more socialist-leaning policy in government. However, the damage done in Ireland during the Fianna Fáil years has made that a hard criticism to level. Furthermore, as Irish economist John FitzGerald told me in an interview, the people who today lead the Labour Party are "well-regarded as having had serious experience while in government" during the Fine Gael–led coalition in the 1990s. People like Ruairi Quinn, Joan Burton (who in 2010 held the finance portfolio for Labour), and the leader, Éamon Gilmore, have earned considerable recognition and respect. Clearly, this party was well positioned to ride the tide of a "throw the bums out" shake-up of the Irish political system heading into elections in 2011. Even better for Labour, the reality of the hard cuts being undertaken had already fallen on Fianna Fáil. Labour (and Fine Gael) would benefit from not having been the ones in charge. As a senior Labour policy advisor told me, "We understand the anger, and it is real—you can sit on the garden wall in our constituencies and you get the real story," especially among the middle classes, the nurses, the teachers, and the police. "Patience has been lost," he said. "We are waiting in the long grass."

The Labour Party had already broken major ground when, in 1990, a well-liked Labour lawyer named Mary Robinson was elected the first woman president of Ireland. Actually, while her background was clearly oriented to Labour, she ran as an Independent with Labour backing, having resigned the party in the mid-1980s over disagreements on Northern Ireland policy. Mary Robinson revolutionized Irish politics, which had been a man's game, then modernized the role of president. As she famously said of being the first female Irish president, "I was elected by the women of Ireland who, instead of rocking the cradle, rocked the system." Nevertheless, by 2010, there were still six men in the Irish parliament for every woman, who make up about 14 percent today, the same percentage as in 1995 and about ten points behind the rest of the European Union members. Still, Mary Robinson inspired a new generation of women to enter into politics in Ireland. One of the twenty-three female members of parliament was a woman who would be a key player in Ireland's new government in 2011.

I was especially keen to meet with Joan Burton because she represented the Mulhuddart area of west Dublin, where I spent considerable time in the 1980s and 1990s. This part of Dublin has seen radical changes. In the 1970s it basically comprised fields where good land could be bought not too far from the city center. By the 1980s, much of that land was being converted into public housing, which, by the turn of the century, was increasingly occupied by immigrant populations. From farmland, to working-class neighborhood, to multicultural community, west Dublin had seen a lot in a few decades. Joan Burton is a good representative of that change. She achieved many of her formative political experiences working as a volunteer and accounting teacher in Tanzania. She was deeply influenced by the election of Mary Robinson and was first elected to the parliament in 1992. While Labour was in coalition with Fine Gael, Burton served as minister of state at the Department of Foreign Affairs.

Joan Burton emerged as one of Ireland's most vociferous critics of government policy on the economy; however, on meeting her, I found particularly interesting her high degree of pragmatism. While clearly channeling constituents' rage at the Fianna Fáil government, her own view was that it was "essential to keep the consensus on the corporate tax rate" and to make Ireland more competitive at selling itself as a "business friendly culture." To her, many of the key problems confronting Ireland were infrastructure oriented. As much as Dublin could be sold as a "fun" place, there was no good transport service from Belfast to Rosslare, thus no link between the two biggest ports on the island. Meanwhile, basic everyday issues in Dublin would turn people off, Burton suggested, "like the lack of parking." When I asked her how she accounted for the rise of Labour in 2010, her answer was straightforward: Labour had developed the "right analysis" of Ireland's core problems as early as 2003. "It was," she said, "less about policy, and more a sense of judgment and credibility as time has proven us right." When I posited that Labour's position seemed ideal because, presumably, the party would join a coalition government after Fianna Fáil had done the really bad economic heavy lifting—particularly making the cuts—I found little disagreement.

Joan Burton was quick to point out the credibility behind Labour's appeal. The party had, urged on by Burton, been warning since 2003 of the dangers lurking in the Irish economy. She had called early for fairness in "tax justice." By 2007, Burton was pointing out in parliamentary debates that "48 of the highest earners in the country paid less than 5 percent on their income tax." She asserted that "Fianna Fáil has presided over a tax regime that has allowed super earners to use a range of tax loopholes and avoidance measures to minimize their tax liabilities—and some millionaires to avoid tax liability altogether—while workers earning at or just over the average industrial wage have had to endure tax rates of 40 percent and more." Also in 2007, Burton called out the growing gap between the new wealth and reality in modern Ireland as average people do not "have the luxury of being exempt from extra fuel and car taxes . . . in the way that ministers are as they're driven around in state cars. . . . So there's a wider gap than ever between what ministers experience day-to-day themselves and the reality of belt-tightening that families will have to endure. . . . People in the ordinary economy in many ways are living in a parallel universe to what ministers in this government are living in."

At the 2007 Labour conference, Burton related the real pain already being felt on the street level in Ireland. Yes, she said, there had been "economic success, but it has not yet given us a successful society." She went on to say, "The woman who has to bring in hot water to wash her mother suffering from Alzheimer's in a hospital less than three miles from here—she knows she's not living in a successful society. Parents whose children are in supersize classes know they don't live in a successful society. Ministers should boast less and listen more." Speaking in October 2008 about expected education cuts, she stated before the Dáil that the highly skilled young people we are educating as teachers will "in many cases no longer have jobs to go to—so we will actually be educating the crème of our young people who are willing to take up a life in education—we are actually going to be educating them to have them once again emigrate to London, to the UK, to Australia and New Zealand where no doubt their skills will be snapped up." The economic collapse, Joan Burton said in a statement before the Dáil in October 2008, "is Brian Cowen's legacy to Irish families. . . . The true costs will hang like a millstone around the necks of our people for years to come." Burton had one searing question for Fianna Fáil: "After 12 years in power, why is income inequality still so deep and why is wealth inequality in assets actually worse than when you took office?"

Joan Burton and her colleagues in the Labour Party were ahead of the curve on predicting Ireland's great fall, and by 2010 they were reaping the benefits of that politically. No one was a greater beneficiary than Labour Party leader Éamon Gilmore. A highly recognizable and charismatic politician, Gilmore was first elected to the parliament with the socialist Worker's Party in 1989, eventually merging with Labour and serving as minister of state in the Department of the Marine in the Fine Gael/Labour coalition government in the 1990s. By summer 2007, he had risen to leader of the Labour Party. I met with Éamon Gilmore in July 2010 to get a sense of what Labour's leader might be thinking. We spent a good part of an afternoon engaging on a range of issues confronting Ireland and the world. There is no doubt that, if one were to want a concise and charismatic person to lead the Labour charge, it would be Gilmore.

Éamon Gilmore acknowledged that Labour had raised alarm bells for the Irish people well before the Celtic Tiger collapsed. He noted with pride a 2007 general election poster that Labour put together with the slogan "But are you happy?" This, he felt, "hit the nail on the head" of where Irish society was at the time. Ireland was seemingly prosperous, but it had lost touch with its values. That 2007 campaign, he felt, was the "start of a reflection on what it's all about" for Ireland—forcing a renewed focus on social justice, equality, fairness, and the importance of education. Éamon Gilmore was especially good at reflecting the mood of the country toward the Fianna Fáil leadership—about which he is clear: "The emperor has no clothes." I was unsure whether to ask Gilmore about the assertion that Taoiseach Brian Cowen had committed "economic treason," but he was eager to expound on it. It was not, as I would have assumed, a well-thought-out or poll-tested statement. Reflecting on the depth of what he called the "double speak" surrounding the property bubble, he "thought of it on the way in. . . . I thought of it that same morning." "It was," he said, "how I felt about it." The statement reflected his personal anger and the outraged mood of his constituents. Gilmore attributed the rise of Labour to a "deep mood for change, the fact that Fianna Fáil was in government for so long," which had created the "deepest sense for change I've ever seen." Of Fianna Fáil, Gilmore said, with contempt, that they were very "superficial" and that "prosperity was their value." Fianna Fáil could focus on growth and claim Ireland was "turning the corner," Éamon Gilmore noted. However, he said this was the "real Achilles' heel in that the government is only hurt when claiming progress because the people are not feeling it."

Core elements of existing economic policy would likely have remained in place under a Labour government, albeit with different priorities. For example, Éamon Gilmore argued that "we will honor the agreement" made with unions at Croke Park. But he also noted that "a national agreement on public and private sector" reform was needed. I was surprised in our meeting that when I asked Gilmore what positive attributes he would sell about Ireland to the world, he provided a fairly stock answer that Ireland was "a great country," "enterprising," a place with "great access—and sports, arts, music." Ireland was "hard working" and a "great place to invest." I was hoping to get a concrete vision of where Labour would take Ireland. But there was a hard, brutal realism in the immediate present. Gilmore summed that up by saying that for Ireland, we are still "recouping our pride." He was optimistic that Ireland would eventually recover and that it would do so "off a different platform" and in a "different world." Tracing his own career alongside major events in Ireland, he reflected that the country had come from what he described as the "nasty sectarian war" in the North to the "agricultural emphasis of Ireland in the 1970s." Gilmore has seen the scope of change as a part of a new generation of Irish leadership, and he has a firm perspective of realism, potential, and patience. On the other hand, for leaders and society on the whole, "expectations are now higher"—but Gilmore seemed very confident that he would be able to rise to the challenge if called.

A critical problem for Labour, looking forward from 2011 is that while it was popular, most of its voting base lay in the large cities. Rural Ireland had been Fianna Fáil domain with its deep patronage networks. Ireland would thus face a test of whether it was in a position to translate sentiment into a new national compact behind a coalition of Fine Gael and Labour. While Labour leaders seemed confident, plenty of independent observers maintained skepticism. Critics were quick to assert that Labour was rising while criticizing Fianna Fáil but not offering its own clear plan to move Ireland forward. A senior Labour policy advisor told me that they were "very well aware that we have to sharpen the message." He said that there was "good reason for wondering whether they could translate current popularity into an electoral mandate from the countryside." Furthermore, if Labour was to eventually form a governing coalition, whom would they do it with? Éamon Gilmore ruled out a partnership with Fianna Fáil in summer 2010—though they would actually be a closer ideological fit than Fine Gael. Even Sinn Féin had come to a point where its leaders were hinting the party could be a possible junior partner in a Labour-led coalition. After their summer 2010 party conference in Roscommon, Éamon Gilmore said, "It is our intention at the moment to stand 65 candidates in the general election, each of whom will be standing to win. That is sufficient to make Labour the largest party in the next Dáil and to lead the next government." That, however, did not happen. Still, Labour did emerge as the second largest party in Ireland.

THE SOCIAL CONTRACT HAS
BEEN SHATTERED IN IRELAND

Labour had peaked too soon, and instead was to be the junior partner to a Fine Gael–led coalition after the 2011 election. Fine Gael was well positioned to regain its footing by early 2011. Despite the rise of Labour, in 2009's local elections Fine Gael won 32 percent of the vote—twice what Labour received. Fine Gael was prepared on details of policy and had presumed that its turn would come at the next general election. In early 2011, polls showed Fine Gael had moved ahead of Labour as the preferred party to govern Ireland, though Labour remained competitive. The rise of Labour, however, initially set off near panic in Fine Gael—so much so that its leader, Enda Kenny, was challenged in June 2010 by Richard Bruton, the party's deputy leader. Kenny, from Mayo, had been involved in Fine Gael politics since the mid-1970s and served as minister of tourism and trade in the 1990s. While Kenny had done much to unite Fine Gael in opposition, there had long been grumblings concerning his ability to excite the party amid qualms about his dry leadership style. For Fine Gael, the key question was thus, "Who could best lead the party into a general election?" The answer, in a secret vote taken by the party on 17 June 2010, was that the leader would be—Enda Kenny. Kenny emerged as a survivor and had demonstrated solid organizational skills, earning him the praise of those who had challenged him. Though tumultuous at the time, the leadership challenge helped Fine Gael work through internal dilemmas well in advance of the next general election. Skillfully, Kenny himself called the confidence vote. This allowed him and his allies to coordinate the parameters of the debate against a powerful but unorganized group of front-benchers led by Richard Bruton. As Kenny said of his internal opposition after appointing a new leadership team (which included Richard Bruton as spokesperson for enterprise, jobs, and economic planning), "There's no long grass; it was all cut a couple of weeks ago."

While Fine Gael would have to compete with Labour for attention, the party was in a strong position relative to substantive policy development. Enda Kenny was frank in stating that it would take at least a decade to get Ireland's economic footing turned around. In an interview with the *Irish Independent* on 13 September 2010, he said there was "no pain-free way" to restore the public sector of the economy. Kenny made clear that he would be asking voters to support a long-term consolidated effort by Fine Gael rather than just "stumbling across the line." He said Fine Gael's goal was to "set a 10-year program to restore soundness to Ireland's finances, and to set out a program of how you can provide services that can really stand up to the best level now—be it in education, the public service, the whole health system, all that potential that exists in terms of infrastructure.

And you cannot and won't do that in five years. We will be setting out a 10-year program." Nonetheless, given the limited policy options available, Enda Kenny's plans seemed little different from Fianna Fáil's. He said Fine Gael would support additional deep cuts from the 2011 budget and would not support raising taxes or cutting capital expenditures. "As a general principle," he said, "we don't see the way forward as increasing taxes. We have said do it on current spending, go back to what we have lost in this country, which is competitiveness and export growth, where there is now serious potential."

Whereas Enda Kenny was less specific on policy detail, his former rival, Richard Bruton, was eager to expand. I met with Bruton at Leinster House as the parliament was headed out on summer holiday in August 2010. The Dáil was quiet, and Bruton was in great form. Although remaining a front-bencher, he had been defeated by Enda Kenny. "I lost," he said. "No regrets." While surely some hard feelings remained, Bruton had told the *Irish Times* on 3 July 2010, "I believe Enda Kenny has proved his steel in that he has won this successfully. . . . We have always had a very strong personal relationship. In my view it was business; what happened was business. It was a professional decision that I took and has proved unsuccessful." In our discussion, Bruton indicated that had a challenge not happened when it did, it "would have come eventually at a far less fortuitous time for Fine Gael." He seemed liberated from politics and eager to deliver a blunt message about the challenges and opportunities facing Ireland.

I was especially curious about Bruton's background. He had done his master's of philosophy in economics at Oxford—and written his thesis on Irish public debt. In Ireland, it often seems that those too closely associated with academia are considered aloof from "real-world" issues. Whether that motivated him or not, I do not know, but Bruton was quick to downplay his impressive academic credentials as an economist. Regardless, he led me through one of the most informed and detailed discussions of economic policy that I have encountered in a politician. The key linkage was the core problem of debt, which Ireland had suffered in the 1980s and was now repeating itself in terms of private debt, combined with the astronomical public debt incurred by the banking crisis. "Debt is the issue" and its "legacy is severe in that it will constrain policy options for any future Irish government," Bruton said. He also noted that other options, like a classic stimulus, were not realistic in the Irish context because of its EU commitments to lower its annual budget deficit and maintain low inflation. Richard Bruton's political sense was keen as to the limits of Ireland's choices given that, regarding the Croke Park deal, "we can't go back to the well again" in terms of pay and maintaining social stability in the country. It is crucial, Bruton said, "that the government play a proactive role in funding targeted areas for infrastructure development"—he pointed to enhancing broadband technology as an example. Bruton was especially concerned that a deepening "culture against risk taking is not good" and believed that the government has a positive role to play in this regard by "rebuilding a culture of lending," especially in terms of supporting small and medium-sized businesses and moving away from NAMA. The tragic reality facing Ireland is that, in Bruton's assessment, absent major governmental reform, "the only thing left is to cut entitlements."

To Richard Bruton, a key way to generate internal savings and make Ireland more competitive and attractive internationally is to reform government and public services. In the context of Ireland's crisis, the "streamlining of government hasn't even started." One of the major advantages that Fine Gael brought to the Irish voter was that its leaders had thought through what would happen if they were to lead a government. Richard Bruton is a clear manifestation of that. Despite the leadership challenge in June 2010, he was certain to be a central figure in the Fine Gael–led coalition in 2011. Bruton is well-positioned to be a primary architect of public-sector reform, which, as he said to me, will be a "major source of economic recovery." In this sense, he noted that for the new government, the emergency will also create major "opportunity to do new things." In particular, Richard Bruton has his eye on how to better use state assets, implement better planning, and reduce waste in government. He said there is "no getting away from having to do more with less." Bruton has embedded within Fine Gael a major slogan of the party's "reform agenda" versus "greed" of the past. He points out that the "health system is dysfunctional, and the pension system is bankrupt." Bruton and Fine Gael conceptualize a government with "a new relationship with citizens" based on a new compact that recognizes there is "no good short strategy." There is also no point in looking back to what he calls the "gleam and glitter of the Celtic Tiger," which was "not authentically Irish in the end."

Speaking in August 2010 at the MacGill Summer School, Bruton discussed in greater detail his concept for major governance reform in Ireland. At the core of what went wrong in Ireland is a culture in which "sectional interests and the self-serving action of insiders have prevailed over the interests of the citizen." To rectify this, Fine Gael might "replace the membership of every State board in an orderly manner within six months of the formation of a new government, giving new members a clear letter of appointment setting out their duties, and requiring them to be approved by the Oireachtas [parliament]." Bruton's MacGill speech stands out as an essential dissertation on the history of Irish economics, politics, and the need for reform. He noted that the founders of the country were "mystical thinkers," like Pádraig Pearse, and a "militant socialist," like James Connolly. He noted how people like Arthur Griffith had developed sophisticated economic theories modeled after German economist Frederick List and "believed that every sphere of public policy needed to be imbued with national ambition." Bruton also noted, "The radicalism of the Democratic Programme of 1919, with its emphasis on the rights of Labour and the subservience of property, is in sharp contrast with the 1937 de Valera Constitution which singled out property as the core part of economic capital to be defended, and the church as the backbone of the country's social capital."

Bruton's MacGill speech was important as it lay the groundwork for serious political reform. Bruton demonstrates a rare quality in a politician—he reflects the fault and responsibility onto both the political system and the national culture. The reasons offered for the economy's collapse, he said, were all too often "convenient explanations for a self-serving establishment which does not want to take a hard look at itself." "The essence of a Republic should be of power, responsibly exercised, properly accountable, in the interests of the citizens. At the heart of our system was a political culture, a system of public administration, of regulation, and of social partnership which no longer enshrined these principles. At critical moments, it was insiders who held sway." The end result, he noted, was a new political culture based on the political desire to live on easy street, the failure to deliver strategic change by the state, the regulatory tolerance of bad practices, and the capture of the reform agenda by sectional interests. Richard Bruton and Fine Gael laid out a detailed plan of public-sector reform, including changes in the role of the parliament, oversight, transparency, and state board membership. Ireland needed a wholesale change in political culture. Bruton said, "The Social Contract between government and citizen, which is implicit in every political system, has been shattered in Ireland. It must be remolded if our country is to be made secure again."

GOOD ORDER IS THE FOUNDATION OF ALL THINGS

Edmund Burke reminds us, in this quote from his 1790 "Reflections on the Revolution in France," of the value of organization, if there must be chaos. Of course democracy is a messy business, and it can be, as Winston Churchill said, the worst form of government, "except for all of the others that have been tried." The collapse of the Celtic Tiger had dramatic implications for democracy in Ireland. At one level, people were acutely aware of how government and economics affected their lives. At a more fundamental level, the Irish people had seemingly lost faith in their government's ability to manage crises and represent the public good. Both Labour and Fine Gael thus saw new opportunities to reshape the political landscape of the country. As to Fianna Fáil, on 21 September 2010, the *Financial Times* laid the problem facing the party bare, blaming it squarely for Ireland's "misguided strategy for dealing with the country's banking sector." The paper called for Brian Cowen to "cut the umbilical cord to the banking system" and noted, "The Irish public has been stoical about austerity but anger is now crystallizing around the banks. Mr. Cowen has a sobering choice: to allow a wipeout of creditors or face wipeout at the next election." By 2011, it might have been too late to devise any serious policy options to confront the deep structural realities confronting Ireland, as Ireland's sovereignty is increasingly in the hands of the European Union and the International Monetary Fund. On 25 February 2011, the Irish people finally had their say. Fine Gael won a strong majority. A change in government from Fianna Fáil to Fine Gael, however, was not major news. In the scope of history, the evisceration of Éamon de Valera's Fianna Fáil and the rise of a strong third force, Labour, was news. Independents and Sinn Fein also scored well. Enda Kenny of Fine Gael would form a new government including Eamon Gilmore as Tánaiste, and as ministers Ruauri Quinn, John Burton, and Richard Bruton. But at the same time, Enda Kenny might have also felt that "winning" in Irish politics is best reflected in the famous lines spoken by Robert Redford at the end of the movie *The Candidate*, when, after winning his election, he asks his key adviser, "What do we do now?"

A poster advertising a protest against former Taoiseach (Prime Minister) Brian Cowen in June 2010. By autumn 2010, Cowen's public-approval rating had fallen to 11 percent, after which he conceded the need to call for a general election in 2011 as his government negotiated deep budget cuts and an EU and International Monetary Fund bailout. In January 2011, Cowen resigned as party leader and announced his retirement from politics.

4

A Million Small Steps

GOOD IRELAND

Former Taoiseach John Bruton suggested that to meet its challenges, Ireland needed to take "a million small steps, rather than one or two big ones." Ireland not only faced serious immediate and long-term crises, but the relative policy options for addressing them were limited and painful: the people were going to have to find ways to lead with new innovation and creativity. The new budget that the government brought forward in December 2010, including €15 billion in cuts over four years, was likely to be deeply deflationary; economic growth was likely to remain stagnant at best, unemployment to be very high, and public services to suffer deep strain from cuts. Ireland was on the verge of undergoing perhaps the most dramatic decrease in relative standard of living in modern history. Still, from this economic devastation, the seeds of the future were still there, underneath the frozen snows of a dark and icy winter. Frank McNally, writing in the *Irish Times* on 24 September 2010, offered a novel approach. Perhaps it was time for a new partition—between "good Ireland" and "bad Ireland." "'Good' Ireland would retain most of the national territory," he wrote, "including islands and seas; all working parts of the economy; success in the arts and sport; a reputation for friendliness; any remaining tours of *Riverdance*, etc." "'Bad' Ireland (BI) would take over the mess left by the construction bubble. In this respect, BI wouldn't be so much a country—at least initially—as an asset company with impaired loans." This perspective symbolized a growing public upset with the situation because, as Liam Doran, general secretary of the Nurses and Midwives Organisation, said to me, "It was just three hundred people and a niche bank that brought this country to its knees."

Irish society had embraced the Celtic Tiger, but it was not average Irish people who broke the country. Increasingly, citizens across the nation were standing up for themselves and—as this chapter shows—working tirelessly to create a future they could believe in. At the core of that process was a major cultural change: no longer are such painful issues subjects that "we don't talk about." Ireland is laying itself bare, which is an essential element of rebuilding, painful as it can be.

WE ARE HERE TO VENT OUR ANGER

Deeply symbolic of a growing desire to stand up to power has been, ironically, the Irish police force, or Garda (in Ireland the police are called the Garda Síochána). A public information video, produced by the Garda Representative Association (GRA), concluded with the following: "Day and night, the rank and file protect the public—keeping a watchful eye on the streets of recession-hit, crime-ridden, modern Ireland. They didn't cause this recession—that was the fault of the government, bankers, and property developers who conspired to increase the wealth of the greedy who don't pay taxes and don't want to support their wider community. The men and women keeping their fellow citizens safe are shouldering the burden of Ireland's journey from boom—to bust." The economic conditions, deep pay cuts, and lack of support for the Garda, combined with a major rise in crime, have left the institution feeling angry, betrayed, and disillusioned. Yet, like so many in Ireland, its members continue to do their jobs with pride in the role they play in society. The Garda, created in 1925, became a source of stability and order in the consolidation of democracy in Ireland. It is a unique national force of twelve thousand based throughout the country. Men and women join the Garda with a basic understanding that they would not get rich, but society would provide job security and operational support.

Despite efforts to head off cuts in the police budget, the Fianna Fáil government came down especially hard on the Garda in late 2009. All public servants' pay was to be cut by 5 percent on the first €30,000 of income, 7.5 percent on the next €40,000, and 10 percent on the next €55,000 earned. This came in addition to levies imposed on pensions, health benefits, and extra income for overtime or high-risk job performance by the Garda. Such allowances were important to encourage people to take on dangerous jobs or to ensure that they might work an all-night shift and then spend much of the next day available for court or office duties. Health contributions by individual Garda were doubled from 2 to 4 percent on incomes of €75,000 or less. Pay-related social insurance ceilings were increased from €52,000 to €75,000, and sustenance allowance and travel rates were reduced by 25 percent. This hit the Garda hard, as 60 percent had a salary under €45,000. Average salary for a ten-year veteran was €894 per week. Additionally, a hiring and promotion freeze, on top of retirements, made for a very young national police force; about 60 percent of its members were in their first ten years of service. The government also recommitted to rules prohibiting police from taking on additional part-time jobs to supplement their incomes, such as bartending, driving a taxi, or working as a security guard while off duty. Average starting salary for a junior-rank Garda was just above social welfare, and many officers incurred substantial debt to complete their training.

On average, the initial cuts meant a reduction of about €200 per month per officer, with a total net cut of 18 percent. The situation was especially bad for junior rank-and-file police working in Dublin, who had to commute as far as one hundred miles to find affordable housing. By law Irish police officers are not allowed to agree to mortgages that they cannot pay back; thus, some banks targeted police for high-risk loans on the idea that they would have to pay them back or lose their jobs. This stuck some of the youngest officers with mortgage and credit debt, loans to repay for their training, and families to support. As Michael Ryan, a thirteen-year veteran of the force, put it, low morale has "impacted on us every day, and you can see it getting worse and worse, and that undermines the job we do. It would be laughable if it wasn't so serious, you know?" Some officers worry quietly that such conditions pose a growing risk of police corruption.

In conducting interviews for this book, I was struck by the depth of anger among the Garda. Their ire is real, palpable. I met at length in June 2010 with Neil Ward, editor of the *Garda Review* (the magazine for the Irish police force since 1923) and spokesperson for the GRA. The GRA represents over 80 percent of the Irish police force. When I first contacted Ward, he grabbed my attention with his quick response that he would be glad to meet and discuss "Ireland's bitter pill." Ward pointed out the "primary success story of the Irish police force" relative to the consolidation of the Irish state after independence. Over forty thousand have served in a "model, world-class police force." To Ward, however, "the force has been betrayed by the government," and by law there is very little they can do about it. The GRA is not a union, and the Irish police do not have a right to strike. "The government," Ward suggested, "has an absolute monopoly" on the destiny of the police, which makes them an easy target for austerity measures. "The only way out," he said, is "to refuse to accept the government's decisions or to resign from the force." The situation amounts to "industrial slavery" for the police, said Ward.

The Garda are clear that they, too, are citizens with rights, and they are standing up for them. In a 2009 survey of all police GRA members (with 5,540 respondents to 11,478 surveys sent out), 93 percent voted for some form of industrial action, and 18 percent wanted to withdraw their services entirely. The situation was not only the responsibility of the Fianna Fáil government, according to GRA general secretary P. J. Stone: "In my view," he said, "all politicians have to share this burden of responsibility. They allowed this country to be mismanaged. They have allowed people like members of the Garda Síochána, who put their lives on the line, to be disillusioned to the extent that they are wondering whether or not it is worthwhile to be employed in the guards because the political system in this country has abandoned them and has let them down." Unlike in the United States, where local communities might band together to support their police, in Ireland the national role of the police force reduces local political costs if the police go unfunded. For example, the police proposed that the government should write down mortgages for junior officers stuck in them; yet, according to Ward, this was "not even costed out by the government. . . . One mistake just seems to pile on another." Consequently, the Irish police felt that their only recourse was to "turn to the media," as Ward put it.

Eventually, the Irish police took off their uniforms—some left them on—and joined public protests of budget cuts. As one Garda member said when interviewed on television at a protest, "We are here to vent our anger." The Garda clarified that they were not striking. Rather, those who were off duty and wished to show solidarity with allied unions could do so. Despite the technicalities, this was the first time in its history that the police force participated in a public action. Ironically, in May 2010, the Garda Public Order Unit was tasked with undertaking special training in riot control, following the breakdown in public order during similar protests in Greece in the midst of that nation's ongoing economic crisis.

A highly professional and respected part of society, the Irish police are deeply cognizant of their responsibility and see themselves as standing up for the people they are charged with protecting. Critics point out that, on average, public servants in Ireland—including the police—are well paid. The average American police officer earned about $49,000 per year in 2010—or about €36,000 annually—without the same generous pensions and health benefits provided by the Irish system. One has to factor in, however, the relative cost of living in Ireland versus the United States, which is substantially cheaper. A house that would cost about $150,000 in the United States would likely cost three times that amount in some areas of Dublin. Still, this is Ireland, not the United States, and these public servants were sending the message that they would stand up for their role in society. They voiced the concerns of people who felt they did not cause the economic crisis but were being asked to pay for it. "How much further can they be pushed before there is a reaction?" the GRA asked. General Secretary P. J. Stone said, "I have to say that if the government was to attempt to move any further on the members of the Garda Síochána, then they simply won't have a police force because people will just simply get out."

POWER TO THE PEOPLE

The social stresses over the depth of public sector pay and benefits cuts became clear in February 2009 when over one hundred thousand people took to Dublin's streets in one of the largest public demonstrations in several decades. These and subsequent protestors understood the need for shared sacrifice on behalf of the nation. They were angry, however, because while wages were being cut, the government was funneling billions of taxpayer euros into the banks. They were paying deeply for other people's wrongdoing. As a sign held by one protestor read, "Banks are bailed out, our pensions are wiped out." A popular slogan was "They say cut back— we say fight back." One small group carrying red Communist Party flags, however, had not gotten the memo on the key lesson of the Beatles song "Revolution": "If you go carrying pictures of Chairman Mao you ain't going to make it with anyone, anyhow!" Unions in Ireland were growing more vocal, but radical action seemed far off. Public-sector strikes were not really on the agenda. People seemed persuaded that having a job was more important than protesting the cuts—for the time being. In fact, only one-third of Irish workers are even in unions. Just 15.9 percent of workers under age twenty-five were in unions (according to the European Social Research Institute). That said, 68.7 percent of public workers are in unions—and that gives them considerable leverage. By 2011, Ireland had not witnessed massive unrest. Still, the Gaelic phrase "póg mo thóin," or "kiss my arse," was taking on a new popularity. This was symbolized when a man drove a cement truck into Leinster House's gates on the first day of the autumn parliamentary session on 29 September 2010. Painted on the truck was "Toxic Bank." Following the driver's arrest, protesters carried signs reading, "Free the toxic truck driver."

Deep divisions over where the cuts in the budget might fall grew steadily across society—and occasionally burst into public discourse. In a budget debate in the Dáil on 11 December 2009, Paul Gogarty, a Green Party TD, said softly to a critic across the aisle, "I respected your sincerity. I ask you to respect mine." Some chatter followed, and TD Gogarty then said, "With all due respect, in the most unparliamentary language, 'Fuck you, Deputy Stagg—fuck you!' I apologize now for my use of unparliamentary language." The parliamentarian convening the debate agreed, "That is most unparliamentary language." Gogarty concurred, apologized, and then said,

"The point is that we are screwed as a country." Gogarty was not formally reprimanded since the Irish parliamentary rules do not specifically ban the word "fuck," which you may thus use; you may not, however, call a colleague a brat, buffoon, chancer, cornerboy, guttersnipe, or yahoo. Gogarty did explain that he was "outraged that someone dare[d] to question [his] sincerity on this issue"—though the issue was that he was bemoaning cuts in social benefits, while also voting for them.

Other sporadic outbursts received national attention. For example, an audience member interrupted host Pat Kenny during a 9 November 2009 airing of RTÉ's *The Frontline* on which Minister for Tourism, Culture, and Sport Mary Hanafin was the guest. He shouted, "It's you, Pat Kenny, who get six hundred thousand a year for doing eleven hours a week, and you have the indignity to speak about people on the social welfare and disability. And then you pontificate against ministers and their corrupt system—your RTÉ do not deserve the money they get, and you need to be confronted for your moralizing and your hypocrisy." I got my own taste of this on a Facebook exchange one evening in September 2010. I am "connected" to Micheál Martin, then minister of foreign affairs. A person criticized an update on his page about a visit to the United Nations, writing that the foreign minister "sure spent a lot of time traveling on other people's money." I added a comment in response, saying that while "there was surely plenty to criticize, this was not the right one—that nearly every foreign minister in the world goes to the UN during the annual General Assembly meetings." I added that Micheál Martin was "also in New York for a meeting with Hillary Clinton to discuss food security—which would save lives in places like Africa and which would benefit Irish farmers at the same time." I got a separate message, unsolicited, from the person who said, "You mind your own fucken business what I say about the ministers ok id love to see you survive on 100 a week from the diole the government are robbin us end of ok." I valued the comment, if not the grammar, because it was an authentic statement of the mood on the street.

On 18 November 2010, Labour TD Pat Rabbitte and Fianna Fáil TD Pat Carey both appeared to discuss the pending international bailout of the Irish banks and economy on the RTÉ program *Prime Time*. The conversation went along typically, until the austere and soft-spoken Pat Carey sought to defend his party against the assertion that it had failed to supervise the regulation of the banks. Pat Rabbitte laid forth an outburst that became an instant hit on YouTube and in the press; it expressed, in effect, another moment of national sentiment. Rabbitte said to Carey,

> Pat, you ought to be ashamed to show your face in this studio after what you have brought our country to penury tonight. And the damage that you have done to people's livelihoods and start the young people emigrating again. You have destroyed this economy, and you engaged in lies over the weekend. You denied it, and then you went on to pretend that it's Ireland coming to

the rescue of Europe. It's about time you went—because you can do no more damage to this country . . . and coming on here with your old palaver, about this and that and structuring and all—you didn't do anything to avoid the crisis that was coming down the tracks at us. You maintained property-based tax incentives until you inflated the bubble that has brought us to the state we're in, and now you come out here, saying somehow, "This is someone else's fault—not our fault." It's the fault of the Irish government [Rabbitte was now hammering on the desk and speaking with shaking emotion], and you ought to be ashamed of where you have brought us tonight.

Carey reacted with genuine astonishment at the tirade, but then listened intently. He responded by saying, "No, I'm not ashamed." To that, Rabbitte shot straight back, "Well, you ought to be! That's the problem with you. You're not ashamed. You don't have any shame!" Rabbitte added, "Like most people, I am crushed by what you have done. I didn't believe it would come to this. But now we are handing over our decision making for the next three to five years to outsiders."

This public debate reflected much of the discussion going on in private settings, around dinner tables and among families. Many people in the private sector pointed out that their wages had been reduced, and they wondered why those in the civil service should not also bear a significant burden. Many public-sector workers noted that they did not make the massive amounts of money their private-sector counterparts did during the Celtic Tiger. This added to growing social divisions—"a civil war even within families," said one union representative, over who was and who should be paying the price for Ireland's woes. Each public service representative I spoke with said this division resulted from a purposeful effort by the government and some media to deflect blame onto a "bloated" public sector. The *Sunday Independent* and RTÉ drew particular attention for what Neil Ward described to me as a "sustained, two-year campaign against public service." They created an image of the public service sector as underworked and overpaid. Eugene Dennehy, deputy general secretary of the Prison Officers Association, addressed this point at a rally of over five thousand people in protest of budget cuts in November 2009: "We are angry that the government and certain sections of the media have deliberately and in other ways brought about a situation in this country where public sector workers providing those essential services have been vilified, have been insulted, have been degraded, as if somehow they are a leech on society. Well, that is a disgrace, and I say shame on you for that!"

When I asked Liam Doran of the Irish Nurses and Midwives Organisation about this vilification, he called it an "absolute, full-frontal assault on public service." Part of this dynamic, he said, stemmed from some media wrongly portraying public servants as having jobs for life and representing an "outdated regime which fueled the fire of uncertainty." An additional issue was even more problematic: there was a "near-complete lack of aware-ness [on the part of] people under the age of forty," deeply ingrained with a strong sense of materialism during the Celtic Tiger, who "didn't understand the word 'no.'" This group turned from "overindulgence to begrudgery," said Doran. In Ireland a tension simmers between those who lived through the 1980s and young people who have never experienced bad times before. There is no doubt that many people aged about twenty-five to forty in Ire-land in 2010—the so-called "Tiger Cubs"—bear substantial responsibility for the thoughtless spending spree. To be fair, a corrupt older generation of politicians and bankers egged them on every step of the way. Still, those under twenty-five had literally nothing to do with any of this, yet will foot the bill for decades. That generation risks being lost—which is tragic, as its members are some of Ireland's most creative and talented resources.

This tension came to the fore on RTÉ's *The Frontline* on 22 February 2010, when Bill Cullen, one of Ireland's leading businessmen (born in 1942), called out what he termed Ireland's "mollycoddled youth." He admonished the youth in the live audience, "You's are way ahead of where we were at your age—way ahead of it. You's have to take that, and use it." He said his generation had not "crippled a generation—we've challenged a generation. . . . We're challenging you with issues that you have to stand up and take on." Prompted by the host, Pat Kenny, he said, "Without a doubt, 'molly-coddled' is the word for it. . . . You guys don't know what tough times are like." A young woman from the audience, a social worker in Clondalkin, responded, "[These] are the very people that want to work, Bill. They just haven't got the opportunities because this government has let them down! [applause of the audience]." This deepening age divide grew clear in 2008, when the biggest group of "no" voters on the EU treaty in Ireland came from those below age thirty-five. The frustration with the situation among younger generations is real. As Elaine Byrne, of Trinity College and the *Irish Times*, explained to me, young people are basically told in Ireland to "go sit down there in the corner and mind yourself."

Liam Doran also pointed to the fact the major public pay cuts had a deflationary impact on spending. One can say, "Dock Liam Doran's pay as a nurse—he can do without getting his house painted for sure," he said. But then there are carry-on effects, Doran added, because then "he doesn't hire that local painter, and that person doesn't hire his supplier, and they don't buy food, and so on." The ripple effects of this deflation were huge at a time when the economy needed spending. The Congress of Trade Unions regularly pointed to the deflationary risks of public-sector cuts. However, it would take the full-on effects of the banking crisis seen in late 2010 for this argument to gain traction. This was especially apparent as Ireland slipped back into negative economic growth as summer ended. By October 2010, the government signaled that much deeper cuts were coming in 2011.

The situation in the health-care sector illustrated the social dilemmas confronting the Irish people. As Irish economist John FitzGerald pointed out to me, Ireland has "huge advantages in terms of export capacity in the health and pharmaceutical sectors of manufacturing." Yet, every politician I spoke with pointed to decline in the quality of health-care provision. Expectations might have been driven high during the Celtic Tiger in terms of what public health care could provide. Ireland did have top-quality health services for those who could afford them. For the rest of the public, however, the system was in crisis and certain to get worse. The Irish Nurses and Midwives Organisation reported in August 2010 that its survey of public health facilities revealed that over fifteen hundred beds were closed in hospitals, resulting in longer wait times; there were very high levels of overcrowding; primary care services were being curtailed or suspended indefinitely due to nursing staff shortages; intellectual-disability services were being curtailed, suspended, or eliminated altogether; and frontline staff in nursing and midwifery were not being replaced as needed, which was compromising quality patient care. As with other public services, the government seemed to be focused on viewing health care through the lens of an accountant, not meeting the primary needs of citizens.

Liam Doran, a highly effective advocate for the nurses and midwives he represents, said that his own time as a working nurse (doing intellectual-disability work) definitely "colors most of his thinking" as he knows the issues that people on the front lines of health care grapple with. Critics fault the union for being unwilling to compromise and refusing to sign the Croke Park deal on wages. According to Doran, this was "not because of changes that would be required, but rather because signing it would have meant accepting a loss of 6,000 jobs in health care." The bottom line for Doran is that, absent public support, "you can't maintain an adequate health service." Health-care providers say they feel a moral obligation to the citizenry for whom they care. In the eyes of union advocates, cuts in health care are really part of a drive to privatize the system. Moreover, during the Celtic Tiger years, people in Ireland came to think that they could have adequate health care without paying for it, suggested Doran. While not signing off on Croke Park, in the end, the Irish nurses and midwives had to accept a 14 percent pay cut nonetheless.

"I have never been more pessimistic about our public health system—it is in a perfect storm," Doran said. He noted that the system, run by the Health Services Executive (HSE), was headed by Mary Harney, who resigned from her position in January 2011 and announced she would not stand for re-election. She seemed "disinterested, had no political ambition to advance her department, and likely wants to privatize the system," said Doran. This statement was, a senior advisor to Harney told me off the record, far from accurate. The senior advisor said that Harney sought to include the data from the private system in public measurements and to work to bring the public system up to par with the private. Still, Doran also pointed out that the country's aging population and the geographic distribution of its citizens would put even more strain on care. Geographic distribution of health provision was especially important. Even in wealthy areas not far from Dublin's city center, if one got ill or injured after hours, the best bet for care could be to trek thirty minutes to a major hospital in the city center. In the west of Ireland, the situation was much worse. A businessman friend in Clare told me the story of a man in Lahinch who had a heart attack. Because no good service existed near him, he had to be taken to Limerick, nearly an hour's drive away, but he died en route. Meanwhile, my friend said, "a friend in Limerick had a baby in early 2010 and was advised to bring her own cleaning products to her hospital room." My friend made clear that "the staff in these places are great—but the facilities are not up to date—and are being closed all around the region." Meanwhile, Mater Misericordiae Hospital in Dublin can have wait times for serious cases as long as nineteen hours. While all of these were crucial challenges needing fixes, in the end, the central issue to Liam Doran was that Ireland needed "mature, transparent, adult, dynamic, and honest leadership."

I asked Liam Doran why the Irish had not taken to the streets more. In his view, civility and a degree of patience were among "the end products of twenty years of social partnership." During that period, the "trade unions were in many ways nullified" and had been especially weakened at the local level. Now, the situation for nurses and midwives, he said, is very difficult, especially as "40 percent of nurses are over forty-five years old." A hiring freeze has been "arbitrary and merciless." Meanwhile, the HSE has put increasing pressure on frontline providers not to support union positions. Doran noted with deep concern that in 2010, sixteen hundred newly qualified nurses would not be getting jobs. These highly skilled Irish workers were likely to head for the United States in search of work. This is especially ironic because, in the 1990s, Ireland faced a nursing shortage and had to recruit nurses from the Philippines, India, and elsewhere. Now, these immigrants are working effectively in the union system to secure their jobs—fair play to them. New Irish nurses, however, are forced to emigrate. Doran estimated that as many as three thousand Irish nurses had left by 2010, mainly for the United States.

There were growing signs by late 2010 that enough was enough. At a public ceremony she attended on 1 November, Mary Harney was covered in red paint thrown by a protester, symbolizing blood. A key Independent TD, Noel Grealish, whom Fianna Fáil had relied on to support the party in government, threatened to withdraw his support over opposition to cuts in health services in the Galway region. At the same time, a group called Galway Says No to Health Cuts held a march of several hundred health-care workers through the city of Galway on 25 September. The problem was, according to the HSE, that growing costs, which had gone well over the budget of €2.1 billion per year, had to be contained. Cuts would have to be mandated—with an additional €50 million coming from Galway services before the end of 2010. The regional director of HSE West, John Hennessey, pleaded his case to the *Irish Times* on 25 September 2010: "Like every public service organization, we have to live within our allocated budget. . . . The simple fact is there is no more money available and every healthcare facility in the country must deliver its agreed level of services within the available budget." Mary Harney, the minister in charge of the HSE, would make no deals to keep Grealish's support. Yet, on his heels came another TD, Mattie McGrath, who made halting potential cuts at South Tipperary General Hospital a condition of his continued support for Fianna Fáil. In the end, Liam Doran said, the social partnership, as it was understood, was dead. On the other hand, the idea of a new social partnership is "needed now more than ever"; Ireland "needs a wider vision" and a clear "path for a better way." In particular, Ireland needs "transparency on what constitutes a social good." Liam Doran added that all sides must work together as "we won't get progress if we go into an old-fashioned box" because "no one side has all the answers." Right now, he said with regret, we are "rowing a boat with one oar."

NOBODY DRINKS IN IRELAND

"Nobody drinks in Ireland. Didn't you know that?" I was asked, one nice sunny day on a beach in Kerry. Of course, I thought, obviously. The fact that I was pretty sure I had a good hangover from the night before notwithstanding, who was I to argue? I have to admit to having a really good taste for the dark stuff. When my wife and I were married in Dublin in 1992, a friend noted in a toast that he knew I had "a sense for Ireland . . . by the way I could love, caress, and admire . . . a finely pulled pint of Guinness." Drinking has, of course, been associated with Irish cultural stereotypes for a very long time. Ireland does rank at the top of the Organization for Economic Cooperation and Development (OECD) in average consumption of alcohol. However, this is actually a new phenomenon. In 1970, according to the World Health Organization, the Irish drank 7.0 liters per capita annually; by 2004 this had reached 13.4 liters. The European Union found in 2007 that the Irish were the largest buyers of alcohol in Europe—spending three times as much as the next-ranked country, Denmark. Even this was, overall, not a huge issue, as many people would enjoy a pint or two, and that would be it. Nonetheless, Ireland has a deepening problem with alcoholism and broader substance abuse. According to the European Union, the Irish were the leading binge drinkers in Europe. Worse, 32 percent of fifteen- to sixteen-year-olds were drunk at least three to four times a month. Still, more Guinness is sold in Nigeria than in Ireland.

Yes, a pint is part of the culture—but being heavily drunk has been historically frowned on in Ireland. Youngsters would often take "the pledge" to avoid drink (and sex), and it was as common to find adults who did not drink at all. Like in any country, a "night on the lash" is part of a good time, so long as it is not the norm. I recall at our wedding party at Finnstown House (a classic country hotel that in 2010 went into receivership) in Lucan nearly twenty years ago, I must have had at least ten pints of Guinness lined up from people. I do not think I ever got to drink one full one though—at least that night. I had, however, come home painted green from my stag party a few nights earlier. We had been out to the Angler's Rest pub at the Strawberry Beds in the country, and friends took me to the parking lot and covered me in green paint. And, yes, there was a wee bit of drink involved—in fact, I had never, and still have not, seen so many empty pint glasses stacked up on each other. Probably my most interesting "cultural experience" was on Christmas Eve in 1991. I was out and about at a pub in Blanchardstown, which typically started slow but ended strong. Most nights that end up as trouble seem to begin with "I'm just going to head up for a quiet pint" and lead to stumbling home many hours later. That particular Christmas Eve, I eventually—unwisely—made it out to midnight Mass in Dublin. While we were standing at the back of the church, a young lad started tugging on me. "Mister, Mister, do ya know that you's are on fire?" My first reaction was to tell him to stop messin' and keep quiet, but then I realized that, in fact, my coat was on fire. I had rubbed up against a candle. This was my penance—for as this was happening, the priest was scolding those among us who only showed up to Mass on Christmas Eve and Easter. At least in my smoldering-jacket case, this was true. I was seemingly bursting into flames (harmless though they were) in church after my night in the pub.

These were the exceptions though, not the rule. For much of the twentieth century, the Catholic Church was an important advocate of abstinence from drink, and abuse was frowned on. In fact, Ireland has among the highest percentage of nondrinkers in Europe—about 20 percent of the adult population. Pubs themselves were traditionally as much social places as they were drinking establishments. They used to close during the "holy hour" at 4 p.m. every afternoon and locked up at 11 p.m. or so each night—maybe a little later in the country. Of course, if you timed it right and had a few pints lined up, you really did not have to leave. You could stay longer if you were familiar to the barman, and if the doors would lock you in, you could join off-duty police calling in for their pints. Probably the best thing about a night out in a pub was that it is really a time to socialize and see friends. The drink was really a secondary element. Often, at the end of the night in many pubs, especially in rural Ireland, when last call was final, everyone would stand up and sing the national anthem. Now, some pubs can stay open through the night or even open early in the morning, when no anthems are sung other than "Show Me the Way to Go Home." The Temple Bar area in Dublin has become Ireland's Bourbon Street, and after certain hours, one has to dodge vomit on the street. Whereas in the 1980s your choices for draft beer were most often just Guinness, Smithwicks, and Harp, now beers from around the world are sold in even the most remote country pubs. I recently noticed that a west Dublin pub had the American beer Coors Light on tap—something I would never drink in the United States. I asked a bar staff about it, and she said it was their biggest seller. "It is cheaper, and a little lighter on the calories for the ladies," she said.

Regrettably, drinking—and the use of other, more serious drugs, such as cocaine and heroin—has gotten worse, particularly regarding younger generations. Merchants Quay Ireland, which provides counseling and other services (including a needle-exchange program), indicated that it dealt with, on average, two new drug users a day in Dublin and also increasingly in the countryside, in areas like Athlone, Portlaoise, Birr, and Longford. Other social ills have increased with the economic downturn, including prostitution. According to the Irish charity Ruhama, the number of women working in the sex industry that it was asked to assist increased by 20 percent in 2010. Their reporting pointed to a major increase in the trafficking of women and an expansion of brothels into the countryside. Ruhama said that "women reported having been punched in the face, the stomach, being kicked down stairs, beaten for refusing to have sex with men, being locked in and refused food, being burned, being bitten." Because of the economy, Ruhama received a 20 percent cut in funding from the government; yet, neither the demand for, nor the cost of, prostitution was affected by the economic downturn.

As to drinking, according to the European Union, average household spending on alcohol a year in Ireland is €1,675. "Hey, on the upside, that is in a year—not in one night!" joked a friend. And, to be fair, he added, "the Irish are also among the top consumers of tea in the world. And, oh, how those sausages and rashers are tasty!" I spent much of June, July, and August of 2010 in Ireland, and one can see the growth—a (sort of) healthy-looking American in early photos turns by the end into a walking vat of sausages and Guinness. In all seriousness, for every story of excess and partying, one finds great stories of healthy activity, from swimming to biking to hiking to sailboarding to running. I used to jog in west Dublin in the 1980s, and people looked at me like I was doing something really weird every time I went out. Now, it is the norm to see people of all walks of life exercising.

As Neil Ward said to me, "Gone are the days of the six pints after work to relax."

While some sectors of society have embraced healthy living and moderation across the board, Ireland is actually the second-fattest country in Europe, according to the OECD. Obesity expanded by 40 percent in the first decade of the twenty-first century. Two out of three Irish women, one in four adults, and one in four children are overweight. To be fair, Ireland was beat out by my home country, the United States. Perhaps this is a side-product from Mary Harney famously saying that Ireland was "closer to Boston than Berlin." The Irish economy spends about €1.6 billion per year to deal with problems related to this serious health issue, such as stroke, heart disease, and colon cancer (according Dr. Muireann Cullen speaking at a Nutrition and Health Foundation conference in Dublin in September 2010). Some hospitals in Ireland were installing oversized MRI machines in order to allow people to fit into them.

The Irish government has been forward leaning, aggressive, and creative in addressing these serious health challenges. In 2004, the government, led on this by Micheál Martin, did what many thought at the time to be unthinkable—it banned smoking in pubs. Ireland was the first country in Europe to do so. Even if one did not partake, smoking was part of the ambiance of the pub scene; thus, the decision came as a surprise. At the same time, many nonsmokers sympathized with the notion that bar staff should not have to breathe other people's smoke. In 2005, the *British Medical Journal* showed that there had been a 17 percent decline in respiratory infections among bar staff since the ban. Another study in *Tobacco Control* showed that 83 percent of Irish smokers thought the ban was a good thing—many said it had helped them to quit smoking. Many pubs also made adjustments by placing area heaters on outside patios, which are quite pleasant whether one smokes or not. Drinking laws in Ireland have also become more stringent in terms of what is permissible. The definition of legal intoxication is 0.08 percent blood alcohol content, which means that two drinks, possibly even one, in one hour might render a person legally drunk, and the police aggressively enforce drunk-driving laws. The Irish government has focused on the marketing of alcohol to youth and enforcing requirements that all children under age fifteen be banned from pubs after 8:00 p.m. Ironically, this creates a problem for families that find the only affordable meal out is pub grub. In a society where cartoon posters saying "Guinness Is Good for You" are an art form, advertising that could appeal to youths is now restricted. Meanwhile, activist groups have sponsored dramatic anti–drunk driving commercials on television with jarring images of the serious dangers involved.

According to the Drinks Industry Group of Ireland, pub sales of alcohol fell by 14 percent in the first seven months of 2010. Overall, Ireland has seen a 25 percent alcohol-sales reduction since 2000. This same group estimates that up to two thousand rural pubs in Ireland will close in coming years. It is odd to walk or drive through Irish towns and see once vibrant public houses now closed. Some pubs, like one I walked through in Ennis on the road to Lahinch, are like buildings in ghost towns. Part of the issue is that alcohol prices in Ireland are 67 percent higher than in the rest of Europe, according to a 2010 Eurostat survey. Consequently, many drink purchases are done across the border in Northern Ireland, where prices are considerably cheaper. A bottle of spirits in Ireland generally costs about €20, as opposed to about £11 up north. Add to that the recession, the smoking ban, and strict enforcement of drunk-driving laws, and many people now take their drinks at home. On the other hand, a row of pubs just down from Connolly train station in Dublin is full each day at 3 p.m. with pensioners and the unemployed, spending their afternoon drinking.

Statistics show that while serious drinking problems are up, overall consumption is down. Demographics have something to do with this. For example, the exodus of Polish immigrants from the failed construction industry had an impact on vodka sales. Many young people aged eighteen to twenty-five, the age group that typically consumes the most alcohol in any society, are emigrating or simply cannot afford big nights out. Kieran Toban of the Drinks Industry Group of Ireland argues that government drinking restrictions are, in fact, hurting industry. He was quoted on 27 May 2010 in the *Irish Times* as arguing that there are "myths and misconceptions in public discourse around alcohol, and one of them is that we are the biggest drinkers in Europe and still growing. . . . We're now in and around the European norm, around the nine litres per capita, around what southern Europeans consume. . . . That's important." In fact, the *Irish Times* rightly pointed out that, in terms of statistics, what really matters is not total alcohol consumption (as Toban was emphasizing); rather the European norm most looked at is liters per adult, on which Ireland remains among the highest in Europe.

The *Irish Times* story also quoted Dr. Fiona Weldon, clinical director at the Rutland Centre (Ireland's leading facility for addiction treatment and study), as pointing particularly to the binge drinking: "A drop of even 7 or 8 percent would still leave us at about 45 percent binge drinking in the over 18s population. We are seeing a change, but the change is in the amount of younger men, aged 18 to 25, and women aged 55 plus, coming in with a much more complex dual drug diagnosis." The *Irish Times* cited Dr. Joe Barry, a public health expert, as skeptical of assertions that Ireland should lay off the drinks industry because it has lost twenty thousand of one hundred thousand jobs in the country. Barry fears that a "government that has lost confidence in itself" will cave to the industry. He said, "This is about big corporations trying to make big profits, and to hell with the consequences." Symbolically, a judge decided in April 2010 to allow pubs in Limerick to sell alcohol on Good Friday for the first time in one hundred years because a rugby match was scheduled for the same day—despite the fact that people could have gotten drinks at home or at the actual match. A T-shirt sold outside the Leinster-Munster match summed up the victory of keeping the pubs open; it said, "Officially bigger than the Catholic Church: Munster Rugby."

Alcoholism, drug abuse, prostitution, suicide—in the past, these social ills were either not talked about or were spoken of only in whispers, tragically often too late to help. Now, the HSE states, "the burden of alcohol-related harm is widespread in Ireland and includes harms experienced by the drinker but also harms experienced by people other than the drinker." According to the HSE, "The burden of alcohol harm to the drinker can be seen in hospitals, on the streets, on the roads, in families, and in lost and damaged lives in every community." In addition to government policy, civil society has engaged in efforts to educate and treat the impact of serious drinking problems. Alcoholics Anonymous, first introduced into Ireland in the mid-1940s, remains active today. Alcohol Action Ireland is one of a number of national charities working on alcohol issues. These kinds of groups have pushed for a shift in cultural attitudes so that rather than "just keeping Paddy off the bottle" a real disease could be identified and treated openly and thoughtfully in society. While it was very funny, a comment by American comedian Jay Leno struck a nerve in Ireland; he said of the "drunken Taoiseach incident," "It's nice to know that we're not the only country with drunken morons, isn't it." The *Irish Independent* quoted M. J. Nolan, a Fianna Fáil TD, on 28 September 2010 as saying, "It's obviously a very popular program in the States and it's not the type of publicity we want for us in the current climate when we're trying to do everything to improve our image internationally," he said. *The Tonight Show with Jay Leno* was even contacted to see if it would issue an apology for the joke—it did not.

Frances Black, one of Ireland's most talented popular singers, is an extraordinary example of the kind of deep change that has occurred regarding substance abuse in Ireland. She was the lead force behind the creation in 2008 of Recovery in a Safe Environment (RISE), which provides support and education for both individuals suffering from alcohol addiction and their families. The goal is to break the cycle of addiction, free families from headaches, rediscover family relationships, change the way people see addiction, and, crucially, reduce associated shame and stigma. This work includes coordinating family education programs in Dublin and raising funds for a retreat center at Rathlin Island in Northern Ireland. As Black told the *Irish Times* on 25 September 2010 about her experiences with the damage substance abuse can cause families, "Every day, they watch someone they love slowly killing themselves. No matter how many times you may have asked them to stop, they just can't hear you. Families are grieving for the person they are losing to addiction."

I sat down with Frances Black just off Grafton Street in summer 2010 to get a sense of how she saw the issue of drink in Ireland change with the culture over time. She spoke straightforwardly about her own addiction experiences, which she went public with following her recovery. Black had been a patient for alcohol and sleeping pill addiction and eventually took the training to become a professional counselor. In her experience, the tradition that "people tend to put blinders on with addiction" governed Ireland's views. The most immediate crisis in Ireland is the degree of binge drinking, because after that, "the next stage is dead," said Black. During her recovery, she came to see that addiction is not just a "weakness" or a "soul sickness on which people do look down." Coming to grips with her addiction and becoming a counselor were "the best things that ever happened to me." And yet, she also noted she had relapsed, which was hard because Ireland can be "an island of enablers with hundreds of years of looking the other way." These kinds of cultural blinders are the "boundaries set for addiction," said Black.

For her work in creating the RISE Foundation, Frances Black was named Social Entrepreneur of the Year for 2010 in Ireland. She told the *Irish Times* on 25 September, "I didn't know what a social entrepreneur was until that's what someone called me." Her ambitions are high; she hopes to raise €2 million for the center on Rathlin Island for families in recovery. But her vision goes well beyond that. Frances Black told me her goal is to be "the heart of cultural change around addiction in Ireland." She hopes to help addicts and their families get "beyond the shame and stigma in Irish society." She says her goal is literally to "change the face of Ireland."

In Ireland, a deep sense of social responsibility cuts against the tendency to turn down the veil on what lies in front. Often people simply do not feel a need to dwell on issues or boast about their actions; they just get busy trying to fix problems. All it takes is a few people to get the ball rolling—with a little bit of money. In summer 2010, a couple of lads ran a marathon a day for a month to raise money and awareness for cancer treatment in Ireland. Vodafone created the "World of Difference" contest, which pays winners a €40,000 annual salary to work with a charity of their choice. One winner, a former fifteen-year-old child bride from Africa, went to work with Plan Ireland, which provides assistance to children in the underdeveloped world. Another, Mark O'Doherty, was a marketing executive who had been laid off. He posted on Facebook about his desire to do charity work and was contacted by Frances Black. Black uses Facebook very effectively to advertise the work she is doing—in fact, it was how we first "met." O'Doherty told the *Irish Times* on 1 June 2010, "If you had asked me last year, I would have said there is no way I could survive on 40,000 euro but when you've lived on the dole, you find you can get by on very little." With his award, he was going to go to work as director of marketing and communications for RISE alongside Frances Black.

Black took on another role as a government protestor—as a featured performer at a major national protest in Dublin on 27 November 2010. She said, "We are saying, 'We've had enough!'" Black sang, "It's legal to rip off a million or two—that comes from the labor that other folks do. To plunder the many on behalf of the few, is a thing that is perfectly legal." Also speaking at the protest, actress Ruch McCabe read excerpts from the 1916 Easter Rising proclamation—on the same platform—in front of the General Post Office. Christy Moore performed "Connolly Was There" about the long line of leaders who had stood tall for the Irish people—and those who had failed them. Singing to the applause of the estimated seventy-five thousand protesters in the freezing rain and snow, he ad-libbed, "They bail out the banks, the bosses, the crooks—the Haugheys and Burkes, the Flynns, the Berties, the Fingletons." He then, on finishing the song, shouted, "The system doesn't work!"

Countless examples can be found of Irish looking out for each other. Some of this impulse derives from personal experience, and much stems from a basic desire to do good things to promote positive goals in society. The 2010 "World Giving Index" prepared by the British advocacy group Charities Aid Foundation shows that 72 percent of Irish people give money to charity. Ireland is ranked as the third most charitable country in the world—even in times of severe economic distress. One key trend to emerge from the collapse of the Celtic Tiger was a new sense of what is important in life—family, friends, and the well-being of others as a measure of one's own personal happiness. Most Irish are determined to not let their neighbors slip through the cracks. Little is new about this—the Celtic Tiger was the aberration with its focus on greed and materialism.

I CREDIT POETRY FOR MAKING
THIS SPACEWALK POSSIBLE

In *Global Security in the Twenty-first Century: The Quest for Power and the Search for Peace* (2011), a survey of some of the world's most entrenched security problems, I conclude with the truism that every challenge has a solution, and it begins with education. The Irish have always understood this. Education was an essential means of keeping Irish culture alive during British rule. When the British system dominated the land, Irish "hedge schools" grew up in the countryside. They taught Irish history, language, and cultural traditions secretly as a way of sustaining Irish identity. The scholarly tradition has also been celebrated in Ireland as poets, artists, and writers have been at the forefront of society. "Education," said William Butler Yeats, "is not the filling of a pale, but the lighting of a fire." Or, as Seamus Heaney said in his 1995 Nobel Prize lecture,

> I also got used to hearing short bursts of foreign languages as the dial hand swept round from BBC to Radio Éireann, from the intonations of London to those of Dublin, and even though I did not understand what was being said in those first encounters with the gutturals and sibilants of European speech, I had already begun a journey into the wideness of the world beyond. This in turn became a journey into the wideness of language, a journey where each point of arrival—whether in one's poetry or one's life—turned out to be a stepping stone rather than a destination, and it is that journey which has brought me now to this honored spot. And yet the platform here feels more like a space station than a stepping stone, so that is why, for once in my life, I am permitting myself the luxury of walking on air. . . . I credit poetry for making this space-walk possible.

Since the 1960s, universal quality education has been a hallmark of governments, economic development, and modern social priorities in Ireland. While some of Ireland's best educated have often had to emigrate for work, in the Celtic Tiger, these people frequently returned home with new skills. Prior to becoming foreign minister, Micheál Martin worked in his previous job as education minister with university presidents and others to reframe Irish education. On his subsequent travels as foreign minister, Martin made tangible links between the "global Irish" and education at home. He told me about a young Irish woman he had recently met in Asia, who had been employed to do food catering for the Beijing Summer Olympic Games in 2008. Her experience, even if linked up through video technology, would be a great asset to "show—here's how I did this, here's what you can do" to Irish entrepreneurs. Micheál Martin was looking forward, seeing direct links between globalization, educational opportunities at home, and economic progress. John FitzGerald, one of Ireland's leading economists, added that export sectors will have to lead Ireland's economic recovery. Ireland must adapt to the global dynamics and demands in the health, pharmaceutical, and software industries. Ireland will need to be adaptive and innovative; it will need to be "educated into a multicultural economy," said FitzGerald. Critical skills for all countries, he told me, will be language, math, science, and engineering with "practical skills in knowledge, research, hard sciences, and international law."

Excelling in education will not solve Ireland's economic difficulties. The ability to manufacture, export, and see the development of small and medium-sized enterprises will be essential. However, there is no question that Ireland has tremendous human capital. If managed effectively, this will create a long-term opportunity for economic and social progress. The

Irish government has launched major initiatives to consolidate and expand gains in science, technology, and innovation. Ireland places this within a strategy to build a "smart economy." Announced in late 2008, the official plan states, "The Smart Economy has, at its core, an exemplary research, innovation and commercialization ecosystem. The objective is to make Ireland an innovation and commercialization hub in Europe—a country that combines the features of an attractive home for innovative R&D-intensive multinationals while also being a highly-attractive environment for the best entrepreneurs in Europe and beyond." Ireland has committed to enhancing university education with an eye toward research and development while doubling the number of PhD students in the country. The idea is that building a smart economy infrastructure will create long-term and high-paying jobs. This will trickle out into the economy via extended service-support jobs.

In spring 2010, Enterprise Ireland, which seeks to promote Irish business and attract investment in the country, hosted an event in Washington, DC, which I attended. The buzz in the room was that Ireland was "going to become the Silicon Republic." Many in the delegation, including Taoiseach Brian Cowen, had just visited the original Silicon Valley in California and seen an opportunity for Ireland to reproduce similar innovation at the geostrategic crossroads between the United States and Europe. Margaret O'Mara wrote on *Foreign Policy*'s website on 16 August 2010 that based on her book about the origins of Silicon Valley, she had been contacted by officials from Ireland as to "how can we duplicate its success?" O'Mara wrote in an article titled "Don't Try This at Home" that this model is not for everyone.

O'Mara says for a Silicon Valley to work, it requires several core ingredients, beginning with "giv[ing] a lot of money to brilliant people—and stay[ing] out of their way." It is further vital to have the engagement of "a top-notch university," and "location matters." San Francisco and its environs worked for the initial Silicon Valley because there was "plenty of open land to build houses, highways, and office parks." Moreover, while much of Northern California is often cloaked in fog, the Santa Clara Valley has "great weather, outdoor activities, good schools, and sought-after real estate—the California Dream." In other words, there have to be other appealing social aspects as well. "As for the rest of what it takes to build your own Silicon Valley," she writes, "all I can say is good luck. . . . Let's face it, not every block can become a new technology hub." Even more importantly, the Silicon Valley did not just come about of its own accord. Much of its genesis had to do with structural investments related primarily to "Cold War spending patterns, sustained GDP growth, and large-scale migration and immigration. It prospered because of unique local characteristics like risk-tolerant capital, entrepreneurial leadership, and good weather. It grew organically." She notes, "Place still matters, and the right ingredients still make a difference. Some of the biggest tech success stories of the past two decades, like India and Ireland, resulted from government investments that came in the form of tax breaks and lowered regulatory barriers to foreign investment—not just building research parks."

An official at the U.S. Chamber of Commerce told me, off the record, regarding American investment in Ireland, "If it's just a building, they could go, 'Costs and infrastructure here are very high.'" Moreover, he said, "everyone always says it's the tax rate, education, and the people—when in reality it's the tax rate, the tax rate, and the tax rate." Still, Ireland has set out substantial ambitions to create an "ideas economy" as its long-term strategic plan for future economic progress. This will include keeping the economic climate attractive to foreign investment, building partnerships with universities, doubling the numbers of PhDs produced, and making large-scale grants for research and development. This is being managed by Science Foundation Ireland (SFI) and includes a €500 million fund for supporting early-stage research and development in small and medium-sized enterprises. SFI hopes, by 2013, to "attract to Ireland a premium cohort of world-class researchers who have been nominated for or secured prizes, awards, and honors that will drive up the international visibility of Ireland to the global research community and the global high-tech business community." Furthermore, it "will foster entrepreneurship, mathematical, science and language skills and prioritize the roll-out of Project Maths." Together, the Irish Development Agency, Enterprise Ireland, and SFI "will develop a marketing campaign" to sell this plan. In total, €2.4 billion of infrastructure development capital has been set aside for the initiative.

I spoke with Dr. Graham Love, who is responsible for promoting SFI and the smart economy, to get a sense of how the program would develop. Love, who holds a PhD in vascular cell biology, asked to go by "Graham." He is a persuasive advocate of Ireland's potential in the area of science and technology. Graham stressed that the smart economy is not a panacea; nor will it happen overnight. He indicated that this is a "textbook chicken-and-egg" scenario in that one needs the foundations to attract the outside capital, which will take patience. It will take decades, but the "payoffs will be well worth it." Graham argued that Ireland "can't rely on foreign direct investment forever" and will need to have its own indigenous paths to competitiveness in the European and global economies. This truly is a long-term strategic vision for which "patience is crucial," he said. "You don't put a cake in an oven, pull it out early, and then wonder why it doesn't taste right." Aside from harnessing ocean energy (which is directly related to the smart economy concept), he argued that this is what Ireland has to run with.

A false image of the smart economy, said Graham Love, paints a picture of "guys in white coats in labs." The core idea behind the concept is to create research, but it also emphasizes development and export-oriented manufacturing. While "not your classic blue-collar job," said Graham, the lab coats will be a "lighter color of blue." He has a particular concern that science and lab workers will be vilified in Ireland's existing economic climate. Furthermore, the declining budgets for restructuring all levels of Irish education raise questions about the ability to sustain the infrastructure needed for a smart economy. Even worse, what if they build it, and no one comes? In that case, Ireland's well-trained people will likely emigrate and apply their skills to helping other countries. Some experts argue that Ireland should just import the high-skilled labor, as that would be cheaper than building an education system. Graham Love and others are ultimately selling a sophisticated argument about how Ireland can develop a niche economy in the early twenty-first century. At the heart of that theory is Ireland's long-standing respect for the value of education. This will, however, require more than just marketing and more than a political system benefiting short-termism. It will also require an economic strategy that stops looking at systemwide cuts through the prism of accountants.

Graham Love described the aftermath of the 2010 budget as a "horrific year" for SFI. Because the money available for grants to attract research and development was cut, approximately three hundred researchers were lost. He indicated, however, that the government had made a sustained commitment, so while SFI would likely not grow much, it would not take deeper cuts. A wildcard would be the new government coming into office—with "a new set of people to persuade," as Graham put it. This will be a sustained sell, especially as members of the Dáil have been pressuring for metrics to measure success. On 8 November 2009 the *Irish Independent* editorialized that the economic crisis had led to a substantial drop in leading science and technology researchers coming to Ireland—they were preferring South Korea, Germany, and the United States. The paper asserted that Ireland had made a "gamble that is beginning to look very shaky indeed. . . . It was a hugely ambitious wheeze. . . . The universities and research centres were to be given billions to train up promising students. They become highly skilled. Ireland has Ph.D.s coming out of its ears. Multinationals fall in love with us all over again. It's the Foreign Direct Investment equivalent of Cheryl Cole giving you the eye . . . and her phone number." The real issue, the paper noted, was that science funding in Ireland "fell off a cliff." Funding was "down 15 percent from 2008 levels. . . . The 2009 outlay [was] around 26 percent lower than what had been planned." The story reported that up to twenty-five leading scientists and researchers in areas of stem cell, semiconductor, cancer, and cellular biology research had refused appointments in Ireland because of concerns about the reliability of funding.

On 3 April 2010, the *Irish Independent* noted that Irish university graduates were beginning their careers on €400 a week or less and that the weakest areas for pay included science and technology graduates: 16.3 percent of the 2008 class of engineers was still unemployed nine months after graduating. In early September 2010, economist Colm McCarthy (who headed the original "Bord Snip" report) told the Richard Cantillon School in Tralee that the only hope for serious employment in Ireland was to create traditional blue-collar jobs in manufacturing, not in the smart economy. The same month, speaking at the Lemass International Forum, executives from major international businesses in Ireland—including Intel, Hewlett-Packard, and Pfizer—all said that Ireland's priority for investment needed to be in engineering and manufacturing, not the smart economy. Christoph Mueller, head of Aer Lingus, told the Leinster Society of Chartered Accountants, "We need to create jobs in the lower wage levels. We cannot dream the dream of the Republic of Ireland becoming a corporate university. That's not going to happen." Summarizing these comments in the *Irish Times* on 13 September 2010, John McManus wrote of the smart economy, "It's clear that business leaders have lost confidence in the approach, not least because of the inability of the Government to sell it with any conviction." This is a view that Graham Love says is "wildly off the mark."

Graham Love knows he has a real selling job to do—and he takes it on eagerly. He pointed out that when Ireland began the process of reforming education and providing universal secondary education in the 1960s, it was strongly opposed as expensive and having no clear benefit. "Similar forces decried the efforts of successive Lemass governments to drive down taxation on companies," he wrote in the *Irish Times* on 27 August 2010. Of the short-term focus on the immediate economic crisis, he added, "It's a measure of the hysteria that to even mention medium- to long-term plans for Ireland suggests one is not aware of the current crises in banking, public finances or employment. To break from the columns of the enraged in this respect is almost heresy." He pointed out that in the first decade of the 2000s, output of scientific study had "accelerated more than at any time in our history" as Ireland had exceeded the average of the European Union and OECD in terms of the output of high-quality scientific publications (which in the 1980s was on par with Bangladesh); quality had improved dramatically as in 2008 "we broke into the top 20 country ranking for scientific quality for the first time"; and the "international standing of our third-level institutions has seen a similar rise." In 2010, global university rankings placed both Trinity College and University College Dublin in the top one hundred. Ireland ranks third in the world in immunology research—not bad for a country with a population half that of New York City. Finally, Graham noted that by 2009, 39 percent of all foreign direct investment in Ireland was in the area of research, development, and innovation. By 2009, SFI-supported scientists were working with 184 multinational companies and 165 small and medium-sized enterprises. SFI researchers were collaborating with counterparts in fifty-six countries.

The smart economy program is potentially Brian Cowen's only major positive legacy as Taoiseach. If it works, it will place him alongside Seán Lemass in terms of innovative long-term planning. According to Ned Costello, CEO of the Irish Universities Association, Cowen has "a personal vision of the theory of the smart economy." Costello was involved with the concept from the beginning, working with Micheál Martin (while he was education minister) to develop a new culture of research in Irish universities that was "so new," he told me. Costello lamented that during the Celtic Tiger, Ireland was the "only place in the OECD where resources per student actually fell." Ireland needed a spark to revitalize its human capital via education. In explaining the development of the smart economy, Costello pointed out that Ireland had been very good at building capital for higher education. EU money was "used creatively" in the 1990s to target technical universities as infrastructure developments "beyond roads." This heralded the "start of seeing the university as more than teaching institutions." Ten years later, a new generation of university presidents came in with more entrepreneurial backgrounds, advocated reform, and committed to the growth of graduate education. This commitment was facilitated by the "big influx of research money," which also made universities "much more part of a global environment." Seeing opportunities for enterprise research-and-development partnerships, these institutions now "viewed themselves competitively," said Costello. Overall, he said, faculty at universities are embracing these challenges, and the false "idea of working six hours and going home" is changing among Irish professors.

The Irish government has established both a minister and a substantial advisory team for building the foundations of the smart economy. Heading up the government effort is the minister of state for science, technology, innovation, and natural resources, who in 2010 was Conor Lenihan. A former journalist, Lenihan is a Fianna Fáil TD from Dublin—and the brother of then Finance Minister Brian Lenihan. He occasionally got into trouble with public missteps. He once told another TD, who was advocating for Turkish workers in the Dáil, that he should "stick to the kebabs." In an interview on TV3, he appeared to fall asleep. He also said in June 2010 that his brother's Finance Ministry had a "lovely axe," which it "sometimes wield[ed] indiscriminately." He argued that the mentality in the Ministry of Finance simply did not "get the link" regarding the value of the smart economy relative to cuts. Most noticeable was a decision Lenihan took to help launch a book titled *The Origin of Specious Nonsense* for a friend and constituent. This self-published book described evolution as a "scientific hoax"—probably not the best public relations move for the minister for science. Lenihan withdrew from the event after much criticism, but only after it became known that the author of the book was the former owner of a pornographic magazine. A professor at the University of Minnesota wrote on his blog, "Lenihan doesn't seem to have any actual qualifications in science. . . . I think he needs a change of title." He was defeated in the 2011 election.

Knowing much of this, I quite looked forward to sitting down in June 2010 with Conor Lenihan. Despite his gaffes, I found him an effective advocate for the smart economy. Lenihan put it simply: it does not take "rocket science" to appreciate the value of what he called Ireland's new buzzword of the smart economy. Lenihan pointed out that new investors would find the size of the country gave people direct access: "It is easy to meet with a minister." "We, in Ireland," said Lenihan, are "not so elitist so that the minister is in the room" when key discussions between investors and Irish representatives occur. In the end, high-tech investors will have to ask "what kind of people . . . they want" when they choose a location, and Ireland has, and will have, a "ready supply of well-educated and highly skilled labor." Lenihan indicated that succeeding will entail substantial challenges, including "persuading policy makers and elites, pointing the science and technology sector outwards, explaining the concepts to the wider society, and ensuring that we have a good pipeline into the higher education system." He also called increasing "growing separation" between the emphasis in the work his area was doing and the broader role of arts and literature "unfortunate." Lenihan pointed to the core relationship between innovation and the arts, citing the "diverse role that da Vinci" played. He suggested that Ireland is in a place of "post-nationalism" and either has to be "in or out when it comes to globalization and opportunity."

The government is well served by a senior civil servant named Martin Shanahan, who, in June 2010, became CEO of Forfás, which provides expert advice on enterprise and science. Shanahan is an expert on the role of human capital, education, and training, especially in the areas of science and technology. We met at his office near the old canal in Dublin, and I quickly recognized him as a real-life example of the smart economy potential. Shanahan's vision is clear: "The smarter you make people, the higher the value" and the "higher the quality of business" that can be built to "drive indigenous enterprise and serve as a beacon for foreign and direct investment." Shanahan and his team have been key players behind the scenes, having "pushed the issue of maths and engineering"—subjects in which Irish students have lagged—with the Department of Education and Skills. Likewise, he argued that Ireland has much room to improve in terms of language issues—particularly Chinese language study. According to Shanahan, a key long-term challenge will be determining "how to translate to policy makers the concepts underpinning the smart economy." Without prompting, he noted that Conor Lenihan's criticism of the Finance Ministry was "a very good comment." Martin Shanahan believes that it can be a challenge to "show a yield return for the long term" when there is strong immediate incentive to invest in hard infrastructure that puts people to work. It is "important that the system maintain faith in the policy." He also noted, pausing with reflection, that during the Celtic Tiger, Ireland had "lost its tendency towards self-criticism" and that it is equally as important "not to go overboard in the other direction today and thus hold the country back from achieving new potential now." Shanahan said that Ireland is really moving back to where it could have been, had mortgage and banking interests not skewed the economy in 2001. "It isn't difficult," he said. "We are going back to the strategy that we were engaged in before the boom—to build a smart, innovation- and knowledge-based economy."

The smart economy concept is not without its critics. When I asked former Taoiseach John Bruton about the smart economy initiatives, he said, "The idea that innovation is all about software is wrong—I don't buy it. What is needed is to make all things more productive—land, labor, and capital." He said that "innovation cannot be confined to the high-tech sector. Innovation is possible in every area of activity." I asked him about reports that showed Irish secondary students were performing poorly in math. He said, "What the Irish need is a change of culture. . . . Whether that means more Plato and Aristotle versus mathematics, I don't know." As to the likely success of the smart economy concept, he is dubious: "I don't believe it. . . . It is really a funding grab by universities." Bruton told me that, in his view, "the universities have got too big a grip on this field. This should be driven by businesses getting help from universities, and not the other way around." Ireland, he felt, needed a major emphasis on development as much as research, whereas the smart economy seemed more about "research and research." Writing in the *Irish Times* on 30 March 2010, he asserted that in Ireland today, "not enough time is given in primary schools to foreign languages, science, and maths, and too much is given to learning the two national languages."

Richard Bruton, the Fine Gael TD, notes that 80 percent of the job losses in Ireland are among the young. As a result, these people will be "building the economic future of Australia, Canada, and other far-flung places," as he said in the Dáil on 29 September 2010. Still, when we met earlier in the summer, he made clear that he "favored the smart economy if it has genuine milestones." Absent metrics to measure its progress, he said, it was only "rhetoric—what are the political institutions to make it happen?" Richard Bruton prefers the concept of the "knowledge economy" and believes that cultivating science and the knowledge economy "is where it's at." Still, the "document advancing it has 794 recommendations! There is no timescale—it's a hodgepodge." Unmet is the need to "find niches and policy tools to encourage them—i.e., broadband and education—cultivating best practices to get technology into the classroom."

Venture capitalist Brian Caulfield is even more skeptical. As we chatted at his office in central Dublin, we both noted the view of cranes not moving, frozen in time in the Docklands from before the construction boom collapsed. To Caulfield, the future "has to be about many innovative products and services—and selling them . . . and manufacturing them." The smart economy is a "long-term play"; in the end, it will not employ many people and will thus be a "drop in the ocean." In fact, he argued that Ireland's task force on innovation had been "hijacked by vested interests with over 60 percent of the advisory group guiding the smart economy being paid by the public purse." "No one from the venture capital community was on the task force," he pointed out.

Stephen Brennan, the highly successful software engineer from the Digital Depot, argues, like John Bruton, that rather than a smart economy, an "entire cultural change" is needed. He sees SFI as but one part of a larger ecosystem and believes that "universities and SFI are not right to do the push." The problem for Ireland is one of "sales and marketing—not an academic one," he said. Really needed are adaptive and innovative skills, and the ability to "talk and connect" is key. The Digital Depot that Brennan coordinates then comprised ninety-seven small and medium-sized enterprises driven by a "more self-reliant generation" in which peers work together at problem solving and rapid-cycle product generation. This was all done with "no grants, no tax incentives." From Brennan's view on the ground, as to the smart economy, "the cabinet doesn't understand what it is." He feels that the government is basically "saying what the large foreign investors want to hear."

Brennan said that the Irish government really needs to "facilitate opportunities to find a customer" for start-up high-tech ventures. He thinks a better investment would be to use public-sector utilities, like Ireland's energy company, to build cooperative public-private partnerships on clean energy production that create "a solution for an Irish market—test it—and sell it to others as a service." According to Brennan, "a smart economy is where every leader is smart." Significantly, as one of Ireland's top technological talents, Stephen Brennan says the smart economy is "not about technology—it is about providing opportunity to others that they otherwise wouldn't have had." A smart economy exists "when every piece of talent has an opportunity if they want to use it." He asserted that Ireland has to invest in and secure its own differences as "the Silicon Valley already exists" (and he should know since the Digital Depot is modeled after it). Anyone can produce a product; "the only difference is the person." Vital to Ireland's future is not only studying Chinese; Brennan says that "the Irish language is important too." Yet, when I asked Brian Caulfield, the venture capitalist, about this, he was blunt: "A [far-away] buyer isn't going to buy something because it was made by some cute, redheaded Paddy. . . . A buyer isn't going to buy it because she sings lovely songs."

GET SMART

The most serious issue confronting the smart economy is the structural problems within the Irish education system feeding into it. According to the OECD, Irish primary schools have the second-highest teacher-student ratio in the European Union. The education budget is heavy in teacher pay and pensions. Like employees in other sectors, Irish teachers endured major cuts and hiring moratoriums. Students, especially in universities, were likely to face increased costs for registration and associated fees. Almost 10 percent of secondary schools had dropped physics entirely as a result of budget cuts, and according to the Royal Irish Academy, 14 percent of schools had dropped science altogether. Meanwhile, Ireland's basic Leaving Cert system had increasingly become (according to critics) a means of securing rote learning and not advancing critical thinking. Particularly troubling for the pipeline into the smart economy, the 2010 Leaving Cert results showed a continued pattern of high failures in maths, sciences, and business. Failure rates were especially high in biology, chemistry, and physics. Only 16 percent of students even took upper-level math exams, and forty-three hundred students failed the math exams at all levels. Overall, the National Adult Literary Agency reports that 40 percent of all Irish adults have serious difficulties doing basic mathematic calculations. In December 2010, the OECD reported that Ireland had dropped from fifth to seventeenth place in its literacy ratings since 2000—the steepest drop among all member nations. It had also fallen from sixteenth to twenty-sixth place in terms of math skills in just three years between 2006 and 2009. Meanwhile, Ireland faced a unique challenge in that the Catholic Church controlled more than 92 percent of the schools in the country.

According to the OECD, by 2010 Ireland was at the bottom of developed economies in terms of what it spent on education—about 4.7 percent of gross domestic product. During the Celtic Tiger, Ireland's investments in all levels of education actually declined relative to economic growth. Only the Czech Republic, Italy, and Slovakia ranked below Ireland in terms of education spending. In August 2010, I took a walk down the Liffey toward the Docklands to meet with some graduate student activists. They had organized a demonstration alongside the replica of the famine ship that sits there to protest their need to emigrate if they wanted work. When I talked to them as they donned the professional gear of nurses, lawyers, scientists, and engineers to make their point, they made clear it was not their desire to leave. One, though, asked me on the side if I could advise him about Ohio State University for further study. These students were angry and frustrated about their limited professional options despite their high skills earned in the Irish system. Increasingly, multinational corporations based in Ireland were having to hire non-Irish to meet their specific, high-skilled employ-

ment needs—especially those involving technology and non-English languages.

To get a sense of these structural issues in education, I spent a morning in
a roundtable discussion with a number of senior civil servants working in
the Department of Education and Skills who were responsible for strategic
planning, curriculum, and budgets. I came into this meeting well coached
about Ireland's horrible civil servants—an assessment that was immediately
proven wrong. These people care about their work, work very hard, and are
some of the smartest and most creative thinkers I have encountered anywhere. They too are frustrated, and they believe that with adequate support,
they could make major progress in the Irish education system. These experts
are frustrated with teachers unions that, they said, have resisted changes in
teacher education. They asserted that teachers unions focus more on numbers of teachers than on whether they are properly trained. They grew especially agitated in pointing out that people who are not trained in math are
teaching math classes (or other courses in which they lack subject-matter
training) in Irish schools. Another key concern is balancing the teaching
of special-needs children, who too often get left behind. A well-intended
desire to treat special-needs children equally has challenged teachers who
are not adequately trained to work with them. Additionally, budget cuts
have reduced the number of special-skills teachers available. This too is a
function, they asserted, of teachers unions that "focus on numbers versus
talent." They argued that teachers in Ireland are very well paid—they have
the fifth-highest salaries in Europe. There is, despite challenges, substantial
pride in the overall approach to education in Ireland. As they reminded me,
unlike in the United States, the system is based on an egalitarian concept.
"Ireland has done very well on using its education system to advance social
justice," said one senior strategic planner.

The Irish teachers unions, not surprisingly, have a different view. I also
sat down with senior policy planners, including General Secretary Sheila
Nunan of the Irish National Teachers Organization (INTO), in July 2010.
INTO represents about thirty thousand Irish primary school teachers. Like
their counterparts at the ministry, these senior union representatives are
some of the most thoughtful and creative thinkers I have met. It is a shame
that the economic climate has put these two groups at odds. The INTO people I spoke with lamented the decline of the social partnership, which was
a "forum where you could make improvements." INTO officials pointed
out that while Irish teachers are well paid, the cost of living is high, and
the workload in the classroom is challenging, given high teacher-student
ratios. Equally difficult are some inattentive parents, who view school simply as child minding. One senior policy adviser at INTO pointed out that
they had with pride taken a senior Australian official to a top-quality Irish
school to show off technological advances. The Australian, however, said

the Irish school "was about five to six years behind where they were." Despite being seen through an "accountant's lens, not an education lens," the Irish schools, INTO officials said, "deliver far more than the initial investment." These people are especially concerned that Ireland not "throw the baby out with the bathwater" as the second-level priorities are "increasingly being hijacked by the university level." A particular worry is that as Ireland streamlines toward a smart economy, it will skew the sound aspects of Irish education—especially in arts, culture, and critical thinking. One senior person at INTO called the smart economy merely "branding." INTO accepted the Croke Park plan, in large part because it felt at the time that it did not, as Sheila Nunan put it, "have the firepower—we didn't have the counterpunch against the exalted position of economists." Like the other union leaders I spoke with, Nunan said that there is "deep anger underneath the surface—as we feel we have been let down badly." She compared the "sense of purpose and hope" that Barack Obama had seemingly brought to the United States with his election as president with Ireland, which was "floundering in the dark." And yet, like the other groups in Ireland who see themselves as protectors of the public interest, the Irish teachers persevere and do their job—"doing a lot with little."

CHANGE YOU CAN BELIEVE IN

From the police, to health-care professionals, to those rebuilding the education sector, to those innovating in the private sector, Irish people are willing to take the million small steps needed to move the country forward. They want to work; they want to innovate. It is not a question of whether they will sacrifice; they already were by 2011 and were about to take even deeper hits. In some cases, the question is whether people, like the police, will refuse to tolerate this situation for long. In other cases, it is a question of whether individuals who take risks and show initiative will be rewarded, perhaps in the areas of health care, social activism, or private enterprise. In other cases still, it is a question of whether Ireland will have the resources to achieve its ambitions—for instance, in the smart economy. Ireland has human resources and natural resources; it has made major progress and has the potential to make much more. That future might come from a new social contract, or a high-tech or health-sector innovation, or from enhancements in education at all levels. It is hard, though, for many Irish to know that, then remember the billions upon billions of their euros being dumped into the Irish banks and their sovereignty being ceded to the European Union and the International Monetary Fund. The future might also lie in what has been cherished in the past—that great tradition of poets and scholars whom Ireland has sent into the world. It was, indeed, the Taoiseach, Brian Cowen, who said on 30 June 2010 that a poet or a writer "can say what others fear to say" and thus "confront what others would rather avoid." At the same time, the Taoiseach called on poets to sell Ireland as a "brand" while also cutting funding for the arts—a move that poet Derek Mahon called "dense and philistine." Sometimes, though, it truly is the artists who will challenge—and change—society. This is why I was especially keen to travel to Wicklow to meet with Sinéad O'Connor.

Start of the Dublin Pride Parade near the Garden of Remembrances at Parnell Square (June 2010).

5

A Post-Catholic Ireland

A MODERN, LIBERAL, AND MULTICULTURAL REPUBLIC

When we met in his Leinster House office in July 2010, Labour Party leader Éamon Gilmore said that Ireland had transformed from being "a very conservative country into a modern, liberal, and multicultural republic." His Labour Party colleague Ruairi Quinn also restated to me his nearly twenty-year-old declaration that Ireland was a "post-Catholic country." The millennial celebrations in 2000 symbolized this reality. While a small candle was sent out to houses to celebrate the birth of Christ, the main commemoration was the building of a spire on O'Connell Street in Dublin with no religious value whatsoever. The church had not gone away, and the vast majority of Irish are Catholics, but the notion that there is an essential cultural link between "being Irish" and "being Catholic" no longer applies. Meanwhile, Ireland has shattered international stereotypes by embracing gay rights and approving national civil-partnership-protection laws. Last but not least, Ireland has become multicultural. Taken together, these three trends tell the story of a society struggling successfully with serious cultural challenges and embracing progress. These major social issues—religion, gays, and race—are no longer "things we don't talk about" in Ireland.

GOD'S CHILDREN, DESERVING TO SLEEP SAFE

The Catholic Church has long been woven into the essential fabric of Ireland. Traditionally, to be Irish was to be Catholic. The church was initially granted a special place in politics by way of the Constitution, though freedom of religion is now guaranteed. The church also dominated the Irish education system. This relationship between the church and society manifested frequently in public policy, including legal prohibitions on birth control, abortion, homosexuality, and divorce, and even church opposition, at one point in the 1950s, to public provision of health care for children. Over time, Ireland reformed most of these social restrictions. In the 1970s, groups of women traveled on trains to Northern Ireland to purchase condoms. They returned to Dublin and handed them out in public protest of the prohibition against birth control, which is now legal. Abortion, however, is not. Women who seek abortion travel abroad while society looks the other way. Still, there is tension in this policy. In 1992, an Irish court prevented a fourteen-year-old girl from traveling to get an abortion after being raped. While the rapist was not arrested owing to a lack of evidence, the girl sued the government for the right to travel. Today Irish women are not barred from traveling under any circumstances. Still, in December 2010, the European Court of Human Rights determined that Irish law continued to violate rights to medical treatment in cases where pregnancy could damage a woman's health. Divorce became legal in the 1990s, though it is difficult to achieve. Amazingly, a woman being habitually abused by her husband could not, before then, seek compensation or justice by dissolving the marriage. Movies like *The Magdalene Sisters* (2002) exposed the treatment of wayward girls sent to live in church-run institutions while working to wash the clothes of priests and nuns and where abuse was common.

Rory FitzGerald, an Irish journalist, wrote for the Huffington Post on 31 March 2010, "Ireland is mired deep in a dark night of the soul." Would soul searching bring purification? That would remain to be seen for, in the words of Patsy McGarry, religious affairs editor of the *Irish Times*, "The Catholic Church in Ireland, as we have known it, is seriously damaged and probably beyond repair. It is sinking and sinking fast." The exposure of persistent criminality among Irish priests has caused a deep, searing pain in Ireland. For decades, child abuse by clergy constituted one of those subjects that "we don't talk about." Known child abusers were relocated by the Catholic hierarchy—not investigated or punished. The first victim to tear aside the curtain on the abuse and its cover-up was a young Irishman named Andrew Madden. Madden, whom I interviewed for this book, is now a prominent advocate for child rights in Ireland. He comes to this having been sexually abused by his local priest in Dublin beginning at age twelve. He detailed his story in *Altar Boy: A Story of Life after Abuse* (2005). The church paid Andrew Madden IR£27,500 to sign a confidentiality agreement, promising not to expose that he was sexually abused for three years by Father Ivan Payne. A journalist for the *Sunday Times* wrote on 28 September 2003 that, when reporting on Madden's initial revelation of his abuse, he received a phone call from a senior cleric who said, "[You are] liars if you print that. That boy doesn't know what he is saying."

As it turned out, Andrew Madden did know what he was saying, and he could prove it. He still had the signed documents, which he took public. Madden described his experience to me as a "microcosm" of shattered social trust. The church preferred to protect its abusive priest, Father Payne—"preferred him to me, they did," Madden told me. He reflected that "the church was supposed to be a refuge of safety." "A mother," he continued, "might spend her day worrying about life for her child—at school, at football—and drive them to church, leave them, and collect them—not aware that the risk was at the church. . . . That was where he needed the protecting." Madden asked, "How can any priest have credibility for talking to anyone about taking responsibility? It beggars belief." And yet, he said, "the government shrugs its shoulders. . . . The state is way behind the people." He is particularly adamant on the need to make it a criminal act not to report child abuse within the church. "If I don't pay taxes," he said, "I'm punished—but if I fail to report abuse I know of, I'm not." Madden said, reflecting frustration, "We live in a state of no responsibility . . . while the government shrugs its shoulders." He told me that when he first wrote to Bertie Ahern as Taoiseach, he found a leadership mostly "mindful of the Catholic vote. . . . The State was even reluctant to ask!" he said passionately. Madden and others work now to promote a constitutional amendment to guarantee children's rights. The Fianna Fáil government, he said, is "Catholic first, Irish second" as they moved very slowly to investigate the abuse allegations. It has been like "having Opus Dei in government," said Madden.

In 2000, the Irish government established the Commission to Inquire into Child Abuse, which submitted a final report in May 2009, known as the Ryan Report. The commission took evidence from over one thousand witnesses from a range of institutions and activities under the purview of the Catholic Church. The investigation found persistent patterns of abuse, as well as failure by the church and government to address the problem over an extended period. Residential reform schools, where wayward children and unmarried mothers were sent, were run like prisons. Thousands of young boys and girls had been terrorized by the Irish Catholic Church that was supposedly there to protect them. Rape was an "endemic problem." In total, thirty thousand people passed through these institutions. Boys were molested and raped. Girls were flogged, beaten, burned, and held under water. The Department of Education knew about these crimes; yet, the government neither intervened nor developed rules to prevent further abuse. Beyond this was the day-to-day abuse that people like Andrew Madden suffered by way of their parish priests.

Another study, the Murphy Report, which investigated the Dublin archdiocese, also concluded in 2009 that there had been persistent "covering up" of abuse by senior church authorities between 1975 and 2004. In many cases, the offending priest was simply moved to another location. The Dublin archdiocese, through the mid-1990s, had been mainly preoccupied with "maintenance of secrecy, the avoidance of scandal, the protection of the reputation of the Church, and the preservation of its assets. All other considerations including the welfare of children and justice for victims were subordinated to these priorities." The church, working under the culture of the Vatican, seemed to embrace the idea that it was essential to remain silent to protect its broader interests. The pope called the Irish bishops to the Vatican, where they kissed his ring. Two Irish bishops resigned; two others tried to, but the Vatican rejected their letters. By 2010, no Irish priest had been punished by the Vatican for covering up abuse. Defenders of the church argued that this is because there was no cover-up. Rather, Pope John Paul II imposed confidentiality in reporting in 2001 and, via an official letter, gave authority to then bishop Joseph Ratzinger (now Pope Benedict XVI) to protect victims. Yet, in 1987, the Dublin archdiocese had quietly taken out an insurance policy against possible legal claims from victims of child abuse by priests and nuns—clearly implying an early awareness of a problem.

Church defenders often do more harm to the Vatican than good. William Donohue, president of the Catholic League for Religious and Civil Rights, a conservative Catholic organization in the United States, said on *Larry King Live* on 30 March 2010, "Al Qaeda suspects are presumed more innocent than the pope," who, Donohue said, had been "libeled" by criticism alleging a cover-up. He suggested that the events in question were decades in the past and that the situation had improved because "practicing homosexuals" are no longer allowed into the priesthood. He continued that what had happened was not "abuse" because the victims were "postpubescent," making these consensual homosexual acts. Even if this unfounded assertion were true, Donohue might have noted that it is statutory rape to have sex with a minor—gay or straight.

In summer 2010, press scrutiny grew of the 2001 letter sent by Pope John Paul II to place direct authority to investigate abuse claims in the hands of then Cardinal Ratzinger. The *New York Times* reported on 1 July 2010, "The Vatican took action only after bishops from English-speaking nations became so concerned about resistance from top Church officials that the Vatican convened a secret meeting to hear their complaints—an extraordinary example of prelates from across the globe collectively pressing their superiors for reform, and one that had not previously been revealed." The article cited new documentation that the authority for the office held by Cardinal Ratzinger to investigate sexual-abuse cases had long been established—dating back eighty years to 1922 and updated in 1962. "But for the two decades he was in charge of that office, the future Pope never asserted that authority, failing to act even as the cases undermined the church's credibility in the United States, Australia, Ireland and elsewhere." When Cardinal Ratzinger's office could have been investigating the abuse crisis, it was more preoccupied, according to the *New York Times*, with "examining supernatural phenomena, like apparitions of the Virgin Mary, so that hoaxes did not 'corrupt the faith,' according to the Rev. Brian Mulcahy, a former member of the staff." Cardinal Ratzinger viewed liberation theology in Latin America—not the abuse of children by priests and nuns—as a "fundamental threat to the church."

The victims of abuse had to wait nine painful years for the Ryan Report, which ultimately held no one specifically accountable. By 2010, the Irish government had nonetheless compensated a total of fourteen thousand people for their suffering, and while lacking justice, they had validation. One woman, Christine Buckley, told the press that the atmosphere and culture at the Goldenbridge Industrial School was one of "almost 24 hour horror. . . . We arose at a quarter past five, we walked around a yard shivering. We went to Mass at seven. Many collapsed because we were not allowed to have a drink after half-four in the day because a lot of us bed wet. I tried to tell the world what was happening to us and I gave a letter to a breadman that, unfortunately, got back into her hands [a nun]. And for that, I received a beating which opened up my flesh on my left thigh." Buckley was in the care of the Irish Catholic institutions from the age of three weeks until she was seventeen. An older gentleman in the audience for an RTÉ discussion on 25 May 2009 grew emotional, saying that when he went to testify, there were "seven barristers there questioning me and telling me that I was telling lies when I told them that I got raped of a Saturday . . . got a merciful beating after it [he visibly tears up and chokes on his words at this point]—and then he came along the following morning and put Holy Communion in my mouth! You don't know what happened there! . . . You don't know what I feel inside me! You don't know the hurt I have!" He went on to discuss a subsequent suicide attempt. Then he said, "They brought a man ninety odd years of age, to tell me I was telling lies . . . that I wasn't beaten for an hour, nonstop—by two of 'em! By two of them! Nonstop! From head to toe without a shred of cloth on my body." He added, "How many times I jump out of the bed at night with the sweat pumping out of me" because he saw the priests calling him to the next room "to rape me, to bugger me, and beat the shite out of me."

An unknown number of children died from this abuse. Survivors suffered lifelong trauma. The Ryan Report concludes, "Witnesses also described lives marked by poverty, social isolation, alcoholism, mental illness, sleep disturbance, aggressive behavior, and self harm. Approximately 30 percent of the witnesses described a constellation of ongoing, debilitating mental health concerns for example; suicidal behavior, depression, alcohol and substance abuse and eating disorders, which required treatment including psychiatric admission, medication and counseling." At one women's institution sold to developers in 1993, 155 bodies of inmates were found dead and buried in unmarked graves. The depth of the depravity was still only becoming clear a year after the Murphy Report was released, when on 6 December 2010 a priest named Tony Walsh was convicted and sentenced to sixteen years in prison for raping one young boy and assaulting two more during the 1970s and 1980s. Father Walsh was known for his impersonations of Elvis Presley, and as he raped one young boy at the alter, tied down with chords from his vestments, he played a record of loud Elvis music to drown out the boy's screams. On 7 December 2010, Mary Raftery, writing in the *Irish Times*, provided an extended quote from the boy:

> When I have a dream, I am basically being raped again and again and again and I could not under any circumstances overstress the world "raped." I am being raped in my sleep. It mightn't happen every night of the week but it happens at least two or three times a week and I just don't sleep because I just, the minute I close my eyes and get back into the sleep I'm getting raped again so I stay awake and I. . . . What they do, they give me drugs to put me to sleep, or I take a bottle of whiskey if I don't want to go near the doctor.

Another child, abused by the priest, reported being beaten by his father when he tried to complain about it to his parents.

The problem of abuse was not simply a moral issue; it was also a criminal one. At the core of that was, to many critics, the appearance, at worst, of a Vatican cover-up and, at best, a deep insensitivity to the issue of child abuse. In January 2011, Irish media reported on a letter sent from the Vatican to Ireland's Catholic bishops in 1997. In the letter, the Vatican's diplomat in Ireland, Archbishop Luciano Storero, warned Irish bishops that the Vatican had decided that the Irish church's policy of mandatory reporting of abuse claims to the police violated canon law and gave "rise to serious reservations of both a moral and a canonical nature." Initially, the Vatican had implied that this abuse of children was mainly an Irish problem. However, similar cases in Australia, Austria, Belgium, Brazil, Germany, Switzerland, the United States, and elsewhere made clear this was also a Vatican problem—though the Irish had suffered immensely. Next followed accusations against the victims . . . calling them liars. Another reaction was to claim the church was the victim of a global anti-Catholic campaign or even conspiracy. Amazingly, the archbishop of Westminster (in the United Kingdom) told the *Guardian* on 20 May 2009, "I think of those in religious orders and some of the clergy in Dublin who have to face these facts from their past which instinctively and quite naturally they'd rather not look at. That takes courage, and also we shouldn't forget that this account today will also overshadow all of the good that they also did." Nothing, though, could top the comments of Pope Benedict XVI's personal preacher in the Vatican, who on 2 April 2010 likened the ongoing criticism of the church and the pontiff over child abuse to the "collective violence" that the Jews had suffered. He quoted a friend who said the criticism reminded him of "the more shameful aspects of anti-Semitism."

Pope Benedict XVI issued a written apology read out to the Catholics of Ireland at Mass in spring 2010. I went to a church outside Dublin and sought a copy. I asked the priest if I could have one, and he said, "Oh, certainly, take as many as you want. We have boxes of them that no one has touched." The pope's apology is an eloquent statement and well worth a close read. It encompasses a lengthy history of the role of the Catholic Church and its unique place in Irish society. The pope indicated that "serious mistakes" had been made as to how the claims of abuse were treated. To the victims, he said, "You have suffered grievously and I am truly sorry." He wrote that priests who were pedophiles would "answer before God and properly constituted tribunals for the sinful and criminal actions they have committed." Still, the emphasis seemed to be on containing the crisis not meting out justice. In March 2010, it was made public that the cardinal in charge of the Irish church, Seán Brady, had been present during meetings in which children signed contracts agreeing to remain silent over abuse in 1975. In June 2010, a survey in the *Irish Times* showed that 76 percent of the Irish public felt that Cardinal Brady should resign. As Rory FitzGerald wrote on 27 March 2010 for the Huffington Post, "The Irish people now feel betrayed by their banks, their government, and their church: the Pope's letter was written to a nation in despair."

A more fundamental issue cuts to the bone of all Irish—the culture of silence, that deep tradition of things "we just don't talk about." This cultural veil was at the heart of the disaster that built up in the Irish Catholic Church over decades. A victim of abuse turned activist, Colm O'Gorman told *CBS News* on 20 May 2009,

> I think there is, frankly, a danger that Irish society may also not be prepared to recognize our collective responsibility for what happened to our children. The children who were put in these institutions were the most marginalized. They were children living in extreme poverty. Children who it was deemed were at moral danger because of the lifestyle decisions of their parents. I mean, appalling subjective judgmental decisions that saw children removed from loving homes and put into these institutions . . . these were the children that nobody wanted to see. And because we didn't want to see them, we banished them to these institutions where they were brutalized, and we have to take responsibility for that.

He added, "It's not just about church. . . . It's about recognizing our collective responsibility for each other—and act[ing] on that." "The things that happen in the world happen because we tolerate them, and it is up to us not to tolerate them if we want to change that," said O'Gorman. Still, the burden rests heavy on the Catholic Church—at all levels. As Mary Raftery of the *Irish Times* said in an interview with television talk show host and social commentator Vincent Browne, "The extent of the depravity and cruelty and the sadism that was exercised against defenseless vulnerable children by people who we put our complete trust and total faith—people who had dedicated their lives to God—in the Catholic Church . . . that they could behave this way, that it was covered up internally within the orders, not just then, but now." Or, as Sinéad O'Connor has said, the crisis in the church was a matter of "God's children, deserving to sleep safe."

A NEW MODEL OF CHURCH IN IRELAND

I felt, as I dove into this material, that it was important to hear from officials in the church. I requested to meet with the archbishop of Dublin, Diarmuid Martin, but he was unavailable. Archbishop Martin had been forward leaning in apologizing and reaching out to victims, calling the way the church had dealt with the crisis a "catastrophe." On 26 November 2010, he stated on the Dublin diocese website, "I see more clearly that the catastrophic manner in which the abuse was dealt with was a symptom of a deeper malaise within the Irish church." "The church in Ireland," he said, "has allowed itself to drift into a position where its role in society had grown beyond what is legitimate. It acted as a world apart. It became self-centered. It felt that it could be forgiving of abusers in a simplistic manner and rarely empathized with the hurt of children." Archbishop Martin said that the church had "deluded itself about the faith of the Irish people." He said of his own diocese that it had "failed not just in its responses to victims and their families. It failed itself and it failed society by trying to keep the evidence within its own structures."

While I could not see Archbishop Martin, his office arranged for me to spend time with Father Ciarán O'Carroll, who heads the parish at University Church at St. Stephen's Green. A scholar of the church, having published *Paul Cardinal Cullen: Portrait of a Practical Nationalist* (2009), he is also the first priest ever appointed in the Dublin archdiocese for evangelization. This was an important position in the church hierarchy because, even before the abuse crisis broke, there had been a marked decline among churchgoers in Ireland. By 2010, on average, only 43 percent of Irish Catholics attended Mass each week. Ireland, long an exporter of priests, was now importing them. Churches were increasingly used for public meetings or aromatherapy sessions, not religious services. By 2010, there were only two Irish priests under age thirty-five in the country. Given the dramatic decline of the Catholic Church in Ireland, I found Father O'Carroll a breath of fresh air. He represents that which is good in the church—past, present, and future. He is thoughtful, with a sense of humor, and realistic about the concerns people have about the role of the church in Irish society. Father O'Carroll says that if you walk up around Grafton Street and ask people, "Do you like the essence of the faith?—they will say yes." But, he said frankly, "if you ask them then, Do you like the church?—they will say no." The Catholic Church, said Father O'Carroll, has to "learn from mistakes." And yet, at the same time he is optimistic, believing "it is an exciting time to be a member of the church." Father O'Carroll says this is "a dynamic time of change, challenge, reflections, and realization." We are "building a new model of church in Ireland."

Father O'Carroll's optimism is welcome and unique. As David Rice, a former Dominican, wrote in the *Irish Times* on 31 August 2010, "The tiny handful of evil-doers among the clergy, along with the incredibly crass, self-protecting decisions of church leaders, all the way up to the Vatican, have made life hell for many priests. . . . Have you noticed how few black suits and Roman collars you see on the streets today? Understandably, for no one wants to be spat at and there are some among the public who would do just that." At a recent service I attended, the congregation, which had already been talking, kept talking while the priest was addressing them. He actually seemed used to it—perhaps he was just happy to have people in the room? On the other hand, as Father O'Carroll and I left our meeting in his private residence, we came into his church (a beautiful Byzantine structure). We hushed our tones quickly as—in the late afternoon on a Monday—a large group of young people was kneeling in intense prayer.

Father O'Carroll places the crisis facing the church in the context of what he calls a "massive, seismic change over time." He points to four historical models of the church in Ireland. The first includes the monastic scholar-priests who dedicated all of their being to Christ. Like St. Kevin and others, they live on today with locations named after them. Father O'Carroll points to people like St. Brigid, who, while not a bishop, "had the symbols of authority" looked to by feminist Catholics today. These devoted followers were "very highly educated and very highly disciplined." Father O'Carroll points to the ancient silver in the national museum today—these monks "were alchemists, they knew how to smote silver." He points out that the *Book of Kells* (from this period) was "written in Latin—not easy to do. They had to study it and know it. . . . From this the whole island was evangelized." A legacy was put in place in which change could occur—from top down and bottom up, derived from study and philosophy. Father O'Carroll points, in particular, to the monastic settlements at the Skellig Islands, off Kerry. He notes that there is "nothing there—it is harsh, very steep and yet they cut steps, gardened, leveled stairs." I had literally just returned from

Kerry and had visited the Skelligs by boat. I knew precisely what he was talking of with these misty rocks a dozen miles off into the ocean. It is like a journey back in time. Where life seemed impossible, these monks thrived on their ingenuity and faith.

For the second model, Father O'Carroll points to the Augustinian and Franciscan monastics. These deeply devoted people gave their entire lives to the church. They performed the same patterns every day as routine was essential to their faith. "They would rise at four in the morning—pray, work, have recreation, dinner, prayer, sleep, and do it again." These devotees too were "highly successful" in their day—which lasted about one thousand years. From this era came the idea of the benefits of routine and healthy living with the pattern of the day, a "very strict rhythm of life—eating well, living balanced." Though strict and rigid, this model promoted a culture of balance and prioritized faith over material goods.

At the end of this period, Henry VIII in England revolted against the Catholic Church over marriage rights and seized lands and assets in Ireland. This led to a third model. When Henry VIII—"a multimarried distant king," said Father O'Carroll—saw that that there was no revolt against the seizing of Irish church assets, the English saw an opening. From this came anti-Catholic legislation. The church had to go underground as penal laws were imposed. Controlling the church became a means of controlling the Irish people. Priests had to hide out, go underground to practice. It was then that the Irish national identity merged with Catholicism. Both the people and the church were at risk of oppression under the penal laws. By the 1700s, Ireland had seen a loosening of its own structures. As Charles Morris writes in *American Catholic* (1998), in the Ireland of that time, "the chastity of Irish maidens was the wonder, or frustration, of travelers. But at the same time, rural Ireland was a highly sexual society, with sexual tensions resolved by very early marriage. . . . Crossroad dancing—nightlong outdoor gatherings of several villages for sexually charged dancing, raucous drinking, and usually a rousing fight—was the despair of reforming clergy."

Father O'Carroll writes in his book about the fourth model—that established by Cardinal Paul Cullen, who made the Irish Catholic Church a unified, structured, and puritan reflection of the faith. In the 1880s, Father O'Carroll notes, Cardinal Cullen set about building a new model in which Catholic education was a primary goal. To Cardinal Cullen, "education was key to a broader sense of purpose." From this, Father O'Carroll suggests, comes the modern social emphasis on the importance of education. Cardinal Cullen even brought Cardinal John Henry Newman to Ireland to help modernize church school curricula. This model came on the heels of the famine that had ravaged the country. Thus, church-driven institution building was a major component of social development. There were positive aspects to this legacy—especially an emphasis on looking out for society's most vulnerable. Education was seen as the solution to social deprivation. On the other hand, this was also the genesis of the idea of building various institutions for orphans and wayward children—which grew into dens of depravity. Father O'Carroll is quick to point to this as a "structural flaw in this fourth model," which allowed some people to join "not for gospel-driven conviction—but rather a means of access to children by those who were there for the wrong reasons." The resultant scandals have "understandably upset the Irish people."

Although Father O'Carroll did not say so, long before the abuse scandals, the church seemed, once it had undertaken this social role, to guard its prerogative and power jealously. For example, Minister of Health Noël Browne advanced what became known as the "Mother and Child Scheme" in 1950. The idea was to guarantee maternity care to all mothers and health care to all children through age sixteen. The archbishop of Dublin, John McQuaid, opposed this concept of social welfare; he insisted that the provision of health care was a private matter for families and that social welfare promoted laziness. If the state were to assume primary responsibility for guaranteeing this kind of social care, it could force the church toward the margins—even if that was not the intended effect. Noël Browne gave the correspondence he received from church officials to the press and exposed a concerted campaign by them to overturn the policy of an elected government. The historical evidence shows that the church played a major role in blocking guaranteed social welfare for children. Noël Browne lost the battle, eventually resigning for failing to implement his government's elected mandate. In a speech to the Dáil on 12 April 1951, he said, regarding the behind-the-scenes manipulations of the church hierarchy, "I trust that the standards manifested in these dealings are not customary in the public life of this or any other democratic nation and I hope that my experience has been exceptional." In his book *John Charles McQuaid: Ruler of Catholic Ireland* (2000), John Cooney quotes a British ambassador as saying to Noël Browne about Cardinal McQuaid (as he passed by in a procession), "What an impressive figure, Noël, would he not make a notable addition to the distinguished company of the Spanish Inquisitors."

Because of the deep cultural impact of centuries of church and society relations, Father O'Carroll said, "The Irish people have an ability to live with ambiguity." He also draws a direct link to the nineteenth-century relationship between the institutional development of church schools and the rise of Republican nationalism. He observes that while St. Stephen's Green is built as a "pantheon of Irish greats," the Irish still do not celebrate their many compatriots who fought and died in World War I—"we don't talk about that." The Irish only just recently erected a memorial by the Liffey for the famine that killed one million and caused one million to emigrate. While a song like "Skibbereen" captures the reality "of people dying by the roadside . . . still there was no commemoration of this for over 150 years—Ireland drew a veil," said Father O'Carroll. Meanwhile, deeply held traditions have blended with popular culture and profit. Today, Father O'Carroll reflects on St. Patrick's Day as a day for Ireland's patron saint. It has, however, become a "pagan ritual—like Mardi Gras—a bunch of Paddy whackers," said Father O'Carroll.

Father O'Carroll optimistically sees Ireland as moving toward an innovative and creative fifth model. This, he believes, is where Ruairi Quinn is right in pointing to a post-Catholic Ireland: the fourth model is gone. According to Father O'Carroll, the fourth model was "an obstacle to fission." There was "much great in it—the hard work of nuns and the many who sought to do good." At the height of the Celtic Tiger, for example, the church was consistently pointing out the increase of poverty while many Irish were getting rich. But he is also clear that the church "has to learn from mistakes." In his view, too many "volunteered not out of love, but to exploit and have access to children—this has to be learned from." He pointed out, for example, that "there is a child protection statement now in every church. This has to be learned and built on." The church has to "recapture the word of God," said Father O'Carroll. His own work is at the core of this effort, seeking to "recapture the Gospel and to evangelize in a new way." He says that there is a growing sense in the church that it is time to reassess its place in Irish education—"to have a role, but not for managing and patronage—we have to lean back." While "debate is the essence of the Catholic school . . . there is a tipping point," said Father O'Carroll, given the multiple faiths emerging in the country. In his own parish, he asks for more community and parental involvement in youngsters' attaining First Communion. The institution, he said, should not be a place "just to drop off the children and leave them to the church." Three parties to his process for each child's achieving Communion include the school, the parent, and the parish. The central challenge of the fifth model is to embrace change. Father O'Carroll notes that you can walk outside his church onto St. Stephen's Green. You will see everyone "all around, together—politicians, immigrants, poor—but all in their own spheres—not in a community." If there is a priest who can bridge past, present, and future, he will be the likes of Father Ciarán O'Carroll.

FIGHT THE REAL ENEMY

Bray is a beautiful part of south Dublin—actually just over the county line into County Wicklow. In summer, it is a place where families go for long strolls on the beach and play amusement games. James Joyce, Oscar Wilde, and leading Irish artists have resided in Bray. A large cross at the summit of Bray Head looks down over the village and out to sea. Living in Bray, under that cross, is a woman who has for decades lived the credo of Bob Marley—that people have to get up and stand up for their rights. Sinéad O'Connor is bold, she is brave, and she is now vindicated for performing courageous acts of protest when a nation sat silent. She once famously said, "I didn't want to be a fucking pop star. I wanted to be a protest singer." She protested the abuse of children in Ireland before the world when she declared on *Saturday Night Live*, "Fight the real enemy!"

At that time, Sinéad O'Connor was a major international talent who had broken big into the American market with the hit "Nothing Compares to U." She has a beautiful, soulful voice. Her career since September 1992, however, has been marked by the moment on *Saturday Night Live* when she ended her rendition of Bob Marley's "War." In a close-up shot viewed live by tens of millions of people, she tore up a photo of the pope. This protest was widely misunderstood in the United States as a disrespectful act against the Catholic Church and the very popular Pope John Paul II. Watching it, I thought it a brave act that breathed life into the stagnant rock and roll of the 1990s—though like most, I also initially recoiled at the symbolism regarding the pope and the photo. It certainly did not occur to me at the time that, nearly twenty years later, we would be sitting in her house drinking coffee and talking about it.

On *Saturday Night Live*, Sinéad O'Connor had ripped off the veil covering Ireland and its church. She had exposed the raw wound underneath for the world to see. Engineers at *Saturday Night Live* refused to turn on the applause sign following her song, and NBC censored her performance in its West Coast broadcast. *Saturday Night Live* music director John Zonars is quoted in Tom Shales and James Andrew Miller's *Live from New York* (2002) as saying, "I think that was the classiest move in the whole history of television—not cueing applause." The show's producer, Lorne Michaels, apparently had a different understanding of "classy": "I think it was the bravest possible thing she could do. . . . To her the church symbolized everything that was bad about growing up in Ireland the way she grew up in Ireland, and so she was making a strong political statement." Still, the next week's host, actor Joe Pesci, said if it had been his show, "I would have given her such a smack." It is fascinating, to be generous, that Joe Pesci (a Catholic) was not condemned for his response, which he saw as justified violence against a woman.

A couple of weeks later, Sinéad O'Connor was a headline performer at a tribute concert at Madison Square Gardens in New York City to celebrate thirty years of Bob Dylan recordings. She was introduced by music legend Kris Kristofferson, who said, "I am real proud to introduce this next artist, whose name has become synonymous with courage and integrity." She was then greeted by this crowd, gathered in celebration of the dean of protest music, with boos. To be fair, there were as many cheers as boos, if not more. And, to be fair, Dylan himself was booed once—though for the lesser infraction of playing an electric guitar. After a couple of minutes of the audience's reaction, a clearly upset Sinéad O'Connor was comforted on stage by Kristofferson, who could be heard to say off mic, "Don't let the bastards get you down." As her band started the Dylan tune they were going to cover, she stopped them and instead went into a powerful rendition of the song that she had performed on *Saturday Night Live*. Sinéad O'Connor, who has since publicly discussed depression resulting from her childhood experiences, said in 1992 of Dylan that growing up she had been inspired by his very religious album *Slow Train Coming*. She had rehearsed to sing at the tribute concert the very spiritual "I Believe in You" off that record. Of Dylan, she said in 1992, "He kept me alive—if it wasn't for him, I wouldn't have survived my, you know, life. . . . He was the one thing that was there to tell me that I wasn't crazy and that I was going to survive and stay alive." And here she was, appallingly being booed by an ignorant audience— blinders pulled down to the reality of child abuse that she alone seemed to have the courage to stand up against.

By spring 2010, Sinéad O'Connor voiced the growing public outrage at the revelations of child abuse in the Catholic Church. She appeared on *Larry King Live*, *The Rachel Maddow Show*, and other major American programs. Even now, however, she is attacked—for many in Ireland and elsewhere find it is easier to dismiss her than to listen to what she has to say. Brent Bozell, head of the right-wing Media Research Center in the United States, berated her, saying, "Sinéad O'Connor is a despicable, hate-filled person who has no business being portrayed as a reasonable voice to discuss the Catholic Church that she has disgraced for the last twenty years." "CNN's decision to have her on as a credible source to bash and criticize the Pope and the Catholic Church is like having the KKK on to criticize President Obama, or Nazis on to criticize Jews. It's disgusting, unacceptable, and disgraceful," said Bozell. It is striking that after all the public reports of what had gone on in the Catholic Church, anyone could so willingly display the views Bozell articulated.

Sinéad O'Connor was right about what was happening in the church and way ahead of her time. Kris Kristofferson penned a song (released in 2009) called "Sister Sinéad" about how her acts of bravery had been misunderstood and how she had "told them her truth just as hard as she could." Sinéad O'Connor represents the essence of what an artist can be—a voice for the voiceless. And she really knows her details when it comes to the Catholic Church. She comes across more as a good lawyer, actually, than an artist. It does make one wonder, though, where the other Irish artists are. Bono of U2, for example, has an audience of millions with a monthly column in the *New York Times*, which he uses well to speak out for the poor of the world. Yet, Bono had, by 2011, little to say about the pain of abuse suffered by his own people.

In March 2010, Sinéad O'Connor took to the pages of the *Washington Post* in a lengthy opinion article addressing the pope's apology to Catholics in Ireland. She wrote, "To many people in my homeland, the pope's letter is an insult not only to our intelligence, but to our faith and to our country." She then told of her own experiences in the Grianan Training Center, a Magdalene laundry, something that many outside Ireland did not fully understand until recently. A nun there actually gave O'Connor her first guitar. She wrote, "Schools for troubled youth have been rife with barbaric corporal punishments, psychological abuse and sexual abuse." She pointed out that in one town of Ferns, south of Dublin, the Irish government had found "more than 100 allegations of sexual abuse by priests . . . between 1962 and 2002. Accused priests weren't investigated by police; they were deemed to be suffering a 'moral' problem." This was, she pointed out, not inconsistent with Vatican policy: "Benedict's infamous 2001 letter to bishops around the world ordered them to keep sexual abuse allegations secret under threat of excommunication—updating a noxious church policy, expressed in a 1962 document, that both priests accused of sex crimes and their victims 'observe the strictest secret' and be 'restrained by a perpetual silence.'" O'Connor spoke directly to an American audience, asking of Pope Benedict XVI, "Now that he sits in Saint Peter's chair, are we to believe that his position has changed? Are we to take comfort in last week's revelations that, in 1996, he declined to defrock a priest who may have molested as many as 200 deaf boys in Wisconsin?" She finds it particularly alarming that the pope's solution for Catholics with doubts derived from these scandals is to "get closer to the church." She pointed out to me that the pope's letter of apology was addressed to the Mass goers of Ireland—not to the people of Ireland. That is an important distinction for, if addressed through the churches, the letter could ascribe the crisis to moral failure—it would have constituted a legal admission if passed through government diplomatic channels.

Appearing on the *Late Late Show* on 2 April 2010 and speaking on Good Friday, Sinéad O'Connor said, "I believe in the Holy Spirit—I don't think that these people do. . . . They are now acting as if they do not believe in the Holy Spirit at all." She told host Ryan Tubridy that, in her view, by not having fired the responsible people who failed go to the police, the pope "really doesn't take [the abuse] very seriously." She added, "These guys cannot take in what they actually did, and we're idiots if we keep on trying to break the door down. What we have to accept is that they don't believe in God, they don't believe in the Holy Spirit, or else the pope has no self-esteem for not firing these guys." Of the Irish people she said, "If we are in a dysfunctional relationship with an organization which is an abuser and is holding the Holy Spirit hostage, and if we believe in the Holy Spirit, we should now stand up and walk away from an organization that does not respect the Holy Spirit." O'Connor's view is clear: as she told the *Guardian* on 10 September 2010, "The Vatican is a nest of devils and a haven for criminals. It's evil, the very top of the toppermost is evil." For the Huffington Post on 20 September 2010, she wrote in an "Open Letter to the Pope" that while he lamented that the church had not acted quickly enough on abuse reports, "church authorities acted extremely quickly and decisively, but in protection of rapist priests and the church, not of children."

To Sinéad O'Connor, the "scandal in the church is the biggest crisis in Irish history." When we discussed her reemergence as a lawyerlike expert on the abuse in the church, she said, "I wanted to be sure that when I meet my maker, that it can't be said that the artists didn't care." O'Connor offers solid advice to the church: "it needs transparency or it won't survive—it has to become a twenty-first-century institution." She calls the new debate over the church in the United States a "gift from God." I could not help but reflect on a degree of spiritual crisis confronting my own country. Images of Abu Ghraib prison and other horrors of war passed through my mind when she said to me, speaking of the earlier situation in Northern Ireland, "The existence of war means you have a spiritual problem." I thought much about this just over a week later when listening to Crosby, Stills, and Nash sing at a concert in Dublin, "God, are you listening, a prayer from a simple man—Stop all this killing in your name," which Graham Nash dedicated to the victims of the conflict in Northern Ireland.

Sinéad O'Connor cherishes the values of truth, unconditional love, and peace that are the heart of the Catholic faith. She said, "The essence of the church is beautiful." In her public role, she said, "[I have] stood for what I knew is real." Most significantly, "it is not that the people have left the church—it is the church that has left the people." She also noted that not all priests and nuns are blameworthy, as many are excellent and deeply caring people—but they work in "a medieval institution." While there is a proven issue of pedophilia, I wondered if perhaps this was a severe symptom, the fundamental issue being hierarchy and power. I told O'Connor that in many ways, the church hierarchy had come to remind me of a desperate clinging to power that many decaying states evinced just before they reformed or collapsed under the weight of their own contradictions. She took the biblical view that "nothing is hidden that won't be revealed."

By 2009 the views that Sinéad O'Connor had been advancing for nearly two decades—and for which she had been ostracized and called a radical—had become mainstream. The *Irish Times* wrote in a scathing editorial published on 1 December 2009, "The days of bending the knee in Ireland to kiss the ring of men who were, at best, indifferent or, at worst, compliant in covering up and perpetuating the abuse of children have passed." The paper concluded, "Abused children have been relegated to the status of distasteful and unwelcome problems. It bears all the hallmarks of a crude, damage limitation exercise. Where is Papal authority and responsibility? In spite of efforts by Vatican spokesmen to put distance between the Pope and the scandals of the Irish church, the buck really does stop in Rome." Maureen Dowd, a *New York Times* columnist, cited Gary Wills, a prominent American Catholic writer, as saying that Jesus "is the one who said, 'Whatever you did to any of my brothers, even the lowliest, you did to me.' That means that the priests abusing the vulnerable young were doing that to Jesus, raping Jesus. Any clerical functionary who shows more sympathy for the predator priests than for their victims instantly disqualified himself as a follower of Jesus. The cardinals said they must care for their own, going to jail if necessary to protect a priest. We say the same thing, but the 'our own' we care for are the victimized, the poor, the violated. They are Jesus."

In 2010, the pope assented—ten years after the Ryan commission began its work and after his public apology—to appoint a team of prelates to investigate the church in Ireland. Still, the official Vatican statement said that the purpose was to "contribute to the desired spiritual and moral renewal." The question of morality versus crime still seemed unappreciated. Ireland's situation was really a case better handled by the police, not the Vatican. Perhaps it was not that the Vatican should be visiting Ireland to find the deeper meaning of the various official studies already done. Rather, Ireland should be sending a team of lawyers to Rome to investigate the Vatican. In her appearance on *Larry King Live* on 30 March 2010, it was Sinéad O'Connor who offered an olive branch, saying, "We should all be willing to open our hearts and our minds to listening to each other carefully here. OK, we've been fighting and fighting now for years. Let's see how do we go forward. . . . Let's unclench our fists towards each other and see how can we actually hold hands and lead each other into trust in the 21st century." Still, as a victim of abuse, American journalist Thomas Roberts, said on the same show, "There are over a billion Catholics in the world. I think they would all like to believe that maybe [the pope] doesn't know anything. But when the priest who abused me confessed and went to jail, it took Benedict three years to defrock him."

I asked Sinéad O'Connor for her views on the future of the church. What key changes did she think were needed? What would a twenty-first-century Catholic Church look like? O'Connor's answer did not match the radical image that her detractors suggest. She offered three commonsense reforms, all oriented toward transparency. First, she argued that "there needs to be a regime change—there has to be a right to get rid of people." She said this can be achieved by making promotion within the church hierarchy open to public scrutiny—"like when someone is nominated for the U.S. Supreme Court." Second, she suggested that priests should be allowed to marry. That priests cannot marry is a relatively new development in the church's history (and, as I suggested to her, it certainly raises questions about their effectiveness as marriage counselors). Third, she said, there must be "women in the hierarchy—women should be priests." On this issue, Maureen Dowd wrote that "stupefyingly" the Vatican "links raping children with ordaining women as priests, deeming both *graviora delicta*, or grave offenses. . . . Letting women be priests—which should be seen as a way to help cleanse the church and move it beyond its infantilized and defensive state—is now on the list of awful sins right next to pedophilia, heresy, apostasy, and schism." Transparency, marriage, and women in the priesthood—these are hardly wide-eyed, crazy ideas. When I left her house and looked up at the cross overlooking Bray, I could not help but think that in talking with Sinéad O'Connor, I had engaged with someone willing to shoulder the burden of change, to challenge Ireland to take ownership of its own destiny. But she and others like her are but lone voices, albeit voices for those who are all too often not heard at all—children.

A REMARKABLE AND RADICAL TRANSFORMATION

In June 2010, after a long day of interviews and meetings, I stopped into a pub in Howth for a meal and a pint. Looking up on the wall, I saw a poster advertising the Dublin Pride Festival. That, I thought, was something you did not use to see in Ireland. I grabbed a pamphlet sponsored by YouTube, Microsoft, and others. It advertised events like "PantiBar Pride," where "Thousands of exquisite Irish queers take to the streets of Dublin." The theme—"We are family too"—was intended to "highlight the fact that LGBTQ [lesbian, gay, bisexual, transgender, and queer] families inhabit a legal limbo without recognition or protection from the State with no legal rights of constitutional recognition." The lord mayor of Dublin, Emer Costello, gave an official welcome: "The Dublin Pride Festival is a welcome celebration of diversity, freedom and respect which I am most happy to support." A week of events included a range of activities, from a "Walking Tour of Historic Gay Dublin" to a discussion hosted by Microsoft titled "Workplace Diversity—Pride at Work."

The culminating event was the Dublin Pride Parade on 26 June 2010. I thought, This we have to see! So, we loaded up the family on the train and headed for the Garden of Remembrance at the top of O'Connell Street. What we saw gave true meaning to the idea that Ireland is a "modern, liberal, and multicultural republic," as Éamon Gilmore had put it. A double-decker bus came down the parade route bearing a big "Labour LGBT" banner, which included a big poster of Éamon Gilmore's head captioned, "Vote Labour." We saw the Lesbian Gay and Bisexual Teachers Group marching. We saw men dressed as women, women dressed as men, and most beautifully, families marching with their children, parents, brothers, and sisters. It was like a family-friendly Fat Tuesday at Mardi Gras. Seeing over five thousand people marching and the streets packed with supporters was uplifting. Truly impressive was how normal and routine it was.

It was not always that way in Ireland: social and religious norms, as well as the law, deemed homosexuality a deviant act. Only in 1993 were laws criminalizing homosexual acts taken off the books. Although these laws had not really been enforced, life for gays and lesbians in Ireland was no easy thing. The law overturning the criminalization had a classic Irish tone: "Any rule of law by virtue of which buggery between persons is an offense is hereby abolished." Importantly, the law also prohibited "buggery by an adult with any person under age 17" (in 2006, the word "buggery" was changed to "defilement of a child"). This law culminated a twenty-year effort headed by a gay senator named David Norris and other activists, including Kieran Rose, a city manager, who founded the Gay and Lesbian Equality Network (GLEN), which he now chairs. The Irish Gay Rights movement emerged in 1974 and, though small, grew steadily. The 1980s, however, saw a decline in gay activism. Kieran Rose told me that one gay pride march had included just a handful of people "with a car whose battery was dying, which made the loudspeaker they had impossible to hear . . . and then we had to push the car . . . an apt symbol for those times." This ended the initial phase of gay activism in Ireland—but a new one began with the government's slow response to the AIDS crisis. Meanwhile, David Norris had initiated in 1977 several legal challenges to Ireland's official discrimination against gays. A future president of Ireland, Mary Robinson, worked as his lawyer. Illustrating how far Ireland had come, by 2011 Senator David Norris was a leading candidate to become the next president of Ireland. If he won, in October 2011, Ireland would have an openly gay president—one who is a scholar of James Joyce and was actually born in the Belgian Congo.

In *Diverse Communities: The Evolution of Lesbian and Gay Politics in Ireland* (1994), Kieran Rose writes, "The perception of Irish people as irredeemably 'backward' on sexual and social issues was an idea that GLEN refused to accept. . . . GLEN knew that there were real and positive traditional Irish values, arising from the struggle against colonialism and for civil, religious and economic rights, which could be activated and the demand for equality was attuned to this heritage." I met with Kieran Rose and Eoin Collins, GLEN's director of policy change, over lunch at the Shelbourne Hotel on St. Stephen's Green in Dublin in July 2010. Ireland had recently passed historic legislation guaranteeing the legality of civil partnerships between gay and lesbian couples. The overwhelmingly favorable attitude among parties in the Dáil had rendered a final vote unnecessary. I was in the Dáil when some of the debates were going on and was deeply impressed by the ease with which Ireland was moving on this matter. I was equally unimpressed by the five protesters—yes, five—outside Leinster House holding bigoted signs condemning gays. I told Kieran Rose, had this been in some parts of the United States, right-wing evangelicals might have mustered tens of thousands or more on the streets.

To their credit, the socially conservative Fianna Fáil had sponsored the bill—having promised in the party's 2007 campaign manifesto to do so. Justice Minister Dermot Ahern said, "Through these legislative measures, the State clearly has shown that people as individuals are entitled to receive fair and equal treatment whether they are gay, lesbian, or heterosexual." Charles Flanagan, Fine Gael's spokesperson on justice, equality and law reform, said, "Ireland is part of a growing trend towards a more rights-driven world that permits and celebrates difference. I am pleased Ireland is moving in that direction." If any concern was expressed, it was that the bill should have gone further. As the Labour spokesperson on these issues said, "The Labour Party welcomes the Bill. It is not the end of the journey, but it is a long way down the path. It clearly does not go as far as the Labour party's Civil Unions Bill." Now, in Ireland gays and lesbians have what Kieran Rose describes in a GLEN document as "a comprehensive set of protections, rights, and obligations for same-sex couples across a wide range of areas including home protections, pensions, taxation, immigration, maintenance, next of kin, social welfare, domestic violence, inheritance, enduring power of attorney and creation of joint tenacities." Rose told me that in his view, this was the "greatest civil rights reform since independence."

Kieran Rose explained to me what he saw as GLEN's success as a network for local and national civil rights campaigns for gays and lesbians around Ireland. The strategy had three key elements. First, he said, "we sought out to win over people." This was done "in a way that people would feel this was working for them—by treading softly and not trashing other people's values." "Our emphasis was on values and equality," he said. Second, "we worked to persuade opposition." The key here was to convince people to see supporting human rights broadly as in their own interests. This approach was essential because, while "winning is important, how you win is equally important." GLEN aimed to ensure that legislation could be supported "no matter what government was in place and no matter what minister was in charge so that it would be seen as a victory for all." The third part of the strategy was "to isolate the bigots." However, the last thing that GLEN wants is a "culture war." According to Rose, one small gay group targets a "bigot of the month," which in the end only highlights the bigot's views and "doesn't help with marginalizing." Rose believes it is far more effective to "talk to the doubter and respect them."

The image in the United States of Ireland as a conservative Catholic country had, to Kieran Rose, become "an embarrassment" and "counterintuitive."

In our discussion, I noted how this false stereotype really says much more about the United States and its view of Irishness than about anything going on in Ireland. He reminded me of the reaction of the Ancient Order of Hibernians, which organized the annual St. Patrick's Day parade in New York City. In his book Kieran Rose describes the scene in April 1990 when a small group of Irish American gays and lesbians applied to march in the parade. The parade organizers, "bolstered by the strongly anti-gay Archbishop of New York, Cardinal John O'Connor, refused to admit them on the grounds that [they were] pledged to uphold the teachings of the Catholic Church, which regards the practice of homosexuality as sinful." The next year, this same request prompted major media coverage. One group associated with the Ancient Order of Hibernians invited about three hundred Irish gays and various supporters to march with them—joined by Mayor David Dinkins. "At various stages along the route," Rose writes, "they were pelted with beer cans, booed, and screamed at." By 2011, the New York parade still excluded gay organizations—the same ones that now march freely to cheers on St. Patrick's Day in Ireland. Irish president Mary McAleese turned down an invitation to be the grand marshal of the 2011 parade in New York City. Though scheduling reasons were cited, Naill O'Dowd insightfully told the *Irish Independent* on 23 September 2010, "I think she made her decision based on the fact that she has a great relationship with gay groups in Ireland and this would be a hugely controversial move for her because of the ban on gays in the parade." President McAleese has been a consistent supporter of gay and lesbian rights since becoming president in 1997.

To Kieran Rose, "The idea that the Irish people are racist is a myth. . . . Ireland has a positive tradition of progressivism." This false image was reflected back on New York in fall 2010 when the Republican Party candidate for governor, Carl Paladino, said, "We must stop pandering to the pornographers and the perverts, who seek to target our children and destroy their lives. I didn't march in the gay parade—the gay pride parade—this year. My opponent did. And that's not the example that we should be showing our children, certainly not in our schools." Paladino said that children "should not be brainwashed into thinking that homosexuality is an equally valid or successful option" (as being in a heterosexual marriage and raising a family). Paladino later defended himself by saying that there was "no difference" between his feelings and those of the Catholic Church. Not so fast, said the head of the Irish American Republicans in New York, Jeff Cleary. Cleary said, "What someone does in their private life is their private life. This is a fundamental right of a free people. If someone is homosexual or transgendered, that's their right, and Carl Paladino was completely out of line. I found his remarks insulting and full of bigotry."

Either way, by 2011 "Catholic Ireland" had more progressive gay and lesbian rights protections than even New York City, a generally welcoming place. In addition to civil partnerships, Ireland had gays and lesbians serving openly in the military. Neil Ward of the Garda Representative Association told me of an organization of gay police officers in Ireland called "The G-Force." Its real name is "Group G," and its goals include providing a forum for social interaction and peer support among LGBT police, assisting in the development of policy on diversity issues, helping police in dealing with the public on LGBT diversity issues, and increasing the visibility of LGBT staff via communications initiatives.

GLEN has been effective at making the case to the government and the private sector about the benefits of diversity in the workplace. "Say you have a merchant banker in New York City who happens to be gay—he would get greater protections if he set up his business in Ireland than in New York City," Kieran Rose said. A 2010 GLEN report titled "Lesbian, Gay and Bisexual Diversity in the Workplace" illustrated the point (it was financed by, among others, IBM). In a forward, Tánaiste Mary Coughlan wrote, "Diversity brings with it an openness to new ideas, more creative workforces, and wider markets and customer bases. . . . Our openness to lesbians, gay, bisexual and transgender people will be a critical part of our success as an advanced, competitive, and 'smart' global economy. The Government recognizes that diversity and equality can be key global competitive advantages for Ireland in developing, attracting and retaining investment, enterprises, key high-skilled workers, and visitors, and is committed to ensuring equality for LGBT people in the workplace and in society." The GLEN report highlighted IBM Ireland: "For IBM Ireland strong diversity policies and an inclusive workplace for lesbian and gay staff is fundamentally about supporting employees to contribute their full potential in an atmosphere of understanding, respect, and trust." According to David Cornick, vice president of IBM North East Europe, "The diversity journey is about leveraging all differences and creating the environment to maximize talent." IBM supports a "Pride/Diversity Month" each June. Meanwhile, Google in Ireland has an annual budget for public pride events, including maintaining a presence in the Gay Pride Parade in June and public displays of support by the executive leadership. Still, deep structural legacies persist. A university employee is quoted as saying, "The University where I work does not have a positive attitude towards LGBT people. For all the 'equality' and 'diversity' legislation and workplace policies in existence, few practical steps are ever taken to deal with bullying. It is more likely that the complainant will be pressurized to leave the workplace."

Kieran Rose is proud that civil partnership remained a vital social and political priority "even in the midst of the greatest economic downturn in state history." I was curious whether there were dissenters—gays and lesbians who might prefer to lose and prove a point or to hold out for full marriage rights. Kieran Rose and Eoin Collins both sighed with a smile.

"Yes, it was a hard sell for some." "It was," they said, "the bane of our life—a family dispute internally. We had to hold our nerve." Early on in the process of building support for the legislation, several members of the Dáil told GLEN leaders that "if they [were] attacked by the gay side, they wouldn't engage, they would just drop it." Furthermore, Rose added, "We never gave up on the idea of marriage—that is the gold standard—and we are close to it." Marriage was not pushed, not for lack of support for the idea but for concern that constitutional impediments might prevent its passage by the Supreme Court. The national referendum on divorce in 1995 had only barely passed, so any national debate on marriage seemed a bridge too far—for the time being.

The GLEN team does not want "to be triumphalist" as its members feel that is bad strategy. Lasting changes have nonetheless taken place within Irish society. A March 2008 public-opinion poll released by the Marriage Equality campaign reported that 84 percent of Irish people supported civil partnership. A solid majority, 58 percent, supported the right to full legal marriage. Still, GLEN's leadership feels there is much more work to do. GLEN employed a consulting group to produce a report titled "Evaluation of the Building Sustainable Communities Programme," which enumerated the organization's larger set of strategic goals. The report (which was shared with me in draft) shows the degree to which GLEN has evolved from a purely voluntary advocacy body into a highly successful organization supported with government funding and staff. A major resource for gay and lesbian issues in Ireland with substantial ongoing goals—for example, working in health arenas and securing safe and inclusive work environments—GLEN has "created opportunities to engage with key decision-makers at the highest level." The group has helped support and shape the conclusions of formal reports prepared for the government. In addition to its expertise and con-sensus building, GLEN is credited with being a "voice of reasonableness and pragmatism." At the heart of its pragmatic approach is success at "shaping the agenda and building conditions for change." GLEN is also skilled at "recognizing opportunities, constraints, and choices" and "does not play a 'zero sum' game—they build on and consolidate achievements." GLEN has become a "trusted voice of LGBT people in the policy and legislative areas," a status earned "because of *how* they engage with partners." The report concludes, "GLEN has successfully combined a 'missionary zeal' to achieve policy and legislative change for LGBT people with an astute professional-ism in how it pursues its agenda."

Homophobia still exists in Ireland. In 2009, the Public Service Executive Union surveyed ten thousand of its members and found that 60 percent of LGBT respondents were not "out" to their immediate supervisor, 53 percent had to be secretive about their sexuality, 53 percent feared unfair treatment, and 60 percent said they were "not free to be themselves." When one talks to Irish people, there is general acceptance of gays and lesbians. Substantial barriers remain, however—socially and legally, for example—to seeing gay adoption as legitimate. At the same time, many Irish argue that if a gay couple wants to provide one of the world's unwanted children with a loving home, then that is what should matter. Still, if this is the kind of stumbling block Ireland faces now, then that marks true progress from the days when homosexuality was illegal and gays were often beaten, shunned, and humiliated in their homes, in their schools, and by their church. Senator David Norris spoke eloquently on the civil-partnership legislation before the upper house of parliament, the Seanad:

> For most of my life, including most of my adult life, I was branded as a criminal by ancient and alien laws for something over which I had as little control as the colour of my skin. I was what was known in those prim days before gay liberation as a "homosexual." At one time I was both technically a known criminal and a Member of this House at the same time, yet I have come through to this week when we shall see the passage of a Bill that will give a degree of recognition to same-sex couples. That is certainly a remarkable and radical transformation to be experienced by any human being.

On 17 January 2011, Glenn Cunningham and Adriano Vilar were announced as the first gay couple in Irish history to have their civil partnership formally recognized by the state. The *Irish Times* quoted Kieran Rose that day as saying, "This is a new dawn for lesbian and gay couples." Also of note, at the same time as Vilar was sorting out his civil-partnership documentation, he was also finalizing his emigrant status—as he is a high-tech worker from Brazil.

NO ONE IS AS IRISH AS MUHAMMAD ALI—OR BARACK O'BAMA

In September 2009, boxing legend Muhammad Ali made what the Associated Press called "a sentimental journey . . . to discover his Irish roots, and met distant relatives during celebrations at a local town hall and a nearby castle." Ali went to Ennis to visit the home of his great-grandfather, Abe Grady. Ali's wife, Yolanda, "said her husband's Irish blood might help explain his legendary ability to bludgeon his opponents with Blarney as well as punches." Ennis made Muhammad Ali a "freeman," which gave him special privileges in the town, including free parking. Having tried to park in Ennis, I can vouch that this is no small thing. And although he is famous for being America's first African American president, there is, it turns out, a song lyric by the Corrigan Brothers that says there is "no one as Irish as Barack Obama." Via his mother, President Obama has ancestors from Moneygall in Ireland. As the song declares, "He's as Irish as bacon, and cabbage and stew. . . . He's in the White House, he took his chance—now let's see Barack do Riverdance." During the 2008 presidential election, as part of the team that advised the Obama campaign on European issues, I did some support work on Irish policy and outreach, including assisting in some research on his lineage. It turned out that Barack Obama's Irish relative, Falmouth Kearney, had settled in Ohio, just down the road from where we live. After the election, I received a package of moving drawings and letters from twelve-year-old schoolchildren in Ennis about what his winning meant to them. We passed this on to Washington, and the school received a package of official material from the inauguration of the United States' forty-fourth president—its first African Irish American one.

Multiculturalism might be the most important lasting benefit of the Celtic Tiger. Irish culture has always had a strand of diversity, despite a general impression that it has been insular and homogenous. First, the Irish have been global travelers over the decades. They have experienced the world and often imparted their experiences back at home. Second, the Irish had their own experience with violent colonialism, giving them empathy for other oppressed peoples. This has translated into a liberal view toward asylum seekers and refugees. Third, the Irish have had a small Jewish Community since the eleventh century. Huguenots came from Germany in the eighteenth century. Muslims came in the 1950s. Fourth, integration into the European Union opened up a new labor force for Irish businesses. Finally, the Irish are indeed a "welcoming people." Still, the degree to which Ireland has been culturally globalized is impressive. Walk the streets of any city, big or small, in the nation today, and you will see Chinese shops, African shops, Polish shops, Arabs, Romanians, Pakistanis, and Indians—Ireland's face has gone global. According to the 2002 census, over 10 percent of Ireland's population was non-Irish.

In July 2010, the Trinity Immigration Initiative published the results of a three-year study titled "Addressing the Current and Future Reality of Ireland's Multicultural Status." The report emphasized that Ireland has done very well in integration, particularly with first-generation "newcomers." However, Ireland increasingly struggles to get "newcomer" children to engage in Irish life—lest they become marginalized among their peer groups—particularly if they lack English language. Often the children of immigrants have been treated as "special-needs" cases, which is ironic as many have parents who are doctors, nurses, and engineers. According to the study, 7 percent of primary school students and 5 percent of postprimary students are international; yet, the government had cut funding for teaching them English. This was serious because "young migrants are highly motivated and have a strong sense of education but face challenges of language, racism, and bullying." I asked Joan Burton, then Labour Party finance spokesperson, about how multiculturalism had affected her area in west Dublin. She pointed out that Mulhuddart had been "transformed by a wave of immigrants." Burton was alarmed, though, that the government was cutting funding for teaching English as the primary language for these "newcomers." "The key is getting them the language skills they need. This is vital for logistical support, for school—as it stands, the children are getting social English—but they really need serious language support." She pointed out that this is crucial because, in the end, the cost of dealing with more serious problems when these people are adults is much higher than addressing them during the less expensive younger years of education. Much of the pressure for support in this area has come from teachers. According to a senior official at the Irish National Teachers Organization (INTO), these children are getting "the language of the playground." This person said that Dublin 15 (Burton's constituency) has become "ghettoized—marginalized." "A lot of the children that need language tuition—refugees and unemployed newcomer families—are not getting it." He added, "There is a danger of creating a downward cycle of alienating a whole group of people." He said, "there is not enough English taught to this new generation to engage them in the curriculum."

Companies like Google and Facebook, already located in Ireland, make clear that they require a multinational and multilingual workforce. According to a leading Irish economist, John FitzGerald, many of the firms that invest in Ireland have a high influx of skilled foreign workers, and many are run by outside management. He pointed out that thirty-five languages are spoken inside the Google Headquarters in Ireland. As a back-of-the-envelope estimate, FitzGerald noted that although many immigrants have left due to the bad economy, "among those who [have] stayed are the highest skilled—doctors, scientists, engineers, et cetera." It will be interesting to see how many of these people marry Irish partners—the coming decades could see "as many as three hundred thousand children" of mixed Irish and other ethnic backgrounds in the country. In a population of 4.5 million, that would be a massive demographic change. Overall, Ireland has adjusted well to this trend. For example, in 2004 there were no cultural liaison officers and multicultural training for police. By 2010 the police, at their own initiative, had over four hundred such officers. On the other hand, the force itself is not integrated to any serious degree. In Britain, for example, one will see police officers of Irish, Pakistani, Indian, and African background; that is not the case in Ireland. Guidelines for teachers titled *Intercultural Education in the Primary School* raise perhaps the most essential question: "Do we need to re-examine our concept of 'Irishness' in order to maintain a cultural identity?" The study asks, "Is racism a problem in Ireland?" According to a senior official at the Ministry of Education and Skills, only a small number of teachers have adequate training in multicultural issues.

Generally, government too often views the issue "as a problem, not an opportunity." Another official added, "It is not a problem of resources, it is an issue of mind-set." There are also private schools in Ireland—some of them are even Muslim—but many people cannot afford them. And privatization brings as much the danger of isolation as the promise of integration among communities.

Liam Doran of the Irish Nurses and Midwives Organisation calls this multicultural change a "revolution. . . . There used to be a 'Chinese wall' in the Irish Sea." This revolution, he said, has been a "terrific shock to the Irish people." People like Doran are concerned that as the economy continues to turn down, the "open arms" that welcomed newcomers might suddenly become less friendly as jobs dry up. In 2005, one hundred thousand people took to the streets in Dublin protesting the hiring of eastern Europeans as cheap labor by Irish Ferries (which was replacing five hundred Irish workers with people mainly from Latvia). The *Irish Independent* reported on 11 April 2010 that over half of all black Africans living in Ireland had experienced racism. This followed on the racially driven murder of a young black immigrant teen named Toyosi Shittabey from Tallaght earlier in the year. The paper quoted Ken McCue, of the group Sports against Racism in Ireland (which was set up in 1997), as saying racism is very real: "We get it on the pitch, from the sidelines, in the dressing room, on the way to games and coming away from games. It just never stops. Our players are very well-disciplined and ignore it. We ourselves get people calling the office and screaming down the phone at us, calling us 'n***** lovers' and about this being a 'green and white' country." The *Irish Independent* quoted an immigrant from Congo who said, "I was on a bus to Tallaght and a man and woman sent their young child to ask me why was I here and why did I not go home. I said to her I was Irish and live in Ireland. She went back and told them and they sent her again. They began screaming at me that I was a n****r and go back to Africa."

To get a sense of how the situation looked from the immigrant perspective, I visited with Eric Yao, a Ghanaian who directs the Africa Center on Lower Abbey Street in Dublin. The center provides intercultural training and cultural activities and emphasizes political involvement by its members—taking credit for a 44 percent increase in voting among immigrants in Ireland. Founded in 2000, the center focuses on what it says are traditional Irish values of antidiscrimination, inclusion, learning, and justice. Yao is a perfect example of the kind of immigrant that has brought a new generation of talent to the country. He has a master's in international relations, speaks fluent Polish, and is married to a medical doctor. His wife had many choices of where she could work but preferred Ireland. According to Yao, as welcoming as Ireland was, "society was not adequately prepared for the influx—and yet many were very talented—doctors, pharmacists, nurses, engineers." "Ireland," he said, "wasn't ready." Immigrant spouses have found it difficult, as he did, to find work given visa restrictions. This has hurt Ireland, he argues, because this is not the case in Australia, the United States, and other places they could choose to live.

Eric Yao believes the government is doing a good job of recognizing the issue of race, but tokenism often replaces serious initiatives. He said when it was revealed that there were two people of non-Irish origin working in the Department of Justice, "they went wild celebrating." He is troubled, though, that when the government did a policy paper on integration, "Africans were not consulted—they had zero role." According to Yao, "Ireland is not a racist country—but there are many incidents of racism." He tells me, for example, that many Irish "refuse to get into a taxi with a black driver and there are certain areas where taxi companies are asked not to send Africans." Yao advised me to walk up to the O'Connell Street taxi lines and see how many cabs had black drivers, which I did. At least on that particular day, there were none.

Former Fianna Fáil TD and government minister Conor Lenihan said people looking to invest in Ireland will ask themselves what kind of people they want. Interestingly, while the Irish benefited greatly during the Celtic Tiger from having an English-speaking population, multilingualism and multiculturalism are now essential elements of human capital. The ability to speak Spanish, Chinese, or other languages in the context of a "global education" is at the core of the smart economy vision. Conor Lenihan notes that today some of the "most skilled in Ireland have been from the non-EU countries—the Africans, the Asians, the East Europeans." Lenihan was the first appointed minister for integration policy, serving from 2007 to 2009 in that position, which was created following a government-led study to create a National Action Plan against Racism, put in place by Bertie Ahern. The study's report places responsibility with the government to ensure that "racism has no place in Irish society." Yet, Lenihan was mostly famous in this position for one of his more colorful public acts—looking to ban Sikhs in the Irish police (of which there was one, a Garda reserve named Ravinder Singh) from wearing the turban. Lenihan said that people coming to Ireland "must understand our way of doing things." This was problematic in that the Catholic cross was actually on the police uniform at the time, and the police organized Masses for its members, which implied official state support exclusively for one faith.

In 1997 the European Union sponsored the European Year against Racism, led in Ireland by a gentleman named Philip Watt, who was then asked to build the National Consultative Committee on Racism and Interculturalism (NCCRI) with government funding. I met with Philip Watt in Skerries, north of Dublin. He spoke at length about the changes that Ireland has undergone. He credited Mary Harney, for example, with working to change rules in the health sector "so non-Irish could run a pharmacy" and also calling attention to "Irish nurses being promoted more than foreign nurses, who yet often came with more qualifications." In one case, a "famous vet was not allowed to practice in Ireland—and yet," Watt noted with exasperation, "his book was on the syllabus at University College Dublin. . . . To be qualified in Ireland, he would have to sit for his veterinary exams again." Yet, by October 2010, the Dublin Institute of Technology was hosting, with sponsorship of the U.S. Embassy, a conference titled "Muslim Entrepreneurship in Ireland," showing how far things had come.

Under Philip Watt, the NCCRI developed into a top-notch resource for information about racism in Ireland. However, it was shut down in December 2008—ostensibly for budgetary reasons. Some in government, however, had taken a harsh view of the organization. Watt paraphrased opponents as saying, "Why pay these people to criticize us?" The group, as a government-funded but independent advisory board, was seen as "left of center politically" and "a threat to civil servants," said Watt. Still, the economic crisis did indeed bring widespread budget cuts. Watt pointed out that the government also cut its antipoverty agency. It had also previously seen "immigrants as draining resources," and the NCCRI had succeeded in changing that attitude. On that score, Philip Watt credited Bertie Ahern, who, he said, "had his ear on the ground, to be fair." But now, he added, the government is "no longer engaged in meaningful dialogue with civil society." The NCCRI, Watt said, fell victim to a "direct campaign against them in the press." The group, nonetheless, had a major impact in developing a proactive architecture for the government to promote, gearing up government agencies for antiracism, and helping develop a clear strategy for the government to develop a national plan.

According to the NCCRI, in 2007 there were 180 reported incidents of racism—up from 66 in 2004. These included damage to property, assault, harassment, and incitement to hatred. In terms of equity issues in society, there had been a 106 percent increase in race-based complaints in the Department of Justice. Watt noted that much of the challenge is to bridge cultures. For example, in Ireland it is expected that people will say "please" and "thank you" as a basic courtesy. In much of the African community, however, "not only is that not expected, it is an offense because people there only say 'please' and 'thank you' to God." Also, in many African cultures, people "don't make eye contact as that can be either a sign of aggression or a come on." But because too many Irish are not experienced with this, "shifty or insincere is how these Africans are seen," said Watt. So, he concluded, this has to be a two-way process: Africans will have to adjust, but so will Irish—they will need, for example, "to be aware not to offer a handshake to Muslims." A key challenge, said Watt, is determining how to promote these understandings "without social engineering" via "interpersonal and interactive conditions." He said that many newcomers to Ireland are surprised by what they find. Many Polish immigrants tell him that they are "surprised how little theater there is, how there are not public swimming pools, and how poor the health care is compared to back home in Poland." He said that many Chinese immigrants also came with high expectations of the Irish theater as a part of society, yet found (in their view) when settling out in the midlands that there existed "no culture or arts."

I became aware in early 2010 of a group called Show Racism the Red Card, a "player driven education initiative harnessing the profile of sportspersons to communicate an antiracism message and promote intercultural activities in schools and communities," according to a briefing provided to me by its program coordinator, Garrett Mullan. Funnily enough, Mullan is the brother of my brother-in-law, something we only realized after the fact. It is a small island. Mullan was excited by a similar movement among soccer players in the United Kingdom when he lived there, and in 2006 he received funding to launch the initiative in Ireland. The program is supported by the Gaelic Players Association, the Professional Footballers Association of Ireland, and the Irish Rugby Union Players Association; Basketball Ireland was added in 2007. Led by Mullan, each year this group distributes sixty thousand posters campaigning against racism in sport featuring fourteen Eircom League of Ireland teams.

Every secondary school and many primary schools, as well as other organizations, received one of four thousand copies of a DVD educational pack the group produced. The DVD features athletes speaking of their own experiences with racism. It shows, at the street level, a group of teens in Balbriggan who one day saw racist graffiti written on a wall. These teens took the initiative to paint it over themselves. In the process they took affirmation from each other and formed the group Balbriggan Youth against Racism, which sponsors international cultural-awareness events and activities in this area near Dublin. The video also shows how Irish soccer players rallied around a black player from Cameroon who was greeted with chants of "monkey" from the stands. In a moving response, his teammates took the field, carrying big red signs reading, "Show Racism the Red Card," which they held up to the fans in the stands. The mission of Show Racism the Red Card Ireland is ambitious: "Our vision is a society which includes and integrates people of all cultures—a society free of racism." In 2009, more than ten thousand young Irish participated in programs sponsored in some part by this group.

In 2010, Garrett Mullan began organizing a summer camp in Donegal. Modeled after Gaelic summer schools, this camp brought together youth from all walks of life in the Republic and Northern Ireland. Mullan said,

"While the Gaeltacht colleges promote Irish culture, our intercultural camp sought to promote learning around different cultures. So as well as learning around Irish, there was also learning of Esperanto, French, Russian, Slovenian, Spanish languages. They learned songs in Russian and Slovenian and dances from Ireland, India, and Russia." He added, "The composition of the camp was half from Irish backgrounds and the other half from non-Irish backgrounds. The non-Irish came from Congolese, Indian, Iranian, Japanese, Kurdish, Pakistani, Polish, South African, Ugandan and Ukrainian families." Also in 2010, Show Racism the Red Card sponsored a competition involving sixty-two schools and youth services from across Ireland. They would watch the DVD and then produce their own response—in videos, paintings, poems, and the like. The winning entry was a comic book from a primary school in Donegal. Mullan told me,

> The teacher, Ms. McMonagle, wrote to me the day after the awards presentation. "We had a fantastic day and I wanted to thank you so much for all your hard work. You have really made a difference in the lives of a lot of people in Raphoe. We arrived home to cars and cars of beeping horns and flashing lights. The whole community were standing out waving. I only wish you could of seen it. Show Racism the Red Card will be talked about in Raphoe for a long time. News spread faster than we even imagined. There were children out in their pajamas waving and requests on the radio. It was brilliant."

Garrett Mullan told me that dealing with racism in Ireland is "often seen as a Pandora's box, something not to be opened or dealt with, and often people feel dealing with racism is all about political correctness. We have a simple message, and that is treating people differently because of their color, nationality, or religious background is not right and should not be accepted." "Diversity is an asset for Ireland," he said, adding, "The Chief Executive of Google Ireland recently said that the reason for locating to Ireland as a base for European and Asian operations was that there was access to a multicultural and multilingual workforce." I was particularly moved by a letter he shared with me from a young girl in the west of Ireland named Yasmina Rahmoune. She writes, "The politically correct term for me is mixed race, as my mother comes from Sligo, and my father from a town called Bousmail in Algeria. Except people (sometimes even teachers) still cannot seem to grasp this. I've been called colored, half caste, black, white, etc. Every time I correct the person, and every time I get the same response of well what do YOU want to be called then, so I say Yasmina Rahmoune. . . . What I see in the mirror is a person, but not everyone sees me that way." She tells of how when she was eight years old, she was compared to a potato and hit in the eye. She says she received more abuse in secondary school: "I would get jeered at, at the school gate, eggs thrown at me as I'd walk home, and my mother would be taunted. They even went so far as to break my windows on one occasion." She says that, as a child, she used to scrub her skin in the bath to try to make other people accept her. Now, with pride, she says, "I am your typical teenager. I love music, going out, shopping, spending time online and talking for hours on the phone. I'm really just like any other Irish teen."

At home and abroad, there are fewer more pressing needs than for the Irish people to learn foreign languages. Yet, the Irish government spends about €1 billion a year for compulsory Gaelic-language training—a legacy from the days of Éamon de Valera. At the Department of Education and Skills, I was told that there is "pressure on the budget" for Irish—and that "it will have to be looked at." One senior official there told me that a survey conducted by the department showed that most Irish like the idea of compulsory Gaelic—but when asked if they ever used it, hardly any respondents said yes. In June 2010, the head of Hewlett-Packard in Ireland, Martin Murphy, said that far too much time and money is spent on Gaelic and that Ireland would do better to invest in the study of Chinese. According to the *Irish Times* reporting on 20 April 2010, only 8 percent of Irish secondary students learn two or more foreign languages, while the European average is 60 percent. When Murphy announced that he would be hiring for Hewlett-Packard in Dublin, he made clear that multiple language fluency was a must. The *Irish Times* pointed to an interview Murphy had done the previous March on *Morning Ireland*. The interviewer had quipped, "No Irish need apply then." Still, when I asked Micheál Martin if the government might consider removing compulsory Gaelic or cutting funding, he said without pause, "That's not going to happen."

While Gaelic is compulsory, a foreign language is not. This makes Ireland the only country in the European Union that does not require all students to have some level of foreign-language proficiency. Only 68 percent of students taking the Leaving Cert in Ireland sit for a foreign-language test. I could not help but reflect on this dilemma at the Crosby, Stills, and Nash concert mentioned earlier. At one point, people were yelling up songs to play. Graham Nash said, "You know, when you shout up like that, we can't hear a word—it all sounds like Gaelic." Then Stephen Stills took to the mic and said, "Yeah, you know, like most Americans, I have a wee bit of Irish in me—but I don't speak a fucking word of Gaelic." When I was once visiting a friend in Dublin, a nice elderly gentleman at his house insisted, "You don't really know poetry until you have heard it in Gaelic." He then commenced to recite, from memory, poem after poem in Gaelic. I did not want to be rude and thus sat there—not understanding a word.

GOD SAVE IRELAND

In our home hangs a framed tapestry with a quote embroidered on it: "God Save Ireland." Today, when one looks beyond Ireland's economy, politics, and the church crisis, one would have to ask, From what? Ireland is now grappling painfully, but honestly and realistically, with generations of sexual abuse by priests. It not only acknowledges gays and lesbians but embraces them. Ireland is no longer a mainly white island off in the Atlantic separated from Europe and the world. Its face is multicultural. These aspects of "we don't talk about that" regarding the church, sexuality, and race are gone. This is change you can believe in—this is today's Ireland. While many Irish people remain uncomfortable, this fundamental change opens major new opportunities for meeting existing challenges creatively and effectively. This includes what were once commonly referred to as "the Troubles" up North.

Derry's welcome sign, where Bloody Sunday occurred. The people of Derry today continue to advance a standard of human rights that defines both Ireland and much of its place in the world.

6

The Jigsaw Puzzle of Peace

HOW LONG TO SING THIS SONG?

In their song "40," U2 asks, "How long to sing this song?" Bono sang that humanity would "sing a new song" one day. Today, in Northern Ireland, a new song is being sung. All is certainly not perfect, but the process of making peace has been accomplished. The process of building peace, however, is only beginning. Like a jigsaw puzzle in the works, the outside frame has been built, but many complex pieces remain to be put in place—and not all fit easily. The people of Northern Ireland have invested their lives in a positive future, and only a small few would turn back the clock. For the vast majority of the people in Northern Ireland, theirs is an extraordinary story of struggle, hope, and spirit. Still, danger lurks below the surface, and if it is left unaddressed, the fragile peace could slip away. Northern Ireland is a hard place. The seas drive the coast, the mountains are rugged, and the people have faced down some of life's most difficult challenges. But the proverbial spring has arrived, and Northern Ireland has a vital message to send to the world. Peace is possible—but it takes constant care.

NO MORE TROUBLES IN BELFAST?

The image of "the Troubles" in the North has beguiled Ireland since 1921, when the island was partitioned. The claims to the North by Catholic rebels and nationalist Republican politicians fed deep divisions within the populace across Ireland. That nationalism reinforced political power in the North and South. As Garret FitzGerald said to me, the Catholic Church

141

gained its unique position in the Republic as a benefit of partition. The church could not have had the same power in a united Ireland with a sizeable non-Catholic population to accommodate. Meanwhile, Protestants led by Unionist politicians and loyalist militants formed a two-thirds majority of the Northern population, and for decades they denied basic civil rights to Catholics. They feared unification, which would make them a minority in a majority Catholic state. Efforts to address Catholic grievances were often seen as threatening to the Protestants. Efforts to reassure Protestants were seen as undermining Catholic rights.

For decades sectarian tensions evolved into mass public demonstrations, and unrest eventually gave way to incidences of barbaric terrorism. The nonviolence of Martin Luther King in the United States inspired early civil rights protests by Catholics in the 1960s, especially in Derry, but violent elements emerged as an upward spiral of violence and terror gripped the North—frequently spilling over into Britain and occasionally into the Republic. A Protestant paramilitary group, the Ulster Volunteer Force (UVF), carried out violent attacks against Catholics, and the Irish Republican Army (IRA) reemerged to protect Catholics. Each act of violence seemed to incite a response, thus provoking more attacks. In 1969, riots in Derry—the "Battle of the Bogside"—led the British government in London to intervene with troops, initially to provide security and protect Catholic minorities. Nonetheless, a radical and violent wing of the IRA, the so-called Provisional IRA (PIRA), emerged to challenge the troop presence, which Catholics soon widely viewed as an occupation. The PIRA sought to protect Catholics, advance civil rights, and use violent tactics to seek Irish unification. Republican nationalism became associated with the political party Sinn Féin. The UVF and other loyalist paramilitary groups gained political empathy from the Democratic Unionist Party (DUP). London governments, seeking to quell violence, sent up to thirty thousand troops, initially to protect Catholics, but in the end to police the North on behalf of British interests. Violent tactics were frequently used, leading to the killing of fourteen innocent civilians on the streets of Derry on "Bloody Sunday" in 1972. The British military used tough tactics and interned Republicans, often without charging them. The more this happened, the more powerful and entrenched grew the IRA. Hatred came to define generations of Catholics and Protestants as a sectarian war commenced.

By the 1980s, the IRA and PIRA had grown into full-blown terrorist organizations carrying out attacks in the North and across the United Kingdom. Catholic prisoners, often brutally interned by the British army and police, would elevate the public relations stakes by going on hunger strikes. This led to the death in captivity of Bobby Sands and nine other prisoners in 1981. These deaths sparked outrage across Ireland and around the world, giving popular legitimacy to Gerry Adams and Martin McGuinness, who had risen up in the ranks of Sinn Féin and were widely associated with the IRA. Unionists like the Rev. Ian Paisley came to define that movement's more radical voices. Caught in the middle were politicians like John Hume (of the nationalist Social Democratic and Labour Party) and David Trimble (of the Ulster Unionist Party), who advocated for rights on each side while eschewing violence. Eventually, Hume and Trimble shared the Nobel Peace Prize in 1998 for their efforts to negotiate peace. In 1985, the Irish government, led by Garret FitzGerald, negotiated the Anglo Irish Agreement with Margaret Thatcher's government in Britain. While not successful in the near term, it laid the framework for achieving lasting peace based on power sharing.

While key figures became polarized on all sides, there were lighter moments. For example, Ian Paisley once appeared in the 1980s, hosted by his daughter, in Dublin on RTÉ. "I never thought I'd see the day, Dad, when you and me would be sitting in Dublin having a chat," said his daughter. Paisley then said, "The first time I came to Dublin was thirty-seven years ago—and I preached at O'Connell Street at an open-air meeting . . . and they didn't like what I said. So, I said to the man who was conducting the meeting, 'What do I do now?' He said, 'You run for it, or they'll throw you in the Liffey.' So I ran for it!" His Dublin audience laughed and applauded. Lest anyone forget, the Northern Irish Protestants (and the many Protestants who live in the Republic of Ireland) are also Irish and enjoy a good laugh.

To many people of Irish-descent outside Ireland, supporting the "cause" of a united Ireland entailed a romantic vision of the IRA that fought for independence in 1916 during the Easter Rising in Dublin. American support for the IRA and PIRA grew in the 1970s and 1980s as the hat was passed for money in Boston, Chicago, New York, and beyond. Groups in the United States, like Noraid (the Irish Northern Aid Committee), would agitate and raise funds in support of Catholic relief in the North. Both the British and American governments accused Noraid of fund-raising for the PIRA. Nonetheless, people in Ireland—North and South—had, by the mid-1990s, grown deeply weary of the conflict. The economy of the North was in ruins, and both sides were deeply demoralized. The people across Ireland, Catholic and Protestant, knew well that their economic progress hinged on changing the perception of the island as a war-torn place. This frustration came to a head when Catholic paramilitaries killed eleven and injured sixty-three civilians at a Remembrance Day celebration at Enniskillen on 8 November 1987. This celebration had been held in remembrance of World War I, a war in which many Irish—Catholic and Protestant—had fought.

A survivor of the Enniskillen blast, Jim Dickson, said, "I remember saying to the surgeon, please hit me over the head with a hatchet—I can't stand it. I felt as if I was dragged into the very crypt of hell. The terror was so real—it would suffocate me with pure fear." Gordon Wilson, who was injured, said the next day of his daughter, Mary, who died, "We were there ten to fifteen seconds at the outside. Bang. Then we were pushed forward on our faces. . . . I was pinned. And then I was aware of somebody squeezing my hand. And Mary said, 'Is that you, Dad?' and I said yes." Mary asked her father if he was alright. When he asked how she was, Wilson says his daughter said, "Alright." "And then I heard her scream," he said. "I asked her again, 'Are you alright?' 'Yes,' she said," and he was sure she was alright, but she was still screaming. "When I asked her for the fourth or fifth time, she said, 'Daddy, I love you very much.' Those were," said a distraught Wilson, "the last words she spoke. . . . I shall never forget them." Wilson went on to become an activist campaigning for peace.

Enniskillen was a turning point—enough was enough. The bombing was condemned universally. Sinn Féin leaders distanced themselves from the attack. The IRA said it had not sanctioned the bombing (though the size of the bomb and the fact that an even bigger bomb was set to go off the same day in another town made this claim hard for many to believe). It had been one thing when the IRA attacked military bases and police stations. Even the targeting of people outside the North in the United Kingdom was tolerated. This was, in part, because the British response was often counterproductive force and further violations of human rights. The no-warning murder of innocent civilians lined up to watch a parade commemorating foreign war veterans in Enniskillen was, however, too painful to bear. U2 took the depth of the nation's disgust to the world when the group performed that evening in the United States. "Well, here we are, the Irish in America," said Bono. Cheers filled the stadium from an audience with a romantic American view of Ireland. Bono went on, "The Irish have been coming to America for years. Going back to the great famine when the Irish were on the run from starvation and a British government that couldn't care less." He spoke of why people left Ireland and how "some [ran] from the Troubles in Northern Ireland—from the hatred of the H-Blocks, the torture—others from wild acts of terrorism like we had today in a town called Enniskillen, where eleven people lie dead, many more injured, on a Sunday Bloody Sunday." The U2 hit song "Bloody Sunday" followed—slowly, retrospectively. "I can't believe the news today . . . I can't close my eyes and make it go away," a pained Bono sang. "How long? How long must we sing this song?"

Bono, often criticized for his preaching and inconsistency, had what is probably his most compelling public moment as an Irishman. Irish artists have an extraordinary ability to express the minds and hearts of a nation when they want to—from Seamus Heaney in his 1975 collection of poems *North* to Bono on that evening in 1987. Halfway through the song, thousands of miles from home, he began talking:

Well, let me tell you something! I've had enough of Irish Americans who haven't been back to their country in twenty or thirty years come up to me and talk about the resistance, the revolution back home, and the glory of the revolution and the glory of dying for the revolution. Fuck the revolution! They don't talk about the glory of killing for the revolution. What's the glory in taking a man from his bed and gunning him down in front of his wife and his children? Where's the glory in that? Where's the glory in bombing a Remembrance Day parade of old-aged pensioners, their medals taken out and polished up for the day? Where's the glory in that? To leave them dying, or crippled for life, or dead under the rubble of a revolution that the majority of the people in my country don't want.

Bono then sang—even screeched—with emotion, "No more! No more! No More!"

In early 1994, Gerry Adams of Sinn Féin was granted a temporary visa to visit the United States for a meeting at the White House with President Bill Clinton. While strongly opposed by the British government and many senior officials inside the Clinton administration, the decision proved a brilliant stroke. A month before, the governments of the Republic of Ireland and Britain had announced a common desire to see Northern Ireland achieve self-determination and said that the majority of the North's population would decide its future. This paved the way for an IRA cease-fire and a commitment to achieve a negotiated settlement to the conflict. On Good Friday 1998 agreement was finalized, with support from the United States, Great Britain, and the Republic of Ireland, to move Northern Ireland on a path to peace.

The peace settlement was based on home rule and power sharing. Northern Ireland would remain part of the United Kingdom but have responsibility for its own future with a new parliament. The paramilitaries on each side would renounce violence and disarm. A schedule for releasing paramilitary prisoners would commence. In 2005, the IRA announced that it would pursue its objectives purely through political means. By 2010, the major paramilitary parties on both sides had disarmed under the auspices of an Independent Monitoring Commission. In spring 2010, a new Northern Ireland police force was finalized. The core architecture of peace had arrived, and it was being sustained and built upon. In a referendum in Northern Ireland in spring 1998, the agreement passed by 71.2 percent. A similar referendum in the Republic of Ireland was passed by 94.39 percent. While a tiny part of the public in the Republic held on to an outdated nationalist concept that Ireland has "thirty-two counties, no matter what," the vast majority of people across Ireland were more than pleased to put the Troubles behind them. In 2007, the first power-sharing executive took office: the DUP leader Ian Paisley was first minister, and Martin McGuinness was second minister, with each holding equal powers within the new Northern Ireland Assembly.

In spring 2010, at a Washington, DC, meeting I attended, which included Martin McGuinness, he made clear that anyone who wanted to go back to the old ways would have to come through him. Given his history, this was a serious warning to dissident Republicans. I met McGuinness briefly just to shake hands, and I can report that he has the strongest handshake of anyone I have ever met. He is very intense at one level—carrying the burden of decades of struggle and now peace. On another level, he is a patient and humorous man who was a teacher and is an avid fly fisherman. Behind the scenes, it was clear that not only is Northern Ireland's leadership reconciled between Peter Robinson (who succeeded Ian Paisley as first minister) and Martin McGuinness, but they are friendly. I was told off the record that when Peter Robinson ran into personal marital problems in early 2010, one of the first to offer support in friendship to help was Martin McGuinness. Nonetheless, the tribal nature of Irish politics applies in the North too, and the deep realities of the past persist. On 17 September 2010, Robinson told the *Belfast Telegraph* that their relationship was "professional" and that McGuinness was "someone you can work with." When asked if he liked McGuinness, Robinson said, "I suppose the factor that makes me slightly different from a number of other people is that I came into politics because the IRA killed my friend. And I found it very difficult to sit in the Assembly chamber, looking across the chamber without that coming into my mind—that the people I'm having to deal with are people who have been responsible for either taking part or supporting the murder of family and friends. Now, that never leaves me." Still, he had confidence in their relationship, which had been tested positively. He said, "It makes it a lot easier for you to be able to sell those agreements because you know you are not going to get stabbed in the back by somebody reneging on an agreement that they've reached."

The political agreement held but was on occasion pushed to the limits. Orange Order marches, which are annual demonstrations by Protestant unionist groups, at Drumcree Church in South Armagh in July 1998 ended when militant loyalist paramilitaries set fire to a Catholic family's house there and killed three children. On 15 August 1998, a new group, the Real IRA, emerged with a bomb attack in Omagh that killed twenty-nine people and injured over two hundred. The attack killed Catholics and Protestants. It killed nine children. This savagery served only to unite those who had worked so hard for peace. It was condemned by Gerry Adams and Martin McGuinness, and dissident paramilitaries remained marginalized. American terrorism expert Audrey Kurth Cronin notes in *How Terrorism Ends* (2009) that unique circumstances allowed the agreement to hold when tested. First, by the time negotiations began, both sides were at a stalemate; no further gains could be made by continuing with the status quo. Second, once diplomacy began, all sides had a vested interest in achieving a successful outcome. Third, sufficient ambiguity in the accords allowed each party to sell them to their constituents. Finally, the external environment was important. Internationally, negotiated settlements were increasingly seen as possible, even between Israelis and Palestinians, and there was a great sense of economic potential. The most essential, and difficult, aspect of the negotiations was the decision to include former terrorists in diplomacy. This was ironic since there is, at least in the American credo, a general refusal to talk to terrorists—which holds true, except for when we do. Even more interestingly, it worked—at least in Northern Ireland.

The conflict in Northern Ireland took a huge toll in terms of lives lost and the deep psychological scars. In *A Secret History of the IRA* (2002), journalist Ed Moloney summarizes the extent of the damage done.

> More than 3,700 people were killed in the violence, an average of just over 2 a week for the thirty years that the conflict lasted. Almost as many people died within a couple of hours in lower Manhattan on September 11, 2001, but to conclude therefore that the Troubles were a petty affair would be a mistake. Had a similar conflict consumed the United States, the equivalent death toll would have been over 600,000; in Britain, 150,000. Nearly 1 in every 50 of Northern Ireland's 1.5 million people, some 30,000, were injured in the violence. The comparable figure in the United States would be 5 million; in Britain, just over 1 million. Very few people in Northern Ireland did not personally know someone who had been killed in the Troubles, and many knew several. There are many definitions of a civil war, but that is surely one of the most compelling.

Today, the Troubles remain hard to look at. The British Museum in Belfast has opened a must-see exhibit on the Troubles—but you have to work hard once in the museum to find it.

INTO THE NORTH

An Irish friend in Dublin tells me that every time he goes into the North, he gets a creepy feeling. Catholics and Protestants in Ireland still feel a sense of unease when talking of the Troubles and their legacy. Every year they are reminded of this during the July "marching season," when "Orange Orders" have parades commemorating Unionist pride in William of Orange's victory at the Battle of the Boyne in 1690. Most parades pass without incident through their own Unionist areas, but some highly motivated orders insist—often viciously—on marching through sensitive Catholic areas up until 12 July. So, I thought, what better time to head North than the week of 12 July 2010. I certainly did not anticipate that my family and I would arrive in the midst of the worst rioting and sectarian violence since the peace accords took hold a decade earlier. Still, one would have to be looking for trouble in Northern Ireland to find it—it is below the surface that the water is simmering. Belfast is even turning the July period into a tourist attraction with an Orange Festival—though many Catholics see this as the time to book their summer holidays outside the North. Overall, in the North, the roads are great, the scenery stupendous, and the people welcoming. One overtly odd thing about the North is how on BBC weather maps, they literally blot out the Republic of Ireland. One can get a great weather forecast for Northern Ireland on the BBC, but apparently the rest of the island either does not have weather or does not exist. On the other hand, when you go to Northern Ireland, you are in another country—with its own money, banks, long-distance telephone charges, and rules. And, both above and below the surface, a living legacy of the past conflicts with a deeply held desire for peace.

The rioters in the Ardoyne and other Catholic areas of Belfast in July 2010 largely used the Orangemen as an excuse for violence. In fact, violence by Catholics in the streets mainly took place after the Orangemen had long gone home—or in some cases where none had marched at all. As I visited the Ardoyne early on the morning after the worst night of rioting, it became immediately clear that the peace is more fragile than it appears from afar, though this would be easy to miss because that fragility is literally at a very local, street-to-street level. The primary target of Catholic street rioters was not Protestants but rather the police—a vital symbol of progress in Northern Ireland. In Belfast and Derry, shots were fired at police, and in one horrific incident, a policewoman was severely injured when hit by a brick in the head. Rioters continued to pelt her and her colleagues as rescuers sought to extract the wounded officer. In another major incident, a young man attempted to take over the Enterprise Train between Dublin and Belfast; he was apparently quite willing to firebomb it and kill women and children. Key is the degree to which the police acted with restraint—refusing to rise to the bait of those spewing hate and violence. Today, the security services are part of the solution, not the problem.

During that July 2010 visit, I took a tour through the rougher areas of Belfast, which was facilitated by some government contacts. My host, who cannot be identified, was a former paramilitary leader. We drove past pubs in central Belfast that used to be either all Catholic or Protestant, but where now they drink together. On the Falls and Shankill Roads, there is peace with no violence in over a decade—though "peace walls" and gates divide the communities from each other. In pockets of divided public housing, however, the divisions remain intractable and unaddressed. Street crime is blatant. We drove by one building where women were lined up in the front—a drug house. A shop front had "PIRA" sprayed on its storefront, while the residue of petrol bombs cluttered the street at the heart of the Ardoyne, where frustrations continue to run high.

We also visited small loyalist Protestant enclaves surrounded like islands by all-Catholic neighborhoods, where Protestant bonfires from the night before smoldered. These people once had a British identity, but now feel they belong to no one. They see themselves as hated by the Catholics that surround them, a problem for the government, and abandoned by London. These Unionist activists believe that Protestants have lost their dominance in the old industrial jobs, which are disappearing. They believe that quotas and better education among Catholics make them attractive in new industries as they hire. These small Protestant enclaves feel they have "lost everything and are stateless." All up and down these streets are Union Jack flags. Many of these houses also fly Israeli flags and have shalom signs on the front step—out of a sense of affinity with Jewish settlers. We drove by a meeting place for former paramilitaries. I was told that were I to return there at 5 p.m., I could walk in and have drinks with former prisoners—murderers. I was also advised that doing so would be a very bad idea. We entered one small street in which the car windows had to be rolled up and no photos could be taken. I was cautioned that we were "being watched here, by people with guns, and that we were allowed two minutes on the street." This was an area where Protestant public housing had been burned out by dissident Republicans. The scars of firebombs remained, as did several row houses where a few loyalist holdouts persisted. We were not really supposed to be there, but my host had made a special arrangement as this small group hoped to get its concerns out to the world.

In Belfast, I also visited an area where the divide remains very open: the Holy Cross school in the Ardoyne. Here the Troubles boil below the surface, and they affect the innocent young. In 2001, Unionist supporters raised flags across the road, causing the parents of the Catholic students to grow concerned for their children. On the route to school, children were harassed and spat at, their parents called "Fenian scum." While the immediate tensions simmered, policing this one location costs over £1 million. The Catholic children today walk to school on one side of the street. A mainly Protestant school nearby has no working relationship with Holy Cross; the youths remain divided. In October 2010, First Minister Peter Robinson challenged Northern Ireland's education system, noting that separation had to change—that it was a "benign form of apartheid." Peter Robinson was right—though his concern applies to public housing as well. Many Catholics, however, saw Robinson's education comments through the old prism. One Sinn Féin leader said, "What we are witnessing is an attack on the Catholic education sector." Second Minister Martin McGuinness warned that Robinson's views risked putting the country on a "collision course which will lead us into a total and absolute mess."

I heard one story of how a film crew came to the Ardoyne a few years earlier to look into the Holy Cross protests and to interview students. The

Catholics sent them a young girl, all dressed up, who said she aspired to be a nurse. The Protestants brought in a kid, totally unprepared for his interview, who wanted to be a gangster. As it was relayed to me, this kid actually strove to become a thug on a street corner. That was more ambition than many youth in the area had. While the divisions in the schools are real, a crucial issue crops up too often when some parents in very small, crucial areas show little interest in their children's future. Ironically, both the Protestant and Catholic communities share this problem. These children have no common experience of the previous Troubles, and today many have few positive role models. The goal for many young boys is to become the top "tough guy," and this can mean proving themselves on the violent streets. Getting seen on closed-circuit television throwing petrol bombs at police is a great achievement in this mind-set; going to prison translates into toughness after release. From this comes a danger that one can paint a flag on a street corner, call it nationalist or loyalist, and suddenly you have people out in the streets—people with nothing better to do—and a slow but growing challenge to the existing peace from the bottom up.

On a street-to-street level, Catholics and Protestants suffer from the same kinds of problems that afflict most major urban populations: gangs, thugs, drugs, prostitution, and other crime. Dissident paramilitary groups still run extortion rackets, and a number of those who fail to pay or get caught up in turf wars have been murdered. In Belfast, however, one can label these crimes political, and suddenly they take on dangerous symbolism that cuts across society. The peace process has left a vacuum in areas where "street justice" dealt with crime in the past. During the Troubles, the paramilitary forces provided street order, and both sides' forces were deeply involved in criminal activity and violence. I took a long look up an alley known to have been used for decades before the peace accords by the IRA for enforcing local rules—which included running protection and extortion rackets against local shop owners. Before the peace accords, when people broke the law or local understandings, they would soon hear a knock on their door. They would be sent up to the alley. As they stood there, a call would go out in advance for an ambulance to come; then, they would be shot in the knee—"kneecapped." Parents had little choice but to turn their wayward children over to this summary justice. For some today who fear the lawlessness on these streets, the peace process has actually brought more danger. As the economy spirals downward, a new generation is coming of age with no idea about what the peace process was or the horrifying events that preceded it. Most of this tension is class based and stems from economic deprivation—though if that were the only issue, we would see rioting in west Dublin too. A combination of factors makes the environment in the North rich for exploitation by those who hold on to outdated ideologies.

The new Police Service of Northern Ireland (PSNI) is vital to bridging these security gaps. It is made up of well-educated, well-trained, and independent public servants with a goal of equal balance between Catholics and Protestants. This is essential for building confidence, especially among Catholics, many of whom saw the previous Royal Ulster Constabulary as an occupying enemy. In Belfast, I visited the headquarters of the Northern Ireland Policing Board, which oversees building the new police force. I met there with a senior official who spoke off the record. The policing board includes power-sharing representation and independent expertise to resolve high-level disputes over policing. Its mandate is to ensure that policing is done within the law and with respect for human rights. The demographics of the police force have worked out well, particularly with an increase in the number of Catholics joining. The force also has to deal with a range of new challenges beyond the peace process. For example, while the focus has been on sectarian concerns, Northern Ireland is becoming increasingly multicultural; yet, multicultural training has not been a sufficient priority. In one case described to me, a Polish-speaking cultural officer was sent into a Romanian house to help officers with translation. When the Romanians made clear that they did not speak Polish, the officers told the translator, "Well, do it anyway." Still, when the police have encountered problems between Indian and Pakistani immigrants, they have been able to say creatively to them, "Well, here is how we do it with the Protestants and the Catholics." Other traditional social problems challenge the police force— very serious issues such as the abuse of young girls on which the "lid needs to be lifted." There have also been issues related to attracting women to the force and retaining them. Still, when the woman police officer was hit in the head with a brick and nearly killed in the Ardoyne riots, "no one was talking of her causing a weakness in the line . . . nothing other than that a police got hit and it was wrong."

Police officials in Belfast tend to see rioters in places like the Ardoyne as guided by a small group of dissident Republicans and thugs. The goal is to "kill a police officer and to embarrass Sinn Féin—basically it is a stunt to show that Sinn Féin is not in control." While there is an ideological tint, organized crime is the real culprit. The general threat from dissident paramilitaries is seen as small but growing. In October 2010, the British government issued a public warning about a rising threat in the United Kingdom from dissident Republican terrorist attacks. According to the official estimate, there were more than six hundred dissident Republican paramilitary members, with the Real IRA (heavily concentrated in Derry) being the most dangerous. There is concern in some quarters that with major budget cuts, some might overestimate the threat in seeking to secure funds. To be sure, as I was told, "events remind people of the need for resources—certainly thus a point to make." Yet, there exists a counterpressure to "play down at

the same time as people want normalization." To the police, it is a matter
of what they could be doing with their time and scarce resources—namely,
working to better the community—instead of chasing down rioters. Matt
Baggott, the PSNI's chief constable, says the July 2010 Ardoyne violence
cost the police £1.1 million. That alone, Baggott said, equates to the "cost
of funding a neighborhood policing team to help out people in Ardoyne
for a period of three years."

The policing commission's oversight role has become an important tool
for building trust and confidence. When I visited the headquarters in Belfast,
Sinn Féin had just taken its seats on the board. This puts them and the DUP
"all in the same room with challenging questions and challenging answers
. . . giving credibility to the police." There is often a disconnect between
what the representatives say in private—which is much more friendly—and
what they say when they appeal to their constituencies in more public settings. There is a "lot of maneuvering for power and jockeying to see who is
left standing." At the ground level, the police have been engaging with civic
groups, both formally and informally. Some civil society groups participate
in police-training exercises. Their activity has largely been a quiet contribution to enhancing police legitimacy. The police have held "no holds-barred
discussions with young people on the Springfield Road—sitting down with
them, informing the training . . . engaging." They have also generated increased respect and goodwill by showing restraint—which was especially
clear in the Ardoyne riots of July 2010. The police did not attack and held
their lines, waiting for the violence to end while closed-circuit television
gathered intelligence on whom to arrest. This approach contrasted with
that advocated by a caller on a radio talk show I heard while driving out of
Omagh who said the way to deal with these people in the streets was "to
take a baton to their heads." The police of Northern Ireland had learned the
hard way over decades that this does not work. In fact, the youth attacking
them with rocks and petrol bombs were clearly hoping to provoke that very
response. The official I spoke with said that "overusing force" would be a
serious mistake—"it feeds right into it. . . . The police acted with incredible
restraint which was very effective and positive."

Another essential success of the peace process has been paramilitary
decommissioning. To get a sense of this, I met with members of the Independent Monitoring Commission established to conduct fact finding
and report on the progress of paramilitary disarming. There are four senior
members—one each from Northern Ireland, the Republic of Ireland, Great
Britain, and the United States. I am not at liberty to say which two I met
with. It is always interesting to begin a meeting being told, "Officially, this
meeting did not happen," but it is less James Bond than it sounds—although the American commissioner is a former senior CIA official. The
reason is that people who go to them with information need to know that

it will be treated in confidence—for my part, I can report what we discussed off the record. For my meeting, these commissioners were gathered in offices deep inside Dublin Castle. I was told that this area of the castle is likely where Michael Collins was smuggled to in order to steal documents during his campaign against British rule. Furthermore, as there was a Brit on the team, this was likely the first time since 1922 that a British official had had an office inside Dublin Castle.

In their assessment of the dissident threat, these commissioners said a very small, known leadership exists of individuals who were once mainstream IRA but became disenchanted with the peace process. The dissidents' goal, they said, "is to prevent a normalization of policy while exploiting a new cadre of disaffected youth." "They claim the flame of true Republicanism," said one commissioner, and in many respects it is an "intrafamilial row." The commissioners reinforced that "certain areas had gone without police for forty years with a brutal and crude code of enforcement by way of shooting and beating." In the eyes of these dissident Republicans, they are the "true legacy of 1916—and yet the context is totally different as the two governments and all the parties are invested in peace." While democracy among all parties has made clear the depth of support for peace, "hardcore, rump Republicans assert their right to take up arms against that agreement. It is totally illegitimate, it is totally antidemocratic, and the basis of legitimacy is totally nonexistent." Still, these dissident Republican groups feel there is "a God given right to a thirty-two-county Irish Republic." These groups are also, the commissioners told me, "a criminal empire." The main target of law enforcement has been counterfeiting and the smuggling of fuel, cigarettes, and, of course, drugs. Dissident Republicans are particularly agitated with Sinn Féin for making a deal to join the Northern Ireland policing process.

I was concerned that the commission's mandate had already been extended, and it was not clear that there would be a similar remit once this group had worked itself out of a job. It was also important to know if the success of the Independent Monitoring Commission could be repeated elsewhere. Aside from the dissidents, nearly all the relevant parties were in compliance with their commitments to the peace process. A central element, the commissioners said, was the American involvement. "You can't underestimate American clout—they were hugely influential." The Dublin participation, publically and privately, was also "highly influential—helped by a good relationship between the [Royal Ulster Constabulary] and the Garda . . . facilitated by John Bruton" as Taoiseach. Serious credit also had to be given to the leadership of the PIRA for investing in peace and renouncing violence to achieve their ends. Crucially, the Independent Monitoring Commission developed an excellent methodology for investigating and documenting disarmament. They studied previous efforts, like that of Richard Butler in the Iraqi weapons of mass destruction disarmament program run by the United Nations. They would "seek out and triangulate" data—"looking for ways to confirm what we were hearing." The willingness to correct publically errors they made was also important to ensuring credibility.

These commissioners are proud of their work; yet, they do not seek public recognition for their essential contribution to peace. Over time, they learned to be "very careful about how to speak" on disarmament issues. Central to their success was their independence and ability to gain trust for "telling it like it is"; people knew their "reports were not the creation of the governments." They were "not succumbing to prevailing winds." In a reflective moment, one of the commissioners told me of feeling proud for rising up through the ranks from the lowest level to be able to build peace in one of the twentieth century's most intractable conflicts. A key challenge was the commission's mandate just to focus on paramilitary disarmament. This limitation could have broader political implications, or political issues could affect the disarmament patterns. Their limited mandate was still "an important piece of the jigsaw of peace." By verifying and reporting the disarmament of the PIRA, the Unionists were reassured that it was worth their political effort to invest in the process. At one point, Sinn Féin sued the Independent Monitoring Commission in court in London on the claim that its members were biased and should not hold public office. After extensive study of the work and procedures, the findings supported the commission, giving it further credibility by way of transparency. The Independent Monitoring Commission was really "done and dusted," the commissioners told me, in 2005—so "why are we still here—and more importantly, what replaces us and based on what criteria?" Perhaps the most crucial lesson that these commissioners provide from their experience is that they proved that terrorist and paramilitary organizations "[can] change, and it was important for us to see that and to record it." Still, there are limits to whether this model might have portability. One of the commissioners pointed out to me, "If you used the same thing in the Afghan conflict, you would have a Pakistani, an Afghan, an American, and a Brit—what would that look like?"

The senior policing official that I met with in Belfast told me, with choked-back emotion, after having been up most of the night in the Ardoyne that week, "We are very proud of how far people have come." We have "forgiven and forgotten—awful things like Enniskillen and Omagh—we can't bear to look at it again." The success story, this person said, is built on the police's ability to grow contacts with the police institution and the population. Support during times of trial from the leadership—especially the fact that Peter Robinson and Martin McGuinness stood together—was key during the Ardoyne crisis. Vitally, this person said, former enemies and combatants were brought into the government—and given a stake in the future. Nonetheless, the legacy of the Troubles persists. As I walked up a street in Belfast, a construction site made a loud bang. People on the street (myself included) jumped. Nerves remain raw. "Small steps have gone so far—but it is still very fragile," said the policing official. This person added one more thought: Northern Ireland has benefited from a "clever state—David Cameron's comments on Derry were very well done—that could have gone very bad."

YOU ARE NOW ENTERING FREE DERRY

On 30 January 1972, the British army challenged a civil rights protest in Derry, opening fire and shooting twenty-six civilians. In total, thirteen died at the scene, and one died later. Several were shot in the back. None of those shot were armed. It became immediately clear that the soldiers who fired had done a horrible wrong. As the Derry coroner Hubert O'Neill (a former British army officer) said in a public statement on 21 August 1973, "This Sunday became known as Bloody Sunday and bloody it was. It was quite unnecessary. It strikes me that the Army ran amok that day and shot without thinking what they were doing. They were shooting innocent people. These people may have been taking part in a march that was banned but that does not justify the troops coming in and firing live rounds indiscriminately. I would say without hesitation that it was sheer, unadulterated murder. It was murder." Commissions would investigate, deflect, and obfuscate while campaigners for those killed and wounded persisted for decades. Officers at the scene insisted that those shot were guilty of acts of violence and that the troops were shooting in self-defense. This was not true.

On 15 June 2010, the Saville Commission, which reexamined massive amounts of evidence on the Bloody Sunday shootings, issued a final report after twelve years and costing £200 million. In one of his first major acts as the new British prime minister, David Cameron read out the results in parliament. In Derry, a crowd estimated at ten thousand gathered at Guildhall Square, where the marchers had been headed on that fateful day in 1972. A massive television screen was up (for World Cup soccer matches), and stark black-and-white portraits of the men killed on Bloody Sunday were draped from Guildhall, looking out at the crowd. David Cameron's remarks were burdened with history and pain, but, if handled well, they carried the potential for renewal. The sun shined bright that spring day in Derry.

David Cameron said the "conclusions of this report are absolutely clear. There is no doubt. There is nothing equivocal. There are no ambiguities. What happened on Bloody Sunday was both unjustified and unjustifiable." At this, the crowd in Guildhall Square burst into emotional applause and cheers. Cameron added the report's conclusion "that the soldiers in Support Company who went into the Bogside did so as a result of an order which should not have been given by their commander." For those looking for statements of innocence, Cameron continued that Saville says, "The immediate responsibility for the deaths and injuries on Bloody Sunday lies with those members of Support Company whose unjustifiable firing was the cause of those deaths and injuries." With this the crowd again erupted into emotional cheers in Guildhall Square. Then, Cameron took official responsibility: "The government is ultimately responsible for the conduct of the armed forces and with that, on behalf of the government, indeed on behalf of our country, I am deeply sorry." At this point, the emotion in Guildhall Square was overrun with appreciation and validation for so many decades of effort on behalf of the innocents lost.

After the prime minister's speech, members of families took the platform. One said, "My brother William [Nash], we've always known he was innocent—now the world knows!" Another said, "Unjustified and unjustifiable—those are the words we have been waiting to hear since the thirtieth of January 1972." Another said, "John Young was going to the aid of William Nash when he was shot. We are sure he was not armed with any lethal weapon. John Young was innocent." Another quoted the official report to the effect that her younger brother was "shot as he was crawling away from soldiers. These shots were not fired in fear or panic. He posed no danger to life or danger of injury. Thirty-eight years, four months, fifteen days— almost to the minute—Kevin is innocent!" While justice would still have to wait, the words of the British prime minister had been heard when he said to parliament, "I am deeply patriotic. I never want to believe anything bad about our country. I never want to call into question the behavior of our soldiers and our army who I believe to be the finest in the world." He went on to say,

> These are shocking conclusions to read and shocking words to say . . . but you do not defend the British army by defending the indefensible. We do not honor all those who served with such distinction in keeping the peace and upholding the rule of law in Northern Ireland by hiding from the truth. So there is no point in trying to soften or equivocate what is in this report. . . . What happened should never, ever have happened. The families of those who died should not have had to live with the pain and the hurt of that day and with a lifetime of loss.

Martin McGuinness was present on Bloody Sunday in 1972. He was identified in the report as having been there, probably carrying a machine gun (which McGuinness calls "ludicrous"), but having done nothing to instigate the attack. He said of the prime minister's speech, "I think the key message out of this, obviously, has to be the heroism and the courage of the families who were prepared to stand for justice for their loved ones—and for the citizens of this city who for almost forty years have been waiting to see those who were shot on that day vindicated." Though addressed to the people of Derry, the prime minister's statement was really one for all of the people of the United Kingdom and Ireland. The undertones conveyed regret, on the part of a new generation of leadership, for the pain that so many, on all sides, in Northern Ireland had felt. Tony Doherty, whose father was shot in the back crawling on the ground for cover, said at Guildhall that bright June day, "When the state kills its citizens, it is in the interests of all that those responsible be held to account. That is not just Derry, or one section of the people, but democracy itself which needs to know, what happened here, on the streets of Derry in 1972. The British people need to know. The Irish people need to know. The world . . . now knows." On 19 June 2010 in the *New York Times*, Bono of U2 wrote, "If there are any lessons for the world from this piece of Irish history . . . for Baghdad . . . for Kandahar . . . it's this: things are quick to change for the worse and slow to change for the better, but they can. They really can. It takes years of false starts, heartbreaks and backslides and, most tragically, more killings. But visionaries and risk-takers and, let's just say it, heroes on all sides can bring us back to the point where change becomes not only possible again, but inevitable."

Not long after the Saville report was published, I visited Derry to meet with Eamonn McCann, who was there in 1972, heard the shots, and observed the panic as he sought safety. He is one of the original civil rights activists and organizers who cofounded the Northern Ireland Civil Rights Association in 1968, which advocated especially for one man, one vote, and nondiscrimination in housing and the workplace. He remains an activist for peace and justice in the world. His book *War and an Irish Town* (1973) is a classic for anyone wishing to understand the complex origins of the Troubles. He brings a vital perspective to understanding them as being as much about class and economic dislocation as about religion. He notes that the original Bloody Sunday served as a major impetus to people joining the IRA—leading to a long history of carry-on effects. He stood by the families for decades, heading the Bloody Sunday Trust, and as a journalist and activist, he publicized their plight. He described his response to the Saville report as "one of unbounded joy."

One has to work to keep up with Eamonn McCann: he rattles off quotes by people from poet Allen Ginsberg to Barack Obama while walking at a fast clip. He was exceedingly generous with his time in meeting me at Guildhall Square. McCann is a vital part of the puzzle of Northern Ireland's past, present, and future. His convictions are universal—and that is really what the story of Derry is about—human rights. For example, he addressed a rally in 2006 in Derry where he said, speaking out against Britain's involvement in the Iraq war,

> Personally, I refer back to a speech made by Chancellor Brown, in the House of Commons in December 2002. . . . What he said was that whatever money was needed in the event of a war on Iraq would be—provided. No conditions. No qualifications. Whatever it took from the taxpayers' money would be made available. Ask yourself this—when have you ever heard a chancellor of the exchequer speak in such terms about poverty, about care for children with disabilities, about the aged, about our health system, about our education system? When it comes to war, its money no object! When it comes to caring for the most vulnerable in our society, its money too tight to mention.

Northern Ireland has seen its politics follow the "same arch as society," McCann said to me. Now that groups like Sinn Féin and the DUP are the government, civil rights in the North have "come full circle. . . . One can't move without the other" in government. Eamonn McCann's class analysis is especially acute when applied to the incidents of that July marching season. Just the night before, not far from where we sat, shots had been fired at the police. Several bombs went off in Derry over the months that followed, targeting police. Eamonn McCann said this is the "economy—the poorest are left behind." These young people today "have no support, no strategy— no hope of a decent job." There is "no way the cops can go at them—it's too dangerous." What is really going on in the North among these youth today is a "search for a sort of dignity," McCann said. This can "result in a carnival of reaction."

Eamonn McCann took me on a walk around the sites where Bloody Sunday occurred. We went past Guildhall, where just weeks before the families of the fallen were vindicated in history. We walked down the side streets of the city where people had been shot and killed—on into the Bogside with its many murals. The murals represent many facets of the Derry story, with the "You Are Now Entering Free Derry" wall at the center. Just behind it is a painting of a young boy in a gas mask; near to that is Bernadette Devlin, representing women, holding a bullhorn and rallying to the cause. The "Free Derry Corner" wall changes with the times. McCann told me that when George W. Bush visited Northern Ireland in 2003, it was remade with a black cloth for the duration of his stay. In 2007, it was painted "all pink" for Gay Pride Week. In 2008, it was drawn with positive "visions of the future"—colors of the rainbow. The murals portray the stories of civil rights and struggle—both peaceful and violent. Eamonn McCann says they reflect a time that was very much a carryover from the civil rights and Vietnam War protest experience in the United States: "it was a significant part of that—a group consciousness that sought freedom of the world." Still, of the mu-

rals, he said, "I really don't like them—if they are too backward looking."
As we walked, he nodded up the hill at the Walls of Derry overlooking the
"Free Derry Corner" wall and the Bogside. These castle walls had also been
written on from time to time, including a statement of "One Nation, One
People" in huge print just before the Church of England steeple that lay
behind the walls.

I could see McCann's point about the murals, but as an outsider, it is
hard not to find them compelling—in both Derry and Belfast. They are a
unique form of political art. That form becomes troubling when it moves
from art and protest into propaganda and control. One sees this in some
parts of Belfast—both Catholic and Protestant. Some murals on the Falls
Road carry a purposeful reminder—such as "Oppression Breeds Resistance:
Resistance Brings Freedom" dedicated to the "women who faced up to
military aggression" during a 1970 Falls Road curfew. One wall on the Falls
Road is devoted mainly to international efforts against oppression. Still,
in the areas where the Troubles persist, murals talk of the loving memory
of people who were themselves vicious paramilitary killers—a fact not
pointed out in these tributes. One mural in Derry catches the eye with a
forward look—in the colors of the rainbow, a dove takes up the entire side
of one building. Just across from that dove mural, a memorial honors those
killed on Bloody Sunday, which McCann took me to see. We then high-
tailed it to the Museum of Free Derry, located in the heart of the events of
both the Battle of the Bogside and Bloody Sunday. The curator and McCann
gave me a walking tour of this extraordinary museum, which testifies to the
events of those days as seen through the eyes of people who were there.
The museum curator said to me, "We know this is our version of what happened—but we feel that those versions have their own meaning to people
and thus it's vital that the story be told." And, as we now know officially,
their version was the true one.

As we walked through Derry discussing a wide range of issues, from
American politics to the church scandal in the Republic of Ireland, Eamonn
McCann caught my attention with a quick mention of how he and a few
others "defeated Raytheon." This, I did not know about. I had noticed on
the castle wall across from Guildhall a plaque reading, "In Memory of all
those killed by weapons systems produced within this city and district."
Just below another sign is dedicated to those "in this city and district who
have lost their lives as a result of war and conflict." When I first saw the
sign about the weapons produced, I had presumed wrongly that it related
to the Troubles. How, then, did a small group—nine people—force one of
the largest defense contractors in the world to close down and bolt from
Derry? The company employed a small number of people in Derry—fifty
in total—and it says that its main work there was software development for
air-traffic control, not weapons design. Incensed, nonetheless, by the Israeli

bombing of Lebanon that summer (2006) and the general state of war in the world, the Derry Anti-War Coalition went active. The coalition saw the values that had guided civil rights activists during the Troubles as having global and local resonance. As Eamonn McCann told me, "If all our rhetoric meant anything, we were going to take a stand on this."

It was a "complicated situation," McCann said, because obviously people in Derry benefited from the jobs provided by Raytheon. But the local activists were upset that Nobel Peace Prize winners John Hume and David Trimble welcomed Raytheon to Derry as part of the "peace dividend" for Northern Ireland. John Hume saw it as part of an effort to build a Silicon Valley in Derry. To Eamonn McCann, this was an affront to the basic sense of justice for which they had fought for so long—"civil rights were not just for ourselves." Noting that even the manufacturing of software by a defense contractor was offensive to many in Derry, McCann asked me rhetorically, "If the KKK gave an order for white hoods, would that be okay?" "This was not a question of when you draw a line—everything is global," he said. Speaking at Guildhall Square on 15 June 2010, McCann read out a statement by the families of the Bloody Sunday victims, which he restated for me in the context of his views of the Raytheon problem: "Bloody Sunday was a great injustice. But the fight for truth and justice has been an inspiration too. It has deepened our sense of who we are. And made us more aware that we are also citizens of the world. Nobody who struggles for justice will be a stranger here. Nobody who dies in the struggle for justice will be forgotten here."

On 9 August 2006, Eamonn McCann and eight others took over the Raytheon building in Derry. As detailed in a pamphlet provided to me by McCann, when they arrived, a short statement was read: "We are here to take a stand against the violence of the U.S./Israeli wars in the Middle East. We must not offer violence to any other person. We will do what we can to get into Raytheon. And when and if we get in, we should leave Raytheon and the political parties of this place with no room for doubt that there are many of us who won't rest until we get this company out of Derry once and for all." The protesters rushed into the building; an initial thirty had been whittled down to nine by the time the police arrived. They threw papers and computers out the windows, then "decommissioned the mainframe" with a fire extinguisher so as to "disrupt Raytheon's internal ordering system and thus hamper production, including production of missiles," while declaring, "Resisting war crimes is not a crime." When the police asked what their demands were, the protestors shouted back, "The removal of Raytheon from Derry!" They then set up a game of cards on the floor, continuing to play as police in riot gear stormed in and arrested them. On 11 June 2008, the Raytheon 9 were found not guilty by a jury on charges of criminal damaging. Eamonn McCann was, however, cited for absconding with some computer software.

After years of pressure, in January 2010, Raytheon announced it was closing its Derry plant. The company had already been cutting staff there and was considering consolidating its manufacturing operations. But the grassroots political pressure calling attention to Raytheon proved more than the company had bargained for. The Associated Press quoted Mark Durkan, a Catholic member of the British parliament, as saying, "People are rightly free to voice their disgust at the violence in the Middle East and the failure of Britain and America to challenge or contain Israeli actions. People are also free to express opposition to the arms trade and the role of a company like Raytheon at a global level within that." Durkan then added, "But destroying property and possibly prejudicing other investment and employment prospects is not the way to register such concerns." The worry was that international investment might now shun Northern Ireland. Eamonn McCann, while fully appreciating this dilemma, made clear to me that "if Derry had come to stand for anything, it had to be for peace."

THE LAST FEW PIECES OF THE JIGSAW?

The Northern Ireland government's move in early 2010 to place authority in its new police force was in many respects the end of the new beginning. As Peter Robinson said at a business roundtable on Northern Ireland that I attended on 16 March 2010 in Washington, DC, "These are the last few pieces of the jigsaw." I attended several events sponsored by the U.S. economic envoy to Northern Ireland, Invest Northern Ireland, and the U.S. Chamber of Commerce built around St. Patrick's Day. I was able to see Peter Robinson and Martin McGuinness up close and in action. To say that they were "on message" would be an understatement. Northern Ireland was at peace, it had outstanding infrastructure and a great education system, and it was attracting high-tech investment. United around economic development, Robinson and McGuinness subtly made an ironic but essential point in their presentations: Northern Ireland was likely a better investment deal than the Republic, given the economic catastrophe there. Its smaller size, top-class universities, non-eurozone status, government willingness to work with companies, and overall infrastructure made the North a great investment. Though the corporate tax would remain high, and the recession had caused significant cuts in services, Northern Ireland was open for business. According to Peter Robinson, it was in a "strong and confident position . . . with an infrastructure that is second to none." The work ethic and business climate would allow "for local companies to compete in the global environment." As one senior Northern Ireland official told me, "It can't go unnoticed that, due to our historic ties to Britain, we do have money in our banks."

In Washington, DC, Martin McGuinness noted how success at the political level had "cleared away difficulties." Now the North was benefiting
from investment across a range of sectors. Even Hollywood—with Universal Studios and HBO—was looking at filming there. Key for McGuinness
was "how to use our own resources for global business . . . building on a
young and well-educated workforce." The first and second ministers introduced an executive from General Electric to discuss how the company's investments in Northern Ireland had paid off—including by creating jobs for
Americans hired to work in Northern Ireland, "engineers and brains" being
the calling card. General Electric was heavily invested in Northern Ireland
via Kelman Ltd., which produces infrastructure for electricity transformers
and power distribution and, according to this executive, was moving power
"from turbine to toaster, which was good for the economy and good for
utilities." He announced that GE had significant expansion plans in the
North, driven by a strong sense that the area benefited from a "pipeline of
talent" generated by its universities, which were producing a "good, cost-
effective, and reliable workforce." To facilitate this kind of investment, the
United States had assigned a special "economic envoy," Declan Kelly, to
bridge common interests in economic progress.

I asked Grainne McVeigh, head of international sales and marketing
at Invest Northern Ireland, a government agency that facilitates international investment, for her take on how economic development related to
consolidating the peace effort. She said the goal is to "sell the image—to
get beyond the dichotomy of what people perceive and what you know to
be [the] reality" of the current environment in Northern Ireland. McVeigh
spoke with pride of the "opportunity and chance to be in a community for
some groups with no choices before." She and her staff "have a passion
and a zeal on a mission" to provide new opportunities for the people of
Northern Ireland. Economic development "brings stability to lives—careers, opportunities. These change people's lives" as they move forward.
She said that because of these efforts, "there are people working now—it
is a powerful motivator." For instance, Seagate set up shop in Derry in
1993 manufacturing computer components. McVeigh said that previously,
"there was nothing there [on the Seagate site]—a green field. There was no
previous history of advanced manufacturing in electronics there." Now,
she said, "one quarter of all computers have a part made in Northern Ireland." Seagate "has touched thousands of families in its fifteen-year history.
Courses are linked into it—it is studied and further expertise is developed."
Asking rhetorically, "Has it been a catalyst for change in Derry?" she answers emphatically, "Yes!" Still, she agrees that there remain big challenges
at the street level in still-troubled areas. For many Catholics and Protestants
across Northern Ireland's society, foreign direct investment has been a big
plus.

There are major bright spots in the area of higher education in Northern Ireland, which is a vital conduit between foreign direct investment and indigenous growth. To get a sense of how the higher education system can facilitate peace building, I visited Queens University in Belfast. I was drawn initially to meet with a leading international security and terrorism specialist, Professor Richard English, who describes the PhD program at Queens as having extensive on-the-ground research networks for the study of peace building and conflict resolution. Students from around the world are coming to Queens to do "peace-consolidation research." The ability to do primary research with people who "know the streets" was attracting a top cadre of graduate student expertise. At the helm of the relationship between Queens University and Northern Ireland's future progress is President and Vice Chancellor Peter Gregson, an innovative and dynamic leader and an engineer by training. I met with him at Queens in July 2010. He began our discussion noting with justifiable pride that Queens now ranks in the top cadre of UK universities along with Oxford and Cambridge.

At Queens University, "the staff and students are connected with life in general," said Gregson. This gives the university a high-profile as Queens is "absolutely committed to serving the wider community." He went out of his way to praise Richard English's work for attracting students wishing to study how peace is built—which in turn helps in the consolidation of peace. In terms of social sciences, Queens has had professors and students working directly in the assistance of writing public policy in the new Northern Ireland government. Professor Gregson said that the university has helped to create spinout companies from research and development in two projects that have created over one thousand jobs in Belfast. He noted that Northern Ireland still needs to move toward even larger investments from the outside, "to move away from a lifestyle economy . . . while also providing for students with the widest possible horizons." Gregson praised the close relationship that Queens has with Trinity College and University College Dublin in the Republic, but he simultaneously pointed out that "being established within the UK is a major asset." Especially advantageous for Northern Ireland, he said, is its relative size as "small size creates access—a habitat for the world in key areas such as health and sustainability" to research and develop initiatives. This, Gregson said, has been especially true in biological research and clinical trials leading to high-quality research in an accessible population. From that kind of university partnership in the medical sphere, three companies employing hundreds have been spun out doing cancer-related research.

According to Peter Gregson, Queens' ability to work with a "private-sector orientation" while being "linked to government funding, but not guided by it" makes the institution unique. There is, he said, a very real "sympathy in the government for education." He also noted that Queens has been eager to remind its funders that Ireland's "history is one of poets and playwrights" and that support for the arts and culture is a vital part of economic development and the "selling of Northern Ireland." There is, for example, a series of major arts festivals in Belfast; "absent Queens, it dies" said Gregson. He tells of a trip to India that Queens organized for engineers to do work on a water plant project. Queens included on its team five poets. They held Irish and Indian joint poetry readings at an associated poetry festival. Queens hosts the Seamus Heaney Centre for Poetry. Gregson points with pride to a study showing that one-third of all poetry read in the United Kingdom is by Seamus Heaney (an alumnus of Queens).

In an area as small as Northern Ireland, a major university like Queens can have a massive impact. I asked Peter Gregson how he saw Queens fitting into the peace process. He noted that the American who was a special negotiator of that process, George Mitchell, had just completed ten years as chancellor of Queens. He left that position to take up a new role as special envoy to the Arab-Israeli peace process for President Barack Obama. Queens had, since the peace process, assumed a "special responsibility to study learning of peace and reconciliation—especially the human dimension," said Gregson. He added that the university "contributes to broader social cohesion," helping to bridge the sectarian divisions of the past. At the professional level, faculty and students are engaged in "planning diverse communities . . . for which education is key."

The peace process, combined with the economic disaster in the Republic of Ireland, has left the North attractive for new business investment. Unable to compete with Dublin on the corporate tax rate (which in the North is 28 percent), senior officials in Northern Ireland point out that mainly left in Dublin are headquarters—there to avoid paying taxes. Northern Ireland makes a different pitch about connectedness, its size and the "ability to be a big fish in a small pond," as Grainne McVeigh put it. She added that while a small investment that hires fifty people in the Republic would have a marginal effect, in the North it would be huge, given the size of the population. Another advantage is that because companies are coming to Northern Ireland for reasons other than the tax rate, they tend to stay. All the benefits of life in the Republic exist in Northern Ireland today. Also, non-eurozone status has served as an advantage while the European Union has struggled with debt crises—as have the historical ties to British banking. Northern Ireland is actually in direct economic competition with the Republic, and in that regard, it is doing well. A bigger challenge in the North, actually, is how to differentiate itself from Scotland or Yorkshire in the United Kingdom rather than the Republic of Ireland. In this case, Irishness sets the North apart. "The people of Northern Ireland," said McVeigh, "are smart. They are welcoming, They are funny and have an edge. They are witty." She said that investors regularly report that "we came for the economy but stayed for the people."

Still, Grainne McVeigh asked of the local criminal on the streets of Belfast, "Can we get that thug to see things differently?" That question remains unanswered—and I began to doubt whether it was something the American government was even considering. I asked this question to Declan Kelly's office directly and never got a response. Serious individuals with decades of senior-level experience in Northern Ireland were deeply concerned that the United States and the leadership in the North were missing out on the essential aspects of peace building. Bill and Hillary Clinton would take occasional victory laps through the North, but in terms of daily routine, Northern Ireland did not rank high on the list of American priorities twelve years after the Good Friday Agreement. Why, some observers would even ask, is the Department of State helping to outsource American jobs to an economy with lower unemployment than that in the United States? Even worse, some say, the United States, the Republic of Ireland, and Great Britain are enabling a culture of dependency in the North. When outside interests invest, that takes away the need for Northern Ireland to develop indigenous growth and political responsibility. When they are not taking care to develop their own industries and labor force, then how can they possibly be taking care of the people of the Ardoyne in Belfast? Furthermore, if those streets are really no different from the streets of Detroit or Cleveland, why not invest that American money in those cities instead?

So long as this process and flyby senior-level attention props up the Catholic and Protestant leadership in Northern Ireland, the politicians there need not build long-term reconciliation. Thus, the serious issues of housing and education go unaddressed. It is here that the great initiatives of Bill Clinton and others are at risk of falling apart—and those who built that legacy do not even seem to realize it. On 19 October 2010, at a U.S.-sponsored economic-development conference in Washington, DC, Declan Kelly said, "In total, we had over a trillion dollars worth of commercial value in the room. And in terms of the companies that had already invested in Northern Ireland, several of them are multi-billion-dollar corporations like Allstate and the New York Stock Exchange, Liberty Mutual, Caterpillar, and so forth." The same day, the *Irish Times* quoted Kelly as saying, "American companies are looking at the pure cold business case. They are not looking at investing in Northern Ireland as a favor—it is if the business case adds up, and Northern Ireland is a very positive region." Yet, it was unclear what this had to do with solving the entrenched problems at the ground level in Northern Ireland.

There is no question that the delivery of jobs in Northern Ireland is an essential aspect of completing the peace process. Furthermore, as budgets are cut across the United Kingdom, the ability of foreign direct investment to pick up the slack in supporting service-sector employment is crucial to reducing dependency on the state. As to the assertion that the United States focus on Northern Ireland is somehow diminished, a prominent Irish American leader told me off the record, "I can hardly think of another region in the world, certainly in Europe, that can boast such attention from the administration. Indeed, is not Declan Kelly's very position unique?" This person added, "Without the prospect of hope for a better life, young people, with no memories of the Troubles, can fall in lure of paramilitaries. Therefore, in parallel with all the community-based programs aimed at achieving parity of esteem and mutual understanding, there must be efforts to generate jobs and opportunity." Still, I left Belfast with the uneasy feeling that these comments would fall on deaf ears where it matters most—on the streets of the Ardoyne and beyond. In fact, it might just make the people there angry.

SESAME STREET TO THE RESCUE

Today, too many young Catholics and Protestants in Northern Ireland share a destiny of nothing. They do not know the horrors of the past and have little reason to think that the peace process produced any benefits. With these concerns in mind, I was especially interested to hear Peter Robinson and Martin McGuinness telling a 16 March 2010 Washington, DC, audience about *Sesame Street*. Actually, in Northern Ireland, the show is called *Sesame Tree* because, well, arguing over what street in Belfast to name it for would cause all kinds of problems. *Falls Street* or *Shankill Street* did not seem promising. A venerable American institution, *Sesame Street* is innovative in adapting its programming for local production to help bridge differences among people worldwide. In Northern Ireland, a centuries-old "fairy tree" served as the basis for the name of the show, which is produced by Sixteen South and Sesame Workshop and airs on the BBC. Via archives, Kermit the Frog, Big Bird, and other classic *Sesame Street* characters make appearances. In Northern Ireland the local stars are Aunt Claribelle, Potto, Archie, and my own favorite, Hilda the Hare.

The *Sesame Tree* concept focuses on promoting good citizenship among children aged three to six. The goal is to encourage positive views of the self, those around us, and our interdependence. The story lines revolve around children's themes to build good self-esteem, empathy, appreciation of differences and similarities, constructive and nonviolent conflict solving, and a sense of responsibility at the local and global level. I spoke with Shari Rosenfeld, vice president for global education at Sesame Workshop in New York City, who is responsible for creating locally produced series around the world. "In developing the *Sesame Tree* project, we worked in collaboration with local researchers, education experts, and production partners in Northern Ireland to create resources which focus on social inclusion, encouraging children to develop as individuals and as members of the larger community," Rosenfeld said. She added, "We feel that its unique combination of entertaining television content and educational and outreach materials will encourage a shared society and make a lasting impact on how children live, learn, work and play together. In particular, *Sesame Tree* will encourage children to be more inclusive of others, help them appreciate similarities and differences, and help foster positive community relations."

I met in Belfast in July 2010 with Fiona MacMillan, who translates this vision into a successful production on the ground in Belfast. An all-purpose project manager and advocate for *Sesame Tree*, she seeks to get every age-appropriate school in Northern Ireland engaged with the program. The team in Northern Ireland has succeeded in getting *Sesame Tree* seen as the primary version of *Sesame Street* in the United Kingdom. Using local writers and puppeteers, the program addresses issues that young people in Northern Ireland might see, but not understand, and reframes them positively. For example, one episode focuses on different kinds of marching bands and how there are all kinds of marches and all kinds of people who might march for all kinds of reasons. MacMillan has a team that goes out into the schools and puts on productions, involving children in puppet making and role playing. Parents, she says, "watch it themselves as they quickly see that this is not just a kiddie show." MacMillan told me that Martin McGuinness attended the public launch of the first program. She said that he got emotional and spoke of his own grandson, wondering what kind of things he would know of growing up.

According to Fiona MacMillan the *Sesame Tree* effort has received some surprising criticism. First, people questioned whether the show would ever even happen; it did. Then, others complained that it amounted to "social engineering." Some critics even argued that it was a new kind of American "imperialism." This, I must say, caught me by surprise—I would never have seen *Sesame Street* as reflecting a kind of "Evil Big Bird Empire." Still, MacMillan said, "people are suspicious of Americans coming in and telling us how to solve our problems." Perhaps more significant was the question of "just how relevant can a show like this be—is it sustainable for the long run?" As with all public television programming, sustainability attracts funding. In this case, the American Ireland Fund has devoted $1 million to support production. A more daunting challenge is the fact that those kids whose parents encourage them to watch the show might not be the ones who most need to see it—is it being watched by those children left behind by the peace process?

Fiona MacMillan pointed out how important it is for "a child to see their culture and surroundings on television." She said she experienced that personally as a child growing up in Scotland—"everything was always about London. . . . It is great to see local environments and someone who talks like them." The team that produces *Sesame Tree* does not see itself as

a silver bullet. Its members know that the "parents want things to be different—not to repeat the past." MacMillan said, "If we can contribute to that
in the smallest of ways, we have succeeded." She shared my concern about
the potential for a lost generation among today's youth, saying, "What
we do is low cost but high payoff." As a society, Northern Ireland needs a
"relatively small investment" in these children. Our system is "brilliant at
the top but poor at the local level—we have traded on that for too long,"
said MacMillan. "As a contribution, ultimately, you have to do something
about where you live." After the peace process took root, MacMillan said
she felt that "as a citizen I did have a contribution and it did not have to be
political—I could be a part in that change as well." Yet, she also reflected,
"it will be thirty to fifty years to get beyond this . . . but anything you can
do along these lines has got to be worth it." "We are," she added, "a little
bit on the way of doing this thing . . . but it cannot be a benign apartheid."
She paused and reflected on how far Northern Ireland has come, saying
with some emotion in her voice, "We have very good change—and the early
young are the foundation for everything else that goes after that." People
like Fiona MacMillan and the team producing *Sesame Tree* form a key part
of the peace puzzle. As Shari Rosenfeld told me, "I'm confident that *Sesame
Tree* will have a long-term impact on how today's young children perceive
the world around them and their own potential role in that world." At the
November 2010 launch of the new season of *Sesame Tree*, Peter Robinson
and Martin McGuinness were photographed together smiling and playing
with a bunch of puppets. Now that's progress.

WASTED

Thousands of pieces of the peace puzzle are being built in Northern Ireland,
each with its own story. Countless people in civil society work every day to
bridge the Troubles—so one should not get the idea that nothing at all is
happening. The real void involves strategy and large-scale progress on key
matters like housing, education, and crime. One group working to fill that
void is Peter Sheridan and the colleagues he leads. Sheridan is the CEO of
Cooperation Ireland. Founded in 1979, Cooperation Ireland is the leading
peace-building charity in Ireland with a mission to "advance mutual understanding and respect by promoting practical co-operation between the
people of Northern Ireland and of the Republic of Ireland." The organization facilitates linkages across communities from schools to youth groups
to local governments and businesses. The goal is to help build a society
established on principles of tolerance and respect for cultural difference.
Before joining Cooperation Ireland, Sheridan spent thirty years as a police
officer in Northern Ireland, rising through the ranks to become assistant

chief constable for the region's rural areas. He was responsible for negotiations in Derry that led to successful agreements on how parades could work peacefully. A graduate of the FBI Academy with a degree in criminology from Cambridge, Sheridan was awarded the Order of the British Empire from the Queen. His last position in the police was as head of the Crime Operations Department. At the time of his retirement, he was the highest-ranking Catholic officer serving in the Northern Ireland police force.

In his first interview as head of Cooperation Ireland in 2008, Peter Sheridan said, "People have this view that the peace is done and it's all over. And to some extent that part of the conflict is over but it's by no means stable yet. Yes, a lot of the engagement has been at the top political level but actually the grassroots hasn't been engaged in it." Sheridan noted that it is harder now to attract media to the long-term peace-building process. He added,

> Do any of us want to be still living in Northern Ireland or Ireland in 30 or 40 years' time with segregated housing still? Is that what we as a society want? And so there's a huge amount of work in terms of mainstreaming government policies and influencing those policies so that actually in 50 years' time we know we're not going to have segregated housing because policies will have been put in place that prevent that. . . . Most people out there since the Good Friday Agreement in working class Catholic, nationalist, loyalist, unionist areas haven't seen their quality of life change to that extent. They haven't got the sense that this has been really to our benefit economically.

I spoke in October 2010 with Peter Sheridan to get his sense of trends in Northern Ireland. Yes, of course, the "conflict has come to an end," he said, "but one has to know where we are now—where you are starting from." Sheridan framed four key phases of the conflict, and he has been a player in each. First was the peacekeeping phase, which required security, seen and unseen, in the time of the Troubles. The overriding question was "how to stop the violence" with "neighbors protecting neighbors." He also said that when working as a police officer, he "never got up in the morning and pondered who to shoot, or kill, or maim—or that there were people out there that would do that to me." The unfortunate reality was that people learned to live with an "acceptable level of violence."

The second phase produced the peacemaking and included the Good Friday Agreement up through the finalizing of policing, which was the "last jigsaw." Still, this phase was mainly an "agreement on a system of government"; it was not peace in and of itself. It is during the third, and current, stage that peace building must occur. Seeking to sustain "normalcy across communities" is just the beginning. But, Peter Sheridan added, it is hard to have that "when 95 percent of the public housing is segregated . . . when there are 88 'peace walls'—soon some will have been there longer than the

Berlin Wall was up. The danger is that we are settling for separation with no sense it will change." A key missing element is some one to drive this vital phase. "Peacemaking had Bill Clinton, it had Tony Blair—but now there are a series of managers" said Sheridan. To him, "if you don't underpin political agreement with agreement at the grassroots level," then there is no firm ground to build on. This is tough work for, as he put it, we are "asking people to live with their abuser." Over thirty years of conflict is incredibly difficult to separate from the psyche of a people who pass on their stories from generation to generation.

Peter Sheridan described the current situation in Northern Ireland as "disparate" with "no strategic direction." Americans like Declan Kelly are doing important work, said Sheridan, but overall "there isn't a strategy at the high level." Yes, he said, "you need economic development to secure peace—but another big bomb wrecks this. The economy needs a peaceful society." Northern Ireland and its international partners "need a collective effort at peace building." Crucially, he wondered, "where are the next generation's Martin McGuinness's? Who will be the peacemakers of the future—and how do we energize them?" This phase, in Sheridan's view, will take generations, but the question of who will lead and toward what is "not even on today's agenda." He used the analogy of a set of filing cabinet drawers. Most of the daily planning is "working in the bottom drawer." On rare occasions, like when Ian Paisley and Martin McGuinness entered into the leadership of the new government, that top drawer is opened. But how to get those middle drawers built into the key issues—like public housing, education—those drawers, if opened at all, just borrow too often from the lower ones.

In the fourth and final phase, Peter Sheridan sees Northern Ireland as having an obligation to give back to the world. While the Northern Ireland peace process might or might not be used as a model elsewhere, people should be able to "come here and learn." There is a range of experiences "for the media, for the church, for the state as to what is good and not so good as to how peace continues to be built in Northern Ireland." Today, though, it was certainly my observation—confirmed in literally every meeting I held and place I visited—that Northern Ireland is just beginning the third phase. The United States, in particular, has been an all-too-silent partner where its help is most needed. Why, for every meeting of a "trillion dollars" was Declan Kelly not engaging persistently and personally on the ground on the streets of Belfast and in other places where the threat to peace grows?

According to Peter Sheridan, Northern Ireland needs a much larger-scale sense of strategy. Piecemeal efforts—a grant here or there—will not cut it. Still, sometimes that top cabinet drawer is opened—like on the day that the crowd gathered at Guildhall Square in Derry to listen to the British prime minister in June 2010. Originally from Enniskillen, Sheridan has lived for three decades in Derry, which he now calls home. He was watching the audience when David Cameron read out the Saville Report. He told me that in the front row were some very hardcore Republicans who "did not go thinking they were going to be applauding a British prime minister." Sheridan said that a moment of warmth and applause spread through the crowd at Guildhall Square much like that at Princess Diana's funeral when her brother spoke. The applause for his eulogy began outside the church and spread, spontaneously, through the crowd with warmth and affection— "it was that kind of moment." The reading of the Saville Report (during which Peter Sheridan helped provide security and support in Derry) was "what was needed—it was done absolutely right." He suggested that it will not do much good for government officials to make the case against dissident Republicans, and he rejected the idea that these people should even be credited as dissidents in the frame of the historical movement. When they blow something up in his town of Derry, Sheridan said, "these are not dissidents—they are anti-Derry, anti-Irish." Instead, the leadership of the Catholic community in the North and in the Republic of Ireland must speak to them and find ways to reach out to those who can be persuaded to invest in peace. For now, though, Peter Sheridan sees a "lack of strategy in nearly every aspect."

Peter Sheridan illustrated to me an example of how Cooperation Ireland is trying to put in place some of the pieces of Northern Ireland's peace-building jigsaw puzzle. As part of its Young Leaders Project, Cooperation Ireland went into a very rough part of Kilwilkie Estate, North Lurgan. Kilwilkie has been a hotbed of youth getting wrapped up in dissident Republican groups like Continuity IRA. Many youths there, hearing of "glory days" and "excitement," fashion themselves as the next generation of combatants in Ireland's struggle. In 2009, two British solders and a Catholic policeman were killed there. This was the first killing of British soldiers in twelve years. On 15 March 2009, the *Scotsman* quoted a seventeen-year-old on the streets of Kilwilkie as saying, "The Irish people can stand again and get the British out of Ireland. [Violence] is the only way Britain is going to move. Britain is making too much money out of this country and that's why they've held on to the six counties. . . . People just got fed up after all the Republicans losing their lives for Irish Freedom and then just laying their weapons down to Britain. We have to fight on."

Not willing to sit still while soldiers were being killed, Peter Sheridan and Cooperation Ireland made the case to the Northern Ireland leadership that it was essential to engage these young people creatively. Going directly into Kilwilkie Estate, Cooperation Ireland recruited fourteen youths via an invitation to write a movie script. Those who participated "didn't believe it" but did engage. They wrote the script, and professionals, including award-winning director Kevin Hewitt, were brought in to work with them on the how-to of producing a short film. Their production, *Wasted*, focuses on life within Kilwilkie Estate for a group of young people, showing how they deal with peer pressure, drug and alcohol abuse, and paramilitary activity. At the debut in June 2010, it was given full, paparazzi, Hollywood-style treatment at the Odeon Theater in Belfast. These fourteen youths, who had first shown up in hoods and gang colors, were now dressed to the hilt and had been taken "outside their bubble." Previously they would have run when told, in the tradition of the Troubles, to "get the petrol, get the rag—but no one asked why," said Peter Sheridan. At the film's premiere in Belfast, Sheridan said, "The rationale behind this challenging project is to reach, reengage, and motivate those young people who may not have the opportunity to use their leadership skills in a positive way. We realize that there are neither quick fixes nor easy solutions, but we are committed to a long-term program geared toward the needs of these young people." These young people have subsequently gone on to internships with Manchester United and leading businesses in the United Kingdom. As great as this is, Sheridan said this kind of program needs to be put in place not just for fourteen but for "one thousand young people—now."

FROM GLEN TO GLEN AND
DOWN THE MOUNTAINSIDE

In March 1995, I joined a small group for dinner and a lecture with John Hume at Mt. Holyoke College in Massachusetts. He said that the essence of peace requires a change of mind-set: "In my own approach, I am a member of the European parliament and am a very totally convinced European. I am a Derryman. I'm known as a Derryman because I am an Irishman. I'm known as an Irishman because I am a European. The world has become a smaller place today with the telecommunications revolution, the technological revolution, the transport revolution. The world is a far smaller place today than it was fifty or one hundred years ago, and that's reflected in relationships between peoples. We don't have independent countries anymore; we are interdependent. We cannot live apart." Hume went on to say, "We spill our sweat, but not our blood, to break down the barriers of prejudice that have divided us for centuries and begin the healing process of breaking down the barriers that divide the people of Ireland. The real border of Ireland isn't a line on a map, it's a border in the hearts and minds of the people. That can only be done by the healing process." Those words still ring true today. Visitors have not truly seen Ireland until they have traveled the North. They cannot understand the depth of the peace-building challenge until they have walked the streets of Ardoyne. They will not have seen the full beauty of Ireland until they have stood upon the Giant's Causeway and looked out on the power of the sea. They will not meet the essence of Ireland until they stand among the people of Derry. As he left active public service, John Hume appeared on Dublin's *Late Late Show* on 29 December 2009 and, at the end of the program, was asked to sing. Sitting with his proud wife, he said, with a crafty look in his eye, "Well, you must know I'm a Derryman . . . because you're not a Derryman, unless you can sing." "Oh Danny Boy," he sang, "the pipes, the pipes are calling. From glen to glen and down the mountainside." Few moments could be truer to the Emerald Isle and its role in advancing peace in the world.

An EU road sign with anti–Lisbon Treaty graffiti, just south of Doolin in County Clare. Though previous referendums failed, the second treaty effort passed just as Ireland was collapsing into economic crisis (July 2010).

7

Éireann Go Global

ALL THE WORLD'S A STAGE, AND MOST OF US ARE DESPERATELY UNREHEARSED

These words, from Irish playwright Seán O'Casey, hold true for all nations—from great powers like the United States to small countries like Ireland. Ireland's history, being rooted in the ebbs and flows of the British Empire, also rises out of global politics. Ireland once formed a vital piece of the British Empire, serving as a rearguard defense against encroachment from competing European powers. The Troubles originated in part from this role as London worried that enemy countries like Spain or France could get a hold in Ireland via ties to Catholicism. By the 1980s, the jealous hold on Northern Ireland was the last nail in the legacy of the British Empire to break. Many hardcore Unionist areas in Belfast today see themselves as the last loyal outpost of Britannia's rule. This chapter shows how Ireland has demonstrated a shrewd capacity to integrate interests and morals in foreign policy while traversing creatively the globalized stage of international relations.

NOT QUITE THE FULL SHILLING SO FAR AS NEUTRALITY IS CONCERNED

Ireland defines its national interests according to a carefully calibrated mix of official neutrality and political, economic, and (increasingly) military alignment with the West. Irish neutrality originally reflected a desire to consolidate and strengthen independence from Britain. Even after independence was achieved in 1922, the British government contested Ireland's right to issue passports, fly the Irish flag on ships, and have its own diplomatic missions abroad. As a small and vulnerable island, the new Irish state had to be creative in foreign affairs. As Éamon de Valera said in 1920 of the relationship between Ireland and Britain, "Mutual self-interest would make the peoples of these two islands, if both independent, the closest possible allies in a moment of real national danger to either."

Dublin often saw cooperation on defense with Britain as providing negotiating leverage on Northern Ireland. Consistently, over time, de Valera's concept of the common interests of the British and Irish would, however, override his aspirations for a united Ireland. For example, Ireland was officially neutral in World War II—much to Britain's dismay. Ireland did allow Allied aircraft a corridor of access over its territory. German pilots who crashed in Ireland were detained, while Allied pilots were allowed to return home. Ireland also made public its coastal detection of German submarines near or within its territorial waters, providing open access to intelligence for the Allies. During World War II, up to forty thousand Irish served as volunteers in the British army to fight the Germans. As many as 180,000 Irish were employed in British military production and related wartime industries. Still, de Valera outraged the Allies when, on the death of Adolph Hitler, he went to the German Embassy in Dublin and signed a book of condolences. Many Israelis still speak of this act today when asked for their views on Ireland. In a biting comment about Ireland's worldview, British prime minister Winston Churchill once said, "We have always found the Irish a bit odd. They refuse to be English."

At the origins of the Cold War, the United States approached Ireland to join as a founding member of the North Atlantic Treaty Organization (NATO) to provide collective defense of the West against the Soviet Union. Ireland responded that it would join the negotiations, but only as a representative of a united Ireland: Ireland would trade neutrality for the North. Washington effectively replied, "It's been nice knowing you," according to Theodore Achilles, a negotiator for the United States, in his memoir *Fingerprints on History* (1992). Still, the NATO treaty was signed in the presence of the Irish ambassador to Washington in 1949. Declassified documents from 1950 demonstrate the United States' conclusion that, while Ireland was "strategically located" and could offer "valuable sites" for air and naval access, the country was "not considered essential at [that] time."

Ireland benefited from alignment with the West during the Cold War—and gained by not paying the costs of that alignment. Taoiseach Seán Lemass said in 1962, "While Ireland did not accede to the North Atlantic Treaty, we have always agreed with the general aim of the Treaty. The fact that we did not accede to it was due to special circumstances and does not qualify in any way our acceptance of the ideal of European unity and of the conception . . . of the duties, obligations, and responsibilities which European unity would impose." Lemass took this commitment beyond words. By the 1960s, Ireland was allowing American planes, including those doing military-support activity, access to Shannon Airport. Beginning in 1955, the CIA received information and cooperation from Irish government sources. Following the Cuban Missile Crisis in 1962, this included Irish searches of planes transiting between the Warsaw Pact and Cuba for war materials.

The Irish Constitution is actually vague on neutrality and mainly stresses rights to independence and self-determination. Article 29 forbids the Irish government from committing to establishing a common defense within the European Union without a national referendum. This too has even been more of a political than operational interpretation; in other words, Ireland uses its assertion of neutrality in a flexible way to advance its interests, but the Constitution imbues the government with flexibility. The lasting characterization of neutrality is a legacy of de Valera, who said in 1936, "I think that the average person in this country wants to make war on nobody. We have no aggressive designs. We want to have our own country for ourselves, as I have said on more than one occasion, and that is the limit of our ambition; we have no imperial ambitions of any sort." He said to the Dáil in 1955, "We realize that, small as our physical resources, there were spiritual ones which were of great value; and we never doubted that our nation, though a small one, in the material sense, could play a very important part in international affairs." He added, "A small nation has to be extremely cautious when it enters into alliances which bring it, willy nilly into [those] wars. . . . We would not be consulted in how a war would be started—the great powers would do that—and when it ended, no matter who won . . . would not be consulted as to the terms on which it should end." De Valera devoted much of his time to building up the authority of the League of Nations—and subsequent Irish leaders would engage deeply with the United Nations—and avoiding military alliances.

Ireland's joining the European Union would prove a major departure, though official neutrality has been maintained. Garret FitzGerald said to me that EU membership was, in his view, a key ingredient to securing Irish independence. While many Irish oppose it as infringing on neutrality, FitzGerald argues that it bolstered Ireland's confidence in dealing with the United Kingdom as an equal player within a European context. In early 2010 I met (in New Orleans of all places) with Irish international relations scholar Karen Devine of Dublin City University. Having done considerable research on how neutrality relates to Irish identity, she says there have been three basic tenants: not getting involved in war, staying independent, and remaining impartial. While Irish elites argued that neutrality was limited to "military alliances," Devine has confirmed via extensive public-opinion research that a broader view is ingrained in the public. Still, the Irish Department of Foreign Affairs published a detailed study of Ireland's 2008 rejection of the Lisbon

Treaty to deepen European integration. It showed that the largest reason for a "no" vote was a general lack of information—with "no" voters often drawing erroneous conclusions about what a "yes" vote meant. Only 13 percent identified loss of sovereignty and independence as a reason for a "no" vote, and only 8 percent saw neutrality and military issues as their main reason for opposition. Among "no" voters, however, 77 percent did agree with the idea that "Ireland should do everything it can to strengthen its neutrality." A major reason for a "no" vote was a false impression among the public that Irish nationals could face conscription into a European military. This view was predominant in the country, despite announced government policy requiring a "triple lock": any deployment of Irish forces would first have to be backed by the government, the parliament, and the United Nations.

Some supporters of EU integration argued that membership would help Ireland do a better job of standing up to the United States, which had gotten itself into quagmires in Iraq and Afghanistan. Agence France–Presse quoted Fine Gael European Parliament member John Cushnahan on 22 February 2008 as saying, "We'll have a more common foreign policy, and we'll be able to counter-balance big powers like the United States." Still, an emotional appeal against militarization of foreign policy in Ireland drove much of the debate over the European Union. Edward Horgan, a former member of the Irish Defence Forces, wrote in the *Irish Times* on 4 April 2008, "The Lisbon Treaty promotes militarism and will mean the death of Irish neutrality," and "the hidden agenda of the Lisbon Treaty is that it is part of a continuum of European and international developments that promotes militarism and erodes neutrality as a peace maintenance option." These views stood in stark contrast to those of advocates Patrick Keatinge, Peadar ó Broin, and Ben Tonra, three of Ireland's leading foreign policy experts, who argued that the purpose of Europe's common foreign and security policy was highly consistent with Irish worldviews. In their assessment, as they wrote in the *Irish Times* on 8 December 2008, the European Union would allow its members to better "promote peace, security, and progress in Europe and in the world." They noted that Ireland was in a unique position—even a morally imperative position—to contribute forces for the "provision of engineers, transportation, field hospitals, [and] bomb disposal experts." By engaging in military integration with the European Union, Ireland would be sustaining a vital strand of Irish foreign policy—a deep appreciation for human rights and support for people seeking self-determination and needing peacekeeping. As the *Irish Independent* quoted Labour leader Éamon Gilmore as saying on 9 June 2008, "Nothing in this treaty provides for conscription or for Ireland being forced into wars or imperialist adventures. . . . Our concentration should be on the responsibilities which we share with our EU partners in contributing to the search for peaceful solutions to conflicts around the world and especially in our own continent." He added that there is "no compulsion on member states to increase their military expenditure."

Patrick Keatinge writes in *Modern Irish Democracy* (1993), edited by Ronald J. Hill and Michael Marsh, "Ireland is not, and never was, quite the full shilling so far as neutrality is concerned." As they advanced Ireland's economic interest in Europe and with the United States, Irish leaders found that pragmatism on neutrality was needed. Furthermore, Ireland also found that neutrality could conflict with its moral commitment to advance human rights and serve as a UN peacekeeper. This became obvious to Irish political elites, including former Taoiseach Garret FitzGerald, who noted that when he participated in European Council meetings, he felt that neutrality forced him to remain silent when security issues were discussed. In *Unneutral Ireland* (1989), Trevor Salmon quotes FitzGerald asking whether it is "in fact necessitated by our military neutrality that we should not utter on such occasions? Are we living up to our own principles, and should not as many voices as possible be raised . . . in every possible arena on issues such as those favoring nuclear disarmament?" As Taoiseach, FitzGerald was no shrinking violet on foreign policy issues. He told me of the tension at a dinner he had with the American president Ronald Reagan, who visited Ireland. FitzGerald had "no reservation laying out his direct opposition to American foreign policy in Latin America" to the popular American president with Irish roots.

THE MOTHER TERESA OF
THE INTERNATIONAL COMMUNITY

In *Defending Ireland: The Irish State and Its Enemies since 1922* (1999), Eunan O'Halpin summarizes the Irish view of the country's place in the world as being "to regard itself as the Mother Teresa of the international community." Frank Aiken, the minister of external affairs from 1957 to 1969, who built a strong and independent voice for Ireland at the United Nations, established and consolidated this image. He and the Irish delegation regularly took stands in support of oppressed peoples worldwide. While principled to be sure, this savvy tactic also reminded the world of Ireland's partition, which was not on the United Nations' agenda. Aiken gave a series of speeches beginning in the late 1950s on the danger of nuclear weapons proliferation, making Ireland the initiator of the process that led to the 1968 Nuclear Non-Proliferation Treaty. In October 1958, Aiken told the UN General Assembly, "The danger of nuclear weapons to humanity, it seems to us, does not merely increase in direct ratio to the number of those possessing them. It seems likely to increase in geometric progression. Those who now possess nuclear weapons are a few great and highly developed states, with great urban populations, with much to lose and little to gain in a nuclear war. . . . The harnessing of nuclear energy for military purposes is bound to become simpler and cheaper with the passing of time. Sooner or later, therefore, unless this organization takes urgent preventive steps, this weapon will pass into the hands of states with much less to lose." Aiken was prescient in pointing to what would become a dominant global security concern of the later twentieth and early twenty-first centuries. He also warned of the risk of dangerous nonstate groups, like today's Al Qaeda, gaining access to such destructive power. He said, "Since local wars and revolutions almost always involve some degree of great power patronage and rivalry, the use of nuclear weapons by a small state or revolutionary group could lead, only too easily, to the outbreak of general war. One obsolete, Hiroshima-type bomb, used by a small and desperate country to settle a local quarrel, could be the detonator for worldwide thermonuclear war, involving the destruction of our whole civilization." Today, 189 countries are signatories to the Nuclear Non-Proliferation Treaty, which was, in its inception, an Irish idea.

Concern and empathy for the downtrodden and those seeking rights arise from Ireland's history, as well as from the vision of modern leaders. In 1992, Mary Robinson abandoned the routine of the ceremonial Irish presidency and went to Somalia, ravaged at the time by civil war and famine. She worked directly with volunteers, feeding children by her own hand. Speaking of this experience at a press conference, she said, "I feel completely ashamed and diminished when I see fellow citizens of this world—fellow women and children—who are so deprived of even a right to a life, to any quality of life." Upon completing her term, Robinson (at that time) became the highest-ranking woman to serve in the history of the United Nations as high commissioner for human rights. Ireland has since provided high levels of foreign aid. By 2009 this meant devoting nearly €1 billion to foreign aid spending, or about 0.58 percent of gross national product (GNP), a nearly 90 percent increase over the past decade. The government had hoped to grow its commitment to UN foreign-assistance programs by devoting 0.7 percent of GNP by 2012. However, in April 2010, the Organization for Economic Cooperation and Development (OECD) published a report showing that Irish foreign aid spending had fallen by 18.9 percent with budget cuts. The remaining budget was €671 million—still a lot for a small nation in economic crisis, but down to pre-2006 levels and likely to fall more. On 14 April 2010 the *Irish Times* quoted Max Lawson of the aid charity Oxfam as singling out Ireland for donors' "lackluster performance . . . [which] is not close to meeting the needs of poor countries, who are suffering now from the impact of the economic crisis. . . . It is a scandal that more than half of rich nations have cut their aid and are giving less of their income than the year before—just 31 cents in every $100."

Ireland also put its soldiers on the line for its values with a deep commitment to UN peacekeeping operations beginning in the late 1950s. By 2000, of all EU members, Ireland had made the third-highest contribution to UN peacekeeping operations outside of Europe—more than the United Kingdom, France, and Germany. Since 1958, Irish troops have suffered eighty-five deaths while serving in UN overseas deployments, including thirty-six killed as a direct result of hostile engagements. Ireland even began shifting its mission toward "peace enforcement" by sending troops into potential combat zones in Somalia in 1993 and Afghanistan in 2002. According to Rory Montgomery (then a senior official in the Foreign Ministry), speaking at EU committee hearings in 2009, "Peace support operations have become the principle raison d'être of our Defence Forces." Ireland has engaged a sizeable percentage of its armed forces in UN peace missions, including operations in Congo, Liberia, and Lebanon, and EU operations under a UN mandate in Central America, Russia, the former Yugoslavia, Cambodia, Iran, Iraq, Afghanistan, Kuwait, Namibia, Western Sahara, Liberia, and East Timor. On average, Ireland has been the sixth-largest contributor to UN peacekeeping operations, and most Irish military personnel do some kind of overseas deployment during their service. Of its 10,000-troop force, Ireland specifically commits 850 personnel to standing ready for overseas service in UN peacekeeping operations. Irish president Mary McAleese stated in November 2008, on the fiftieth anniversary of the country's role in UN peacekeeping, "For Ireland, as a neutral and non-aligned country, this method of military participation has proved itself to be a worthy and invaluable channel for our armed forces to lend their considered, measured and subtle military expertise to calm, stabilize, and help to pacify some of the world's most troubled regions."

In 1996 Ireland began building a relationship with the American-led military alliance NATO via its Partnership for Peace program. In 1999, the Irish government backed the NATO war in Kosovo—even though that war was fought without a UN mandate. In 2002, Ireland, sitting on the UN Security Council, voted to approve the resolution that paved the way for the American-led invasion of Iraq to overthrow Saddam Hussein. The reality of Ireland's position on neutrality was still often seen as free riding on other countries' hard military contributions to international security. Stanley Sloan, in a 1998 U.S. Congressional Research Service report, said, "Among the former European neutrals, Ireland probably has the least defensible argument for remaining outside the emerging cooperative defense framework in Europe. . . . Having largely enjoyed a free ride on security throughout the Cold War, other Europeans as well as U.S. officials question the justification for Ireland's position." I concurred. In a 14 December 1998 *Wall Street Journal* op-ed piece titled "Bringing Ireland into NATO's Fold," I argued for Ireland's joining NATO's Partnership for Peace program of outreach to European countries that sought to associate themselves with, but not necessarily join, the military organization. I wrote, "Ireland can gain from the Partnership for Peace by dispelling a growing perception that it is the free-rider of Europe, using neutrality as an excuse not to contribute or help pay the costs of the security burden in Europe." Dan O'Brien of the *Economist* wrote on 4 August 2009 in the *Irish Times*, "Where the Swedes and the Swiss committed resources to their militaries, Ireland left itself undefended because it knew that its allies would protect it. . . . That is called free-riding. No Irish person should be proud of it." O'Brien was especially critical of Ireland's not having developed a serious professional class of expertise on foreign affairs, with the current foreign minister being "a school teacher. . . . His four immediate predecessors were, respectively, a solicitor, a solicitor, a barrister, and Ray Burke [who was found guilty of corruption and sent to jail]. None had any background on international relations or diplomacy." He concluded, "No other developed country entrusts its foreign relations to unqualified amateurs with no experience of the world."

Ireland has since bridged many of its historical constraints and is now a contributor to EU Battlegroups, which will eventually form a key part of a sixty thousand EU rapid-reaction force. Ireland agreed in 2006 to join the battlegroup concept combining combat and support troops, which train, equip, and stand ready for the rapid deployment of at least fifteen hundred soldiers. In 2008, Ireland joined the Nordic Battlegroup, which had a total of twenty-seven hundred troops, along with contributions from Sweden, Estonia, Norway, and Finland. Ireland sent one hundred army personnel, most of whom actually remained in Ireland, except during a six-month standby activation. Swedish brigadier general Karl Engelbrekston, who commanded the Nordic Battlegroup, sought out the Irish forces for their ability to work with the dangerous improvised explosive devices used by insurgency movements in conflict zones. He requested the Irish troops after working alongside them on peacekeeping operations in Kosovo. "Following on from this request we assembled what is essentially a hybrid unit comprising of an [improvised explosive destruction] capability. . . . This is built around an Engineer Special Search Team (ESST), which is a specialized combat engineering team, developed from past experiences at home dealing with the 'on island' threat," said General Engelbrekston.

Ireland's participation in these EU battlegroups was, in the view of strict adherents to neutrality, a bridge too far. Critics allege this is part of a "militarization" of the European Union. The Green Party officially called the country's participation in these plans "the final assault . . . on what remains of Irish neutrality." Sinn Féin likewise stated that it "has consistently cautioned against the deployment of EU battlegroups. . . . We believe the increase of military missions will further boost the militarization of the EU, in turn becoming a blueprint for future EU military interventions, enhancing the introduction of the military aspect." Roger Cole, head of the Irish Peace and Neutrality Alliance (PANA), was less restrained in his assessment in a press release: "The integration of Ireland into an Imperial, militarized neo-liberal European superstate allied to the U.S. will ensure the full and active participation of all of Ireland in the resource wars of the 21st century." Cole called the battlegroups "shock troops, regiments of the emerging empire." Nevertheless, the major political parties were united in support. In fact, Billy Timmons, then the defense spokesman for Fine Gael, mainly criticized Ireland's not going far enough to shed its neutrality image: "From the point of view of Ireland's participation in an EU battlegroup, the 'triple lock' will continue to act as a barrier to Ireland's participation in an EU battlegroup." UN Secretary General Kofi Annan's visit to Dublin on 15 October 2004 confirmed Ireland's argument that these trends in foreign and defense policy were consistent with its deep commitment to the United Nations. Annan said in his public comments, "I want to leave you in no doubt of how important strengthened EU capacities are to the UN. . . . The EU is in a position to provide specialized skills that our largest troop contributors may not be able to give us, and to deploy more rapidly than we can."

THEY ARE ALL REDMONDISTS

I met with Roger Cole, the founder and leader of the Peace and Neutrality Alliance, in Dùn Laoghaire over lunch in August 2010. I had not visited this lovely seaside area since 1992 and was stunned by how much it had been developed. Then again, when I noted the degree of change to an elderly man working in a shop who had lived all his life there, he declared, "Imagine what it looks like to me!"

When I told Cole of the range of people I had been interviewing, he quickly said, "They are all Redmondists! All those elites who think they know the best interests of the Irish people—they are not Irish—they are European!" Cole added, "They want Ireland to be a rather insignificant region of the European Empire." John Redmond was an Irish politician who, prior to 1916, had worked within the British system to negotiate "home rule" for Ireland. Redmond also backed the British effort in World War I, urging Irish men to volunteer for the British army. In 1914, he said in a speech, "The interests of Ireland—of the whole of Ireland—are at stake in this war. This war is undertaken in the defense of the highest principles of religion and morality and right, and it would be a disgrace forever to our country and a reproach to her manhood and a denial of the lessons of her history if young Ireland confined their efforts to remaining at home to defend the shores of Ireland from an unlikely invasion, and to shrinking from the duty of proving on the field of battle that gallantry and courage which has distinguished our race all through its history." To Roger Cole, advocating EU and Irish military cooperation with the United States and NATO is just another step in this "Redmondist" tradition—which he sees through a nationalist lens of colonial subservience.

Roger Cole and PANA are significant players in Irish politics. They managed to get an estimated eighty to one hundred thousand people onto the streets of Dublin (when only twenty thousand were expected) in protest of the U.S. plans to invade Iraq in February 2003. They were also a major element in efforts to defeat national referenda on Ireland's integration into the European Union. The residue of that effort remains. I was recently driving up a road in Clare, not far from the musical and fishing village Doolin, when I saw a sign advertising that the European Union had helped to pay for the road. A large *X* had been spray-painted through it, along with the words "Lisbon 2: Same Question, Same Answer" (referring to the defeat of an earlier referendum). This time around in voting, the measure passed—as the economy was cascading into meltdown. Many people, comparing the situation to the economic collapse of Iceland, asked what the difference was between that country and Ireland: the answer was "an E and a U." If Ireland's economy completely disintegrated, its only hope would lie in international institutions like the European Union and the International Monetary Fund. This perceived risk to sovereignty is at the core of what drives Roger Cole and his allies. Cole is blunt in his assessment: "I don't like empires." He sees his movement as part of a tradition going back to Wolfe Tone and Michael Collins—in his view, these new international commitments are a new kind of threat to Irish freedom. "My views are deeply rooted in 1916—I'm a match to it," said Cole. He added, "Going into empire is a high lack of confidence. . . . Collins, etc., they did not lack confidence—and one needs a lot of confidence to take on the biggest empire in the world today!" Cole and PANA now coordinate a computer mailing list that can reach up to two hundred thousand people, upgraded with top-drawer software to target particular audiences.

PANA is not isolationist. The group is pro–United Nations and believes Ireland's foreign policy should be focused there. Roger Cole also sees himself as pro-American, noting that a majority of Americans now opposed the ongoing wars in Iraq and Afghanistan, as did he. Cole also rejects criticism that he is anti-European: "No. My mother was Portuguese—how could I be?" Roger Cole is discouraged as he believes the "Redmondists have won," which he feels has undermined democracy in Ireland. While a majority did eventually vote in favor of the European Union, he says that the media, especially the *Irish Times* and RTÉ, would "put on headbangers, not me." In the first EU referendum, which was defeated, the government had facilitated town hall debates across the country with all sides represented. The successful referendum did not include such debate, and Cole and PANA felt the government had marginalized them purposefully. The Irish elites "don't believe in democracy; they believe in wiseheads," said Cole, "which is what happens when a ruling elite is isolated from the façade of democracy." The elites that govern Ireland, he said, "are all nice, smart people—who are collaborating with mass murderers!" A PANA-commissioned public-opinion survey showed that, on issues such as access to Shannon Airport by American military aircraft, 58 percent of Irish were opposed. According to Cole, the major Irish press ignored this poll. Anyone can vote in a less scientific poll at Dublin's Collins Barracks museum (which highlights the history of the Irish armed forces). A machine has three buttons to choose from as to what Ireland should be doing with its armed forces. On the day I was there in July 2010, it read, "UN Peacekeeping (5948); Defend Ireland (505); Fighting Terrorism (1611)."

Among the most significant policy challenges to the Irish conception of neutrality has been an intense discussion of any role that Ireland might have played in "extraordinary rendition" by the United States of terrorist suspects. The basic assertion is that Ireland either knowingly or unknowingly allowed CIA planes to transit prisoners through Shannon Airport en route to third-party countries with looser interrogation standards than those allowed by law in the United States. The allegations were made by different "watch groups," who identified markers on planes allegedly owned by CIA front companies transiting through Shannon. The most official of various investigations into this question came from the European Parliament (on 23 January 2007), when a temporary committee concluded, "Secret detention facilities in European countries may have been located at U.S. military bases," and "there may have been a lack of control" over these bases by the European host countries. The European Parliament did not implicate the government of Ireland directly in active support of rendition but rather indicated that evidence existed of associated flight cases involving Ireland. In a final report released on 14 February 2007, the European Parliament accepted a formal resolution of 382 to 256 (with 74 abstentions) concluding that it was unlikely that European governments (including Ireland) were unaware of rendition activities on their territories. Opponents of Ireland's shifting foreign policy during the war on terror seized on these and other reports (i.e., one from Amnesty International on 5 December 2005, which concluded that there were at least fifty landings of CIA transport planes at Shannon).

The allegations regarding CIA flights were never substantiated in terms of actual cases of known rendition. The Irish government and United States confirmed this position officially. The American ambassador to Ireland wrote on 18 May 2006 in a letter to the Irish-language newspaper *Lá*, "We have not brought detainees through Irish airports or Irish airspace in violation of Ireland's sovereignty. There is simply no evidence that we have done otherwise and the Irish government has spoken very clearly on this subject, that it has not granted permission for such flights. This is a non-issue promoted by activists with a political agenda and there is simply no real evidence to support their claims." He added that if it were the case that there was intelligence cooperation between the United States and European friends, then it was likely that Irish lives had been saved as a result. Still, the popular mood was restive on this issue. American antiwar polemicist Noam Chomsky said in January 2006 to a packed Dublin audience, "If Shannon was being used by the CIA to transport prisoners, Ireland would be participating in a war crime as defined by the Nuremberg Trial."

Equally challenging to Ireland's conflict over security cooperation and neutrality has been the long-standing agreement to allow American planes transporting soldiers to stop over and refuel at Shannon Airport. For many soldiers returning from the Persian Gulf, this was their first bit of respite. While precise figures are difficult to attain, just in the first five months of 2006, an estimated 177,741 American troops transited through Shannon—mainly en route to or from Iraq. Official Irish figures, reported in the *Guardian* on 21 January 2006, showed that 330,000 total U.S. troops transited Shannon in 2005—twice the number that went through in 2004. This arrangement was estimated to inject about €37 million into the local economy around Shannon. Still, war profiteering did not sit well with Ireland's self-image. Speaking in opposition to this, Brian Meany of the Green Party stated to the *Guardian* on 21 January 2006, "You can't allow an airport's future to depend on selling sandwiches to soldiers. . . . People have a notion of Irish neutrality, and they think it is being undermined and sold out." An activist group called Shannon Watch used the airport's transit role in campaigning unsuccessfully against the October 2009 second vote on the Lisbon Treaty. Shannon Watch argued in its literature, "Up until 2003, Irish governments upheld the 1907 Hague Convention on Neutrality which states that 'belligerents are forbidden to move troops or convoys of either munitions of war or supplies across the territory of a neutral Power.' . . . But then the Fianna Fáil led government agreed to support the build-up of U.S. troops in Kuwait to invade Iraq by providing Shannon as a transit base."

The claim to neutrality was a double-edged sword in the war on terrorism. It would be naïve to think that Ireland, as part of the West and a member of the European Union, would not be a target of radical Islamic terrorism. Given Ireland's neutral status and the general sympathy under its laws for refugees and humanitarian gestures, in summer 2009, Ireland was asked, as a test of its friendship with the United States, to house two former terrorist detainees from Guantánamo Bay in Cuba. Taking such individuals was consistent with Ireland's humanitarian role in world politics; however, despite its opposition to activity at Guantánamo Bay and the treatment of prisoners there, the country risked a backlash of accusation that it was once more doing the great powers' bidding. Ireland seemed stuck between participating in the war on terrorism and thinking that neutrality would somehow shield it from danger.

THE (NOT) FIGHTING IRISH

I spent an afternoon in late July 2010 at briefings put together for me at the Irish Department of Defense with senior officials, including the new chief of staff of the armed forces, Lt. Gen. Sean McCann. I had arrived to meet with defense officials at a tough time. A long-serving and beloved former chief of staff, Lt. Gen. Dermot Earley, had just passed away, only ten days after standing down for health reasons. He was a former Gaelic football star from Roscommon who had served Ireland around the world in risky assignments. Lieutenant Generals McCann and Earley walked in the shoes of Michael Collins, who had shown that when they have to be, the Irish are warriors; however, they far prefer peace. Dermot Earley's funeral procession and Mass were attended by thousands on 26 June 2010 in Roscommon. Monsignor Eoin Thynne, the head chaplain of the Defence Forces, said during the funeral Mass, "In Lebanon or the Golan Heights, he would practice regularly by kicking a ball into the air and fielding it. . . . There were Arabs and Christians who didn't know what to make of him." In his eulogy, Lieutenant General McCann said, "I cannot speak of Dermot without the word indomitable coming to my mind, as it does now; as well as inspirational, talented and in the military and non-military sense, supreme. His 44 years of distinguished service in the Defence Forces are replete with examples of his sheer brilliance. . . . He was our chief, he held us together, informed us, inspired us; told each of us what work we ought to be doing and motivated us to do it." Lieutenant General McCann added, "Who is the happy warrior, who is he that every man in arms would wish to be—that man was Dermot Earley."

Ireland has a very small military and spends the least of all EU countries on defense as a percentage of GNP (about 0.5 percent, or about €900 million by 2010). There is a total of 10,460 active forces and 14,875 reserves. The army is the primary focus of the defense forces with 8,500; the navy has 1,100, and the air corps 850. Ireland's twelve thousand police officers are the lead element of internal security, but the military provides them with logistical support. In addition to the European Union, the Irish army also has a history of joint engagement with the United States. Indeed, the original impetus for creating the army came from a study conducted in the United States not long after independence in the 1920s as the young Irish state was consolidating its core institutions. In the 1960s and 1970s, elite Irish army forces attended courses at the U.S. Army Ranger training center at Fort Benning, Georgia. These special forces brought the concepts they learned back to the Irish army, and in 1980 the Irish Army Rangers Wing was created. Ireland also joined in bilateral engagements with militaries from Britain, France, Luxembourg, Holland, and Italy during the Cold War years. Given the military's relative size and existing charges of free riding, defense experts became concerned when in 2009, the An Bord Snip Nua recommended major cuts in Irish defense spending. This would reduce from fifteen to a just a few the number of overseas missions the defense forces could engage in and end Ireland's UN mission in Chad. The Army Equitation School, a national symbol of Ireland and its horses, would be cut, along with jobs for five hundred soldiers and twenty civil servants. This included a cut of two-thirds of the Reserve Defence Forces. Total cuts would be €53.4 million. The headline in the *Irish Independent* on 17 July 2009 read, "Budget Would Hit Our Image As a World Peacekeeper."

At the Defense Department, I received a briefing by an outstanding young army captain from the Operations Directorate. His PowerPoint slide presentation was as good, indeed better, than most that I have seen at the Pentagon or NATO Headquarters. His overview of the history, development, and current operations of the Irish military was a testament to the professionalism in this small but stellar force. During the off-the-record discussion with senior defense officials that followed, a number of key issues became clear about Ireland and its defense forces. First, while Ireland faces a benign external environment, a great deal of its military's expertise has been gained from experiences with the "internal threat on the island" during the Troubles (which persists, from the military's point of view). Dealing with border checkpoints and disarming explosives tested the armed forces and gave them essential skills to export as peacekeepers. Second, neutrality is important, but the operational tempo of the military is served by overseas missions. Third, the Irish navy and air corps play an important role with search-and-rescue operations, piracy concerns, and drug-smuggling interdiction, working in a support role with the police. In this capacity the army provided twenty-five hundred troops for security during a major EU ministerial meeting held in Dublin. Fourth, the Irish military is deeply engaged in supporting the lead role of civilian capabilities and is thus an important operational model for how militaries think about counterinsurgency. As one officer put it to me, "What is the threat—the tank or the lady with a pram covering a bomb?"

Ireland has a very small contingent—less than a dozen troops—doing a peace-support mission in Afghanistan. When I mentioned the Irish in Afghanistan during an interview I did with RTÉ in June 2010 about the war there, officials were quick to remind me that Ireland is in that country in a UN, not a NATO, role. That the army has to "keep quiet" about its very small role in Afghanistan and distinguish between the United Nations and NATO is significant. It raises concern among senior military leadership about a growing detachment between the armed forces and society. The public does not hold high-profile national events celebrating the armed forces, there is no sense of engagement, and the public is not well informed about the role the military plays at home, in Europe, and beyond. Consequently, in times of serious budget crises, it is that much harder to make the case for spending on defense. For example, the government will give approval to procure long-needed naval patrol vessels but insist that funding come within the existing budget. As a result, in 2010 the forces were struggling to put down even a deposit to buy a long-needed navy ship. At this rate, Ireland will eventually have a hard time sustaining its commitment to contribute to UN peacekeeping operations. In 2011, Ireland began negotiations with the United Nations to send to Lebanon a new force of as many as four hundred troops. However, at the same time, the 2011 budget added a 4 percent cut in Irish defense spending. Still, because of high unemployment, there was no problem with recruitment. In 2010, twenty-five hundred people applied for just thirty cadetships in the defense forces. These highly educated applicants included former stockbrokers, lawyers, teachers, and engineers. In fact, because of higher demand and fewer positions, the number of Irish signing up for the British military had increased sevenfold by 2010.

Absent an overseas mission, there is serious concern that the Irish Defence Forces will stagnate and suffer lasting damage to morale. Ireland's military is increasingly "oriented around what we can get, not what is needed for the mission," said one senior civilian planner. All in the room shared a serious concern, given the already low spending on defense forces, as to what would happen if Ireland took an approach like that which Britain was implementing with major cuts in military spending. Such an approach in Ireland would be "devastating to the defense forces." These officials understand the need for near-term cuts—but in the long run, they are not sustainable. Worse, politically, the military, like the police, has "no natural constituency of support." The officials I met with take great pride in being frugal in their spending. They build their budgets based on requirements, not wish lists, and regularly deliver within their allocations. "All of our purchases are mission relevant," said one official. "There are no $500 hammers here." Also, like the police and other parts of society, the military has "major deficiencies" in foreign languages. It works with universities to do cultural training before deploying overseas but often depends on others to provide costly translation services. Meanwhile, the Irish armed forces are well trained in human rights and are setting an example for other countries on how to integrate with civilian nongovernmental organizations.

HOW TO CRACK GLOBALIZATION

When I met with Ireland's then minister of foreign affairs, Micheál Martin, in July 2010, he quickly noted that the key challenge in representing Ireland abroad is "how to crack globalization." How can Ireland make the realities of globalization work to its advantage? At the same time, how does globalization challenge Ireland with new vulnerabilities? To Ireland's president, Mary McAleese, China forms a key part of the challenge. She visited Beijing and delivered a speech at Renmin University in June 2010 to celebrate thirty years of diplomatic relations between Ireland and China. President McAleese emphasized that the 115 Irish companies now doing business in China represent a tripling in five years and that the two countries do about €4 billion in annual trade. She said, "Irish companies are investing in China and Chinese companies have begun to invest in Ireland, which is a gateway to the European Union." She drew parallels in her speech between Ireland's integration with Europe and the world dating back generations and that now being done in China. Both countries share a common interest, it would seem, in moving from being an agricultural economy to one based on higher education, high technology, and software. Meanwhile, a growing number of Chinese are living and working in Ireland. To John Bruton, former Taoiseach and EU representative to Washington, DC, Ireland should approach globalization by not being overly ambitious. Rather, he emphasizes "building on the small strengths—in the United States and Europe—the parts we know best." Certainly, he notes, in the long-term, places like China, India, and Brazil will be the leading new markets. However, he sees Ireland being best served by working with the United States and within the European Union as a "platform for China and India." This raises an interesting question about how Ireland should prioritize—for example, should it emphasize Chinese language study or maybe Spanish instead? Or, given the role of the European Union in Ireland's economy in 2011, perhaps French and German?

These kinds of questions lie at the heart of how to target the future smart economy in the context of globalization. Martin emphasized to me that "Chinese will happen" within the Irish educational curriculum. He reflected on the evolving role of China in the world and how it might affect Ireland from the outside in. He noted, in particular, how the West has evolved to have rules regarding "labor, health, safety, human rights in our system." China remains "out of this." So, for countries like Ireland, the interesting question is "how to leverage best from China" and engage in a way that advances national interests while also being consistent with these Western principles. Martin said, in the context of China and beyond, "no doubt, we have to be more global."

Under Micheál Martin, Ireland furthered its deep commitment to humanitarian values by serving as the architect of a Hunger Task Force study and cosponsoring with the United States a major UN food-security conference in New York City on 21 September 2010. Addressing a UN General Assembly meeting on global development goals, Martin stated, "Today, with the U.S. administration, we hosted a meeting of international leaders committed to building a partnership which will focus on nutrition in the vital first 1,000 days of life, from pregnancy to second birthday." In introducing the presentation of the Hunger Task Force, Taoiseach Brian Cowen said,

> When my Government decided to establish a Hunger Task Force in September 2006, it was on the basis that hunger is the single greatest challenge facing our world today. One hundred and sixty years ago, Ireland experienced firsthand the trauma and devastation of famine—losing more than one quarter of our population (some two million people) to death and emigration—and that scar has never been fully erased. . . . It is unthinkable and unacceptable that in this century, as we pride ourselves on huge technological advances and global interconnectedness, hunger is still the reality for at least 860 million people—and that number continues to rise.

Taking a lead on food security was consistent with Ireland's history and principles, and its manufacturing and agricultural base had something to contribute to helping solve this global challenge. Once again, as with Frank Aiken and nuclear weapons, Ireland was in the vanguard at the United Nations.

Micheál Martin also played a unique role in the international community by engaging Ireland in Israeli-Palestinian issues. In 2010, Martin was the first European leader to visit Gaza after Hamas's electoral victory there. He told me it was quite an operation and that he was not there to meet with Hamas. Rather, he crossed into Gaza from Egypt in a UN humanitarian aid truck. To Martin, Irish diplomacy toward the Arab-Israeli conflict is uniquely "informed by the experiences of Northern Ireland." There is empathy in Ireland for the Palestinian cause, which is viewed through the prism of Ireland's quest for independence. There is also a similar sense of appreciation for what Israel confronts in the region. Based on the experiences of Northern Ireland, Micheál Martin points out that any policy that uses too forcefully the kinds of tactics that the British did will only bolster rebellion and undermine the desire for peace. The British learned this over time and their experience might thus inform how Israel approaches its security. On 2 December 2010, the *Jerusalem Post* reported that leaked diplomatic cables showed that during the 2006 Israeli intervention in Lebanon, the Irish government sought restrictions on the transit through Shannon Airport of American equipment that could go to support the Israeli war effort. A cable from the U.S. Embassy in Ireland explained, "Segments of the Irish public see the airport as a symbol of Irish complicity in perceived U.S. wrongdoing in the Middle East." Apparently, the American ambassador warned the Irish government that such restrictions would cost the Irish economy millions of dollars as the United States would seek other airports for transit.

For peace negotiations to work in a similar framework as in Northern Ireland, there would also have to be "conditionality on contacts" mandating certain behavior regarding groups like Hamas, said Martin. "It was the Provisional IRA cease-fire that was the catalyst" for peace in the North, he said—and that is currently missing in the context of Hamas. Ultimately, Micheál Martin said, "Israel needs good neighbors—we relate to that. Same goes with security. But there is also a question of humanity and the need to be moderate on both sides." American journalist James Traub summarized this dilemma in an article published on *Foreign Policy*'s website on 27 August 2010. Traub quoted an Israeli official as saying, "The IRA was looking at the end of the day to negotiate with the British, which you can't say of Hamas, and of Syria and Hezbollah and other parties to the conflict." At the same time, Traub wrote, "Israel's position constitutes an equal and reciprocal obstacle to peace. Israel is the occupying power in Palestine, as Britain was in Northern Ireland. . . . Neither the [Israeli] government nor the broader public has proved willing to make concessions, above all on settlements, that would strengthen" the ability of Palestinians who want to negotiate.

In June 2010, Ireland found itself caught in the middle of a major international crisis involving Israel. After his visit earlier in the year, Micheál Martin had called on Israel to lift its existing naval blockade of Gaza. This concern became serious on 31 May 2010 when Israeli troops boarded on the high seas a Turkish-flagged aid flotilla that was carrying humanitarian supplies to Gaza. Israeli commandos killed nine activists, and many more were wounded. Six Irish nationals were on this flotilla, and two were injured. A week later an Irish-flagged vessel, the *Rachel Corrie*, was to arrive with one thousand tons of medical and educational supplies and building cement for delivery into Gaza. Israeli foreign minister Avigdor Lieberman said on Israeli radio on 5 June 2010, "No ship will reach Gaza. The *Rachel Corrie* will not reach Gaza." On 4 March 2010, the Israeli ambassador to Ireland, Zion Evrony, had written in the *International Herald Tribune* that on a recent visit to Northern Ireland, "I could not help feeling a pang of envy, as well as a hope that a similar change may one day happen in the Middle East." As the *Rachel Corrie* steamed toward Gaza, Sinn Féin president Gerry Adams called for Ambassador Evrony to be expelled from Ireland. Micheál Martin called the ambassador into the Foreign Ministry and reminded him of Israeli obligations to international law and treatment of Irish citizens as well as to honor free access on the high seas.

Israel did have a case regarding enforcement of a blockade and a right to inspect ships (which Ireland suggested could be done by the United Nations), but that only applied to a legal blockade of contiguous territory. Martin had already called into doubt the validity of the Israeli blockade of Gaza earlier in the year. The toughest words for Israel came from Taoiseach Brian Cowen, who warned in the Dáil on 1 June 2010, "If any harm comes to any of our citizens, it will have the most serious consequences." He also called for a "full, independent international inquiry into yesterday's events, preferably under UN auspices." "Israel," Cowen said, "must listen and respond to the clear concerns of the international community on this issue. To do otherwise will only serve to reinforce the position of the extremists on both sides and jeopardize the hope of achieving some urgently needed political progress in the region." It should be noted that the *Rachel Corrie* was named after a young American woman who was crushed to death by an Israeli Defense Forces bulldozer when serving as a human shield to protect Palestinian homes.

In the broader context of globalization and state power, Micheál Martin does not worry extensively about how globalization might lead to a brain drain. He said with confidence that "they come back"—and when they do, "they bring experience and skills with them." Martin initiated a special program targeting the "Global Irish"—children, grandchildren, and great-grandchildren of Irish from around the world who would be granted substantial fee reductions to come study in Ireland. Martin also put in place a program by which people of Irish extraction around the world can buy a "certificate of Irish heritage," which gets them discounts when traveling in Ireland. This idea of linking the estimated 70 million people worldwide with direct Irish lineage was a significant step in enhancing Ireland's place in the world. Martin said of this program at its launch, "The reach, power, and influence of many members of the diaspora can provide Ireland with an important competitive edge."

Paul Cullen of the *Irish Times* wrote on 26 June 2010 in praise of this and other programs reaching out to the global Irish. He was surprised that many people in Ireland immediately criticized the certificate program as some kind of tacky, meaningless gesture. Cullen wrote that, outside Ireland, it was seen as a wonderful way to connect people with their origins. Cullen asserted, "The gulf in views mirrors a wider gap in attitudes to Irishness. In Ireland we have the passports and the citizenship but look disparagingly at any initiative mooted to get us out of our present wretched state; those outside the country, in contrast, yearn for a connection to Ireland and are happy to admire the view through rose-tinted glasses." He added, "What isn't in dispute is the huge interest among people of Irish descent about their origins. Every day an average of 20 or 30 people turn up at the National Archives in Dublin looking for help to trace their family history;

while some are from Ireland, many are from the U.S., Britain and many other parts of the world."

These global sentiments toward Ireland are real and exist at all levels in the United States. In March 2010, during St. Patrick's Day activities in Washington, DC, I attended a black-tie dinner hosted by the American Ireland Fund honoring U.S. Secretary of State Hillary Clinton for her work on Irish issues. The elite of Washington's Irish American society was there, as was a planeload of Irish, including the likes of Brian Cowen and Ryan Tubridy. Barack Obama's campaign had actually criticized then senator Clinton for exaggerating her involvement during the Northern Ireland peace process. Obama's senior foreign policy adviser Greg Craig released a memo just before St. Patrick's Day 2008, which read, "Senator Clinton has said, 'I helped to bring peace to Northern Ireland.' It is a gross overstatement of the facts for her to claim even partial credit for bringing peace to Northern Ireland. She did travel to Northern Ireland, it is true. First Ladies often travel to places that are a focus of U.S. foreign policy. But at no time did she play any role in the critical negotiations that ultimately produced the peace." He added, "News of Senator Clinton's claims has raised eyebrows across the ocean. Her reference to an important meeting at the Belfast town hall was debunked. Her only appearance at the Belfast City Hall was to see Christmas lights turned on. She also attended a 50-minute meeting which, according to the Belfast *Daily Telegraph*'s report at the time, '[was] a little bit stilted, a little prepared at times.' Brian Feeney, an Irish author and former politician, sums it up: 'The road to peace was carefully documented, and she wasn't on it.'"

Nonetheless, Bill and Hillary Clinton are very popular in Ireland and do have a unique sense of Irishness. Hillary Clinton had also energized the American electorate as a candidate for the Democratic nomination and was doing a highly regarded job since becoming secretary of state. I noted, sitting just thirty feet or so away from former president Bill Clinton at the dinner, that when a local school choir performed "Danny Boy," he sang along quietly to himself, knowing all the words. Secretary Clinton finished her speech with a story about their daughter, Chelsea.

> And I remember the first time our daughter set foot in Ireland. She was a teenager. We were not even actually going to Ireland, but we were again shopping [corrects to "stopping" to laughter] in Shannon to refuel. And so as we got off the airplane, she went up to one of the officials standing there to greet us, and she was engaged in very serious conversation. And I didn't know quite what she was talking about. And then she came back and she said, "They're going to let me do it." And I said, "What are they going to let you do?" And she said, "They're going to let me leave the airport and go out and actually touch the ground of Ireland." Wow. So she did. And she gathered some soil from Shannon Airport, and she placed it in a bottle, and she brought that home with her to the White House, where it resided until she went off to college, and she has kept it ever since.

Wiping a tear from her eye, Secretary Clinton said this was a small story, but it represented metaphorically the connection so many have to Ireland and its future. I noticed that Bill Clinton too wiped away a tear during this emotional retelling of their strong personal connection—to their daughter, to each other, and to Ireland.

Another example of enthusiasm for Ireland is the growing number of American students wanting to study at Irish universities. A number of my students have done semesters at University College Cork and thoroughly enjoyed and valued the experience. An important program, the Mitchell Scholars Program, run by Trina Vargo, a former senior aid to Senator Ted Kennedy, brings a group of talented American students to Ireland each year to study at the master's level. These students are chosen for leadership potential and academic quality, and the Mitchell program pays their expenses (it is named for former U.S. senator and Northern Ireland peace negotiator George Mitchell and funded by the U.S., Irish, and Northern Ireland governments as well as private donations). This program is important to Ireland because it sends future leaders back to the United States with a warm appreciation for the country. While some politicians in Ireland are critical that their government helps to pay for this, in 2010, the Oireachtas (parliament) passed, by unanimous consent, legislation to match anything up to €20 million that Vargo can raise toward an endowment for the program. Micheál Martin told me that government support for the Mitchell Scholars Program is strong. He personally praised Trina Vargo and the work of the Mitchell scholars. Illustrating the attention these scholars can get, in the midst of the economic crisis, Fine Gael leader Enda Kenny took time in late 2010 to meet and greet the current Mitchell scholars.

A survey of the one hundred students who have completed this program showed that all of them would recommend it. Four out of five would recommend their Irish universities to other students. There are, however, some caveats. Vargo told the *Irish Times* on 28 September 2010, "The most serious complaint from Mitchells is that their programs aren't challenging and often repeat what they learned as undergraduates. . . . Early on, we realized that if we were to convince some of the brightest students in the U.S. to spend a year in Ireland and Northern Ireland—students who can as easily go to Oxford, Cambridge, Harvard, Yale—we would have to design a scholarship program that offered more than academics alone, since we couldn't compete on the basis of university rankings." Ironically, as Irish students tended to go home or to visit old friends on weekends, the Mitchell students also note that the sense of campus community they are accustomed to in the United States is lacking. This struck me as an interesting perception for the welcoming nation of which Trina Vargo said, "The Irish are more likely to have the same friends from cradle to grave [and] seem slower than Americans to take on new friends." In an important observation relative to the smart economy, the Mitchell scholars actually tend to prioritize other areas, according to Vargo, such as "conflict resolution/peace studies/terrorism/human rights because of Ireland's prominence in these fields. Scholars also report that the Equality Studies program at [University College Dublin], the Immunology and Global Health program at Maynooth, and the Music Therapy program at [Limerick] are programs that they cannot get at home." The students surveyed generally viewed the experience as "life changing," and one said, "I feel personally tied to Ireland and Irish issues in a way that I was not before the experience and could not have become without it. Professionally and personally, I see myself as an advocate of sorts for Irish affairs."

While globalization creates new opportunities, Ireland also faces a serious brain drain crisis. Micheál Martin and other officials I spoke with were optimistic, seeing the positive side, in that Irish go abroad, get skills, and come back. The economic foundations of this new wave of emigration, however, suggest that Ireland risks losing some of its most skilled labor. In past waves of Irish outward migration, all skill sets could go abroad—to Australia, Britain, Canada, Europe, the United States—searching for work. Now, however, in the United States manual-labor jobs are going to Americans needing work or other immigrants (particularly from Latin America). Yet, 39 percent of all U.S. jobs that require a PhD are held by non-Americans—meaning that the very best educated of Irish have real opportunities to bolt the country and apply their skills in the United States and elsewhere. By spring 2010, Micheál Martin's Department of Foreign Affairs had a backlog of forty thousand passport applications waiting to be processed. Ironically, budget cuts prevented Ireland from processing passport applications as quickly as they were coming in.

By 2011, 5,000 Irish were emigrating per month; in total, an estimated 120,000 Irish emigrated between 2010 and 2011. This is especially frustrating to the many talented Irish who were lured home with promises of great days to come during the Celtic Tiger. It is even worse for the generation under twenty-five who had nothing to do with the Celtic Tiger's collapse and yet either have to emigrate or spend much of their lives paying for another generation's mistakes. A survey published in December 2010 by the *Irish Examiner* showed that up to one in three Irish between the ages of eighteen and twenty-four were making plans to emigrate over the coming year. One example, from a report in the *Guardian* on 2 March 2010, illustrates this dilemma: Julian Tung graduated as a civil engineer from Trinity College in Dublin in 2008. As this was just before the economic collapse, he walked right into a job with a top engineering company—but within nine months had been laid off, along with the entire Dublin office. He said, "I quickly realized that there was no chance of finding another engineering job in Ireland so I packed up and headed to London." Between January and August

2010, at least sixty-three thousand people had left Ireland for work. On the other hand, unemployment in Ireland would be even higher if these people had stayed.

Today's emigration differs from historical waves out of Ireland in an important sense. Because of globalization, one does not necessarily face the same deep pain brought by previous waves. When my wife left Ireland in 1986, she left parents and grandparents whose generations were accustomed to saying good-bye to children leaving on ships or planes and never seeing them again. That is not the case now as jet travel, e-mail, Facebook, and Skype all allow people frequent contact with loved ones. Still, technology cannot replace the joy of being together—even if the distance is not so far in the mind. It would be tragic in the end if Ireland's emphasis on building a smart economy, in its effort to "crack globalization," ended up training highly skilled Irish to go overseas and invest their talents in building other countries. Many economists in Ireland rightly point out that building the export sector is key to Ireland's eventual economic recovery, but once again, one of its major exports today is its talent.

SHAMROCK DIPLOMACY

The special relationship between Ireland and the United States is deeply rooted. As President John F. Kennedy (the first sitting U.S. president to visit Ireland) spoke before the Dáil in June 1963, his Irish roots were more than well appreciated. So was his declaration of the common destiny the two countries shared: "And so it is that our two nations, divided by distance, have been united by history. No people ever believed more deeply in the cause of Irish freedom than the people of the United States. And no country contributed more to building my own than your sons and daughters." In a phrase that could well apply to today's situation in both countries, President Kennedy said, "It is that quality of the Irish, the remarkable combination of hope, confidence, and imagination, that is needed more than ever today." When I first traveled to Ireland in 1987, I visited homes with two pictures over the fireplace—one of the pope and the other of John Fitzgerald Kennedy. Today, one would be hard pressed in both countries to find anyone who would put a politician's portrait up in his or her home. Yet, the relationship between Ireland and the United States remains vital to Ireland—and of interest to many Americans.

The contemporary Ireland–United States relationship "needs new anchors," former Foreign Minister Micheál Martin told me. New demographic realities in the United States, including the rise of a major new immigrant influx of Hispanics—all part of globalization—mean that Ireland has to work hard to sustain its presence among American foreign policy priorities.

Martin told me that during the 1970s, Irish representatives were "often left out, even heckled, at diplomatic functions in the United States," which had to strike a balance between its empathy for Ireland and its vital relationship with Britain over the last hundred years. Woodrow Wilson, a U.S. president deeply committed to the ideals of self-determination, paid little heed to the concerns of the Irish during World War I—even while Éamon de Valera was in the United States after 1916 working to advance the Irish cause. Today, however, deep cultural ties and important economic links bind 40 million Americans of Irish descent with the Republic. In 2010, 230 Irish companies with stakes in the United States employed eighty-five thousand Americans. The annual trade in goods and services between the two countries is over €50 billion. Each year 1.5 million people travel between the two nations. In addition, intense political battles in the Irish American community revolve around the question of immigration. Should Irish, for example, get special status in immigration access to the United States because of this special relationship? Or should they be treated like any other group coming to the United States? Meanwhile, American business interests in Ireland have lobbied very hard for the country to keep its very low 12.5 percent corporate tax rate, lest they lose money. Some have even threatened to leave Ireland if it goes up. Even if Ireland raised its rate to 20 percent, it would remain among the lowest in Europe. Moreover, companies like Dell have already left due to high labor costs, and the low tax rate could not persuade them to stay. Pulled between Europe and the United States, Ireland by 2011 faced the dilemma of cutting aid to blind and disabled people or helping American businesses continue to get rich in Ireland.

A serious challenge for Ireland is to deepen and sustain its relationship to the United States beyond the annual big event of St. Patrick's Day—which all too often becomes more pomp and less substance. Each year at that time, Irish politicians and other leaders converge on New York, Chicago, and, especially, Washington, DC. This provides a chance for Americans with Irish roots to fly the Irish flag with pride. This is especially true for leading members of Congress and major Irish interest groups, who have the chance to be seen with the Irish political leadership. Likewise, it is a chance for the Irish leadership to be seen with the president of the United States, the Speaker of the House of Representatives, and so on. Needless to say, this does not always go according to plan. In March 2009, Taoiseach Brian Cowen visited the White House and delivered a traditional bowl of Shamrocks. In his official remarks, Cowen began to read from the teleprompter. The problem was, he realized well into his speech, that he was not reading out his prepared text. Rather, he was reading the same speech that President Barack Obama had just delivered. With a laugh, during his 2010 visit, Cowen began his remarks saying, "I made one solemn promise to myself when I've come to the White House for the second time: I intend reading my own speech tonight." This time, the United States' first Irish-Catholic vice president Joe Biden made the gaffe: while talking about Cowen's family connections to the United States, he told his audience, "His mom lived in Long Island for 10 years or so, God rest her soul, although . . . wait . . . it's your dad passed. God *bless* her soul."

St. Patrick's Day certainly holds a special place in the United States—where the idea of celebrating Ireland's patron saint with parties and parades actually emerged. The 7 a.m. drinking and green beer—neither of which would go over well in Ireland—never cease to amaze me. In terms of diplomacy, it provides a unique opportunity for one of the smallest countries in the world to gain exceptional access to the highest levels of American government. As Denis Staunton, a Washington correspondent for the *Irish Times*, wrote to remind his Irish readers on 17 March 2009, "St. Patrick's Day in the U.S. is, above all, a cultural event and an opportunity for Americans to connect with part of their national story, shared by many with no Irish origins—the experience of fleeing poverty and oppression in search of dignity and opportunity." In effect, this is an American holiday; thus, one should not expect it to reflect a real understanding of Ireland or the issues facing people there. Irish Americans care about Ireland, but they also have their own concerns, like jobs, health care, war, and so forth. While people in Ireland might think that their problems should be high on Americans' radar, they are not. If Ireland registers at all, it is in terms of the North, and that concern is now scarce, given the appearance of stability there. The key thing that Ireland really brings is, as Denis Staunton wrote, that diplomatically the country "can serve as a valuable bridge between Washington and Europe, a role that could be enhanced now that the U.S. has a president who is popular in Ireland and an administration with foreign policy goals that are closer to Ireland's."

The economic crisis in Ireland has been, however, a serious diplomatic burden. It did not help Ireland when, at the dinner I attended for Secretary of State Clinton, Taoiseach Brian Cowen indicated that a strategy for recovery was in place and that the deficit had been stabilized. Six months later, it was clear to the world that this statement simply did not reflect reality, and in the end it seriously damaged Irish credibility. In repeated trips to the United States during 2010, Irish leaders put on the best face they could to sell Ireland—but these efforts simply did not connect to the realities on the ground. It is understandable why the Irish government would stretch the truth. However, in diplomacy, credibility is a commodity difficult to recover once lost. Lisa Hand of the *Irish Independent* wrote of meetings I attended in the nation's capital during St. Patrick's Day 2010, "It was a glorious day in Washington, D.C. The temperature had soared overnight into spring warmth, and the air was bright with talk of the 'Luck of the Irish.'" I could not help but see a huge disconnect between Washington's celebration of Irishness and the realities of life in Ireland. A March 2009 review of Irish American relations by the Irish Embassy in Washington, DC, asserted, "Ireland has thus probably one of the best 'brands' of any country in the United States." While this is true, the ability to deal frankly with the economic crisis was a test of whether that brand would continue to sell—especially as the United States had billions of dollars exposed in some form or another to Irish bank losses. An Irish friend who had just immigrated to the United States reminded me of this when he said in October 2010, "If I had a dollar over here for every time I hear 'luck of the Irish,' I'd have a deposit for a house."

Denis Staunton suggests that the most important gains Ireland can make by engaging with the United States are cultural: "Irish cultural products and the cultural identification of millions of Irish-Americans with Ireland are the most powerful drivers of American goodwill towards Ireland. . . . As our poets, musicians, dancers and other artists perform this evening at a White House event that makes bigger countries writhe in envy, it is time their importance to our national interest is more fully recognized at home." Ireland has made major investments in the United States, such as a grant for $3.5 million to help build a new Irish Arts Center in Manhattan. Keenly aware of the need to further embrace the arts as a means of securing the Irish brand, in March 2010, Ireland announced that actor Gabriel Byrne would be named the country's "cultural ambassador." On his appointment, Byrne said that American audiences hold a "very limited view of Irish art. It's Druid [theater company], Brian Friel, the Anglo-Irish stew of Yeats . . . and there's U2. There's a whole other life—great young conceptual artists, film-making, people writing who wouldn't have written 15 or 20 years ago. Right now, there are four major Broadway productions that are Irish." He went on to say, "America is a giant market for Irish culture. And it speaks English, and it receives us with tremendous good will. To a great extent, our culture is what defines us."

CÉAD MÍLE FÁILTE—SERIOUSLY

Ireland is widely seen through the Gaelic phrase "céad míle fáilte" as being the land of "one hundred thousand welcomes." For generations, the country has thrived on attracting visitors from around the world; tourism typically accounts for about 4 percent of Ireland's economy, generates 128,000 jobs, and is worth about €1.5 billion in tax revenue for the government. The ability provided by globalization to market Ireland to visitors has made tourism all the more important during the extended economic crisis. Seeking to remind world travelers about Ireland, on St. Patrick's Day 2010, Tourism Ireland spent €1 million to cast green floodlights onto major international landmarks, including the London Eye, the Sydney Opera House, the CN Tower in Toronto, and the Empire State building in New York City. Not simply part of a celebration, this was, in some ways, a cry for help. The *New York Times* quoted the CEO of Tourism Ireland, Niall Gibbons, as saying, "It's a response to the difficult climate we found ourselves in. . . . It's going to be a long hard road in 2010." The same article quoted John Power of the Irish Hotels Federation: "It's been pretty horrendous. . . . We are a long way from being out of the woods yet." Being competitive in attracting tourism is a vital piece of the question of "how to crack globalization," and it is a challenge. As Gibbons said, "We are coming off the back of one of the most difficult years for the Irish tourism industry in living memory. . . . If we don't go out and sell hard, other countries will take our space."

The problem is, as the global economy collapsed, so did tourism to Ireland—dramatically. Between 2007 and 2009, Ireland saw a reduction of about 20 percent in overseas visitors (including a drop from North America from 1.034 million in 2006 to 892,000 in 2009). By May 2010, Ireland had experienced an additional drop of 20 percent from the same period in 2009. Not only were Americans not coming, but there was a decline of 30 percent among British tourists as well. Interestingly, the relative number of people visiting from non-European and non–North American countries remained steady with about three hundred thousand visiting from Australia, New Zealand, Japan and Asia, Africa, and Latin America. Those still coming to Ireland increasingly visited places that were free. For example, the National Gallery of Ireland, which charges no entrance fee, saw an increase in visits between 2008 and 2009 of 40,137, while visitors to the Guinness Storehouse declined by 19,744 in the same time period. The *Book of Kells* at Trinity College lost 63,060 visitors, the Cliffs of Moher, 44,552, and the Blarney Castle, 40,000. Not only does the *Book of Kells* cost a lot to see, but often the lines at the Trinity College location are so long, it is not deemed worth the bother (wrongly, in my view) if there are other places to go. I have always enjoyed a visit to the Cliffs of Moher, but in July 2010, I kept driving when I saw they wanted to charge me to visit nature. On the other hand, when we drove into the lovely fishing and music village of Doolin nearby, entrance was free—but the town was so crowded, there was nowhere to park.

Former tourism Minister Mary Hanafin asserted in the *Irish Times* on 27 August 2010 that Ireland's tourism agencies fight "for every bit of business" and are trying to "get the message out that there has never been a better time to visit Ireland both in terms of the value for money on the ground and the quality of our tourism offering." For an American coming to Ireland today, the economic downturn has its advantages. The dollar-to-euro rate was, by 2010, better than it had been in as long as I could remember. A rental car for two to three weeks cost 50 percent less than it did in 2005. Top-quality hotels were booking rooms at cut-rate prices. Even a pint seemed to cost less than it had in ages. Ireland has a large government-supported agency, Fáilte Ireland, which is responsible for providing targeted support within Ireland to the tourist and hospitality industry. I met with Fáilte Ireland's chief economist, Caeman Wall, who indicated that while the agency has faced cuts, its budget of €100 million has a high-value return.

Fáilte Ireland targets much of its work internally, toward the Irish who take holidays at home. About 25 percent of Fáilte Ireland's effort is returned into the Irish economy—feeding the "staycation culture—that kind of craic," said Caeman Wall. Thus, he said, the agency is invested to "promote Ireland in Ireland." Fáilte Ireland has seen itself as a "child of the peace process" as more people have shown interest in visiting the North and South of the island. However, it is also perfectly willing to go head-to-head with the North in competing for events that will attract visitors. For example, Fáilte Ireland successfully sold Volvo (over competitors, including Northern Ireland) on hosting an ocean race in Galway. Fáilte Ireland spent €8 million to secure Volvo's participation, and that money spent led to a €56 million return with Fáilte Ireland as a cosponsor. Caeman Wall said much of the agency's investment goes into training and helping Irish infrastructure better facilitate delivering on tourist expectations, while surveying tourists to learn how Ireland can better perform in this area. A draft report for 2010 showed that the primary reasons people come, and return, to Ireland are—surprise—the "beautiful scenery" and the "friendly, hospitable people." The lowest-rated rationale was that the "country is suitable for touring," which, even with improved roads, is still a difficulty. As anyone who has driven them knows, many Irish roads are dangerous and require constant alertness. These kinds of assessments, said Caeman Wall, are crucial, given that the consecutive years of tourist trade downturn were "a shocker." It is all the more important that "when people visit Ireland . . . they leave happy." Furthermore, he noted that not all of the downturn is attributable to the global economy (of which the relative drop in international market share is not that high for Ireland). Ireland, said Wall, needs "better and cheaper food that people can access easily." It also needs to lose its image as "rip-off Ireland," where some prices are, in fact, much higher than in the rest of Europe.

GLOBAL IRELAND

"Irishness" is a high-value commodity among global brands—if it were stock, I would buy it as a (very) long-term investment. The evolution of its global engagement has shown a nuanced and creative balancing of Irish interests and values. The country has punched way above its weight on issues from nuclear proliferation to peacekeeping. It has been at the core of the rise of globalization for decades, long before the Celtic Tiger. It continually works to find its place in the evolving global system—from China to the Middle East to Washington, DC. The Irish brand has, however, been seriously tarnished by the economic crisis and political mismanagement, which risks overshadowing the good that the country brings to the international stage. Some additional damage to that brand was self-induced during the drive to modernization. In the name of development, Ireland built over Viking ruins in the Liberties in Dublin. It built the M3 motorway, creating a major commuter exchange just over a mile from the sacred Hill of Tara, the spiritual home of early Celtic kings, now considered one of the world's most endangered heritage sites, according to the Smithsonian Institution. To be fair, as poet Seamus Heaney writes, "Whether it be in a matter of personal relations within a marriage, or political initiatives within a peace process, there is no sure-fire-do-it-yourself-kit." Or, as a friend in Dublin frequently says, "God loves a trier." Despite its setbacks, Ireland does a lot with little and brings a place to humanity that can make Irish at home and abroad proud.

A horse photographed in rural County Kerry in summer 2010. Ireland's attempts to move forward will in many respects require renewing faith in core aspects that make Ireland great—its land, its people, and its traditions.

8

Tales from the Promised Land

ORDINARY RICHES CAN BE STOLEN, REAL RICHES CANNOT

Spray-painted on the sidewall of a building of abandoned and rundown apartments is the phrase, "Tales from the Promised Land"—referring to the struggle facing the Irish people. Despite its hardships, Ireland is reinventing itself and, in so doing, reinventing the very meaning of a promised land. Oscar Wilde's quote about "ordinary riches" reminds us of where that renewal begins—within each person. Each Irish person, each American, each global citizen can take one of the million steps moving the world toward a better place. The initial rise of the Celtic Tiger teaches us that economic progress is achievable when a creative and spirited people is given the opportunity. The Celtic Tiger's collapse teaches that greed, materialism, and a politics detached from the people's interest serve no one. The power for positive change now rests in the hands of creative, innovative people willing to roll up their sleeves, work hard, and dream big. As George Bernard Shaw said, "You see things; and you say, 'Why?' But I dream things that never were; and I say, 'Why not?'" It took Ireland twenty-five years to get to where it is at today, and it might take another twenty-five to dig itself out. But Ireland's long-term story is one of renewal—of Celtic revival.

GETTING BACK THE CELTIC MOJO

Ireland today is in a far better position than it was for much of its history. One need not retell stories of famine, civil war, economic isolation, and mass emigration to understand that. In a speech at University College Dublin on 1 October 2010, former U.S. president Bill Clinton made this point to his Irish audience: "And every one of us, the truth is, if we were flat broke and had to start again tomorrow with nothing would have a better chance than half the people alive on the planet Earth today, and they too share our future. The legacy of the Irish in the modern world is you have proved you can make peace, you can prove that we can make prosperity, and you have proved that we can make a difference in the lives of people we will never see half the world away." It would do a profound disservice to Ireland's contributions to humanity not to appreciate its blessings. At the same time, it does not help a person without a job or a family burdened by someone else's debt to say, "Hey, it could be worse."

All things are, nonetheless, relative. People in the developed part of the world in which Ireland exists have good reason to think positively about the future. The two billion people in the world who live on less than $2 a day, who worry not about whether there will be jobs but about whether their children might live past the age of five—they have it bad. The fact that ten million children in the world die every year from preventable and curable diseases like tuberculosis and malaria—that provides real perspective. Even in the wealthiest of nations, especially my own country, the United States, too many fellow citizens are simply left behind. An Irish nun from Belfast, Sister Maeve McMahan, published *Riding Out the Hurricane* (2010) based on her experiences as a schoolteacher during Hurricane Katrina in Louisiana in 2005. Sister McMahan said in an interview with the Irish-Central website on 25 October 2010, "I heard incredible human stories of courage and faith and experienced the loss of all material things myself. All of my friends, black and white, were affected, many losing everything. I just couldn't get my head around the fact that the richest country in the world had let its own people down while often children were displaced from their homes and schools by Hurricane Katrina."

I recall as recently as 1992, when asking for driving directions from Dublin Airport to Clonsilla, being told to "turn right at the horse at the big roundabout." I did, three times, only to find myself, twenty minutes later, back in the exact same spot each time! Today, the roads are better, the infrastructure is improved, and the education system is modernized. The people have proven that the Irish can work hard, innovate, and be highly productive in the global economy when given the opportunity. The Celtic Tiger was built upon solid initial foundations, which persist, albeit under the weight of massive debt today. As Bill Clinton told his audience at University College Dublin, "If we try to build an interdependent world where the positive forces outweigh the negative ones, and we make sure that the next time that we make an economic mistake, at least it's a new mistake—we don't do the same thing all over again—we're all going to be just fine here. We're going to be just fine. Get your confidence back. Get your mojo back. Take the bitter medicine you have to take. But this is not the drab, horrible story that drove starving immigrants to the shores of the United States almost two hundred years ago. This is a story of prosperity gone awry. . . . We just have to get our mojo back, and we are going to do it."

I decided to have a little contest to name this book among some friends on Facebook. I was struck by how focused on the immediate narrative—the negative story of Ireland's collapse—the suggestions were. Then again, I offered for first prize a pint of Guinness and for second prize a share of Ireland's sovereign debt—so I probably had stacked the decks. The answers I got back were creative, to be sure: *Modern Ireland: The Good, the Bad, the Ugly*; *Modern Ireland: What the Fuck?* (actually I got three variations on this from three different friends in Ireland); *I'm Only Ten and I'm Broke*; *Our Beautiful Country Gone Bad*; *IMF—On the Way*; *Ireland: We Can Bail Out YOUR Banks Too!* As I am a big fan of the writer Cormack McCarthy, I especially appreciated *Ireland: No Country for Young Men*. Others that caught my eye were *Ireland: We Have Turned the Corner—and Hit a Brick Wall* and *Ireland: Last One Out, Please Turn Out the Lights*. I also got *I-Wrish We Didn't Have So Much Debt*; *Irish Politics: As the Sli-Go*; *Why Irish Eyes Aren't Smiling*; and *Who Pissed in the Whiskey?* Others came in the original Gaelic: *Ní sheasann sac folamh* (which means something like "an empty sack won't stand"); *Is minic a rinne bromach gioblach capall cumasach* (something about an awkward colt eventually becoming a lovely horse); and probably most appropriate for the author of a book, *Gura slán an scéalaí* ("May the bearer of the news be safe," or "Good luck to the storyteller").

Ireland needs to be positive to get its mojo back. But this cannot happen without a brutally frank assessment of the realities that face the nation. As Bill Clinton said in his 2010 talk, "It's good to have a market, not good to turn it into a gambling house." At the same time, dwelling endlessly on existing negative realities is not helpful as it can have a reinforcing effect on investment and business start-up—creating a self-reinforcing dynamic. Nonetheless, reality is inescapable—Ireland in 2010 was only at the beginning of its economic dislocation, and while a general election in 2011 would bring major change, this was only a very preliminary first step—as necessary as it was. Whatever the future of Ireland's political developments, the country faces sustained economic difficulty. By November 2010, IMF tables showed Ireland's sovereign debt holdings as being so massive that they literally went off the charts: the actual numbers had to be written in as the chart on the page did not go high enough. With the IMF and European Union coming in 2011 with an €85 billion bailout at a very high 5.83 percent interest rate, Ireland was in a bind. Its ability to pay down this long-term debt was highly in doubt, and an eventual default seemed a very plausible and highly destabilizing outcome. Cuts in the budget of €15 billion would likely not be enough—at the same time, they risked being highly deflationary in the economy, stunting growth and employment for years to come. Especially frustrating, with hindsight, is Ireland's failure at every single turn to have done something to ameliorate or avoid its present situation when it had a chance, going as far back as 2001.

There was reason for concern that Ireland might still sugarcoat its bitter economic pill. Just as the government was putting forward a €15 billion, four-year plan of additional, painful budget cuts, data showed they would likely be woefully insufficient. Ireland had a commitment as an EU member to get its fiscal debt down to 3 percent of its economy as part of the eurozone. Realistically, though, the sinkhole of the sovereign debt would make meeting this budget target much more difficult than even the most austere of cutters in the government were telling the public. On 7 November 2010, Megan Greene of the Economist Intelligence Unit told the *Sunday Independent* that the cuts "should be closer to 9 billion euro for 2010 and around 20 billion euro in total." She added, "I think the Government is being pretty optimistic and I don't share its view." Greene said of its forecast of gross domestic product growth (GDP) of "0.25 per cent for 2010, 1.75 per cent in 2011, and 2.75 per cent on average over 2011–2014 . . . I expect real GDP to have fallen by 1 per cent in 2010 and 0.8 per cent in 2011, but to grow by an average of 1.1 per cent in 2011–14." Even worse, Greene said, "I don't think this is the end of the bank bailout. The property market hasn't found the floor yet, which means further write downs on loans." EU leaders would repeat that Ireland was going to turnaround, as did the political leadership, but the numbers showed something very different, reflected in the continued very high costs of borrowing. "Come June the Government will have to raise money and it won't be able to on the bond markets. It will have to turn to the ESF [European Stability Fund]," Greene said. Greene was, in fact, off by about six months as the debt crisis had spiraled beyond Dublin's ability to manage its own affairs by December 2010.

The worst part for Ireland was that it really could do very little to change its circumstances. The *Telegraph* quoted Colm McCarthy on 3 November 2010 as saying, "We cannot do 'fiscal stimulus', nor can we devalue our exchange rate, since we do not have one. It is perfectly reasonable to ask how we got into this mess, to allocate blame and to demand retribution. But no amount of ranting can expand the limited range of choices available to the Government." Ireland's core economic problems were structural; policy adjustments were not going to change this, and some, like deep budget cuts, could propel a spiral of deflation leading to even slower recovery. This was especially frustrating as Ireland was being productive in terms of exporting goods and services. Ireland continued to benefit from globalization. Contrary to the predictions of Thomas Friedman and his admonition to follow the "leaping leprechaun," however, the economy was not benefiting from globalization in a way that would drive a recovery—the overall dent in employment and revenue was insufficient. The most crucial indicator was that in November 2010, the rate Ireland paid to borrow money rose to a record high of over 9 percent on ten-year bonds. Ireland was paying a very high price to attract people in global markets to buy its bonds in order to remain solvent as a nation. It was on the verge of losing complete control over its fiscal policy, while its people were facing deep reductions in their standard of living.

Ireland really only had three realistic options by the end of 2010. The first would be to stay the course and make even deeper cuts in the budget, raise the corporate and personal tax rates, and effectively cross its collective fingers and hope for the global economy to recover fast. In a best case, this would mean a decade or more of stagnation or decline. A second option was simply to default on its debt—to walk away from it and stop financing the banks. The problem with this was that so much had already gone to Anglo Irish Bank alone that the damage was done—it was too late. Defaulting would also do severe damage to Ireland's international reputation and make it a very bad place for future investment. This left only the third option—a massive debt bailout by the IMF or the European Union. At least the "good part" of the Irish economy could get moving forward while the burden of the bank debt was made manageable and paid down over several decades. In reality, this approach was really about stabilizing the banks; indeed, it would substantially increase and draw out the average Irish person's economic pain. Other options existed but were not really in the cards politically. One interesting option would have been for Ireland to quit the eurozone entirely and peg its currency to the noneurozone British pound. Nonetheless, as Ireland moved toward the hundredth anniversary of the 1916 Easter Rising, ceding national economic sovereignty to Britain would seemingly be a bridge too far. Even wilder ideas included Ireland's seeking to become America's fifty-first state. This too was not in the cards. These wilder options really showed that wherever this small nation turned, its independence was seriously diminished. Perhaps, most realistically, Ireland needed not a bailout of its banks by the European Union and IMF but rather a restructuring plan for the entire country's public and private debt carried out over a significant period of many decades.

In each scenario, Ireland would likely eventually have to raise its corporate tax rate, personal taxes, and fees, as well as continue massive cuts in public services and pensions and face long-term high unemployment. Any major growth in the Irish economy would, for the foreseeable future, have to go to paying down the nation's debt. On 26 September 2010, the chief economist at Société Générale, James Nixon, a highly respected analyst of sovereign debt, told the *Sunday Independent*, "Unless Ireland significantly accelerates its fiscal consolidation, its debt dynamics will ultimately be unsustainable." This state of affairs, he added, "probably dictates that ultimately, however reluctantly, Ireland will be forced to seek additional funding from the European Financial Stability Facility." "I think," Nixon said, "if the IMF are called in, there will be many pounds of flesh extracted of which corporation tax will be only one." Nixon indicated that Ireland needed to seek up to €80 billion from international lenders to prevent a "long, slow death." Writing for the IrishCentral website on 27 September 2010, Christopher M. Quigley laid out the problem succinctly: "As each month passes the government borrows an additional 2.6 billion just to fund day-to-day expenses. . . . Soon government borrowings will be over 100% of GDP and with exploding interest charges, increasingly taxes are simply being used to pay off foreign bondholders. Increased taxes are contracting the economy further and so the death spiral of debt is squeezing the life out of day-to-day commerce. Business is collapsing under a deflationary depression."

To be sure, the IMF/EU package was not a good one for Ireland. As David McWilliams wrote in the *Irish Independent* on 1 December 2010, by using the entire IMF/EU funding, Ireland could "add 85 billion euro to the current outstanding 90 billion of debt. That will leave us with a national debt of 175 billion by the end of 2014. The interest on this will come to about 8.6 billion euro per annum. This, of course, is the optimistic scenario. . . . Anyone who has watched in horror as the cost of Anglo has risen from zero to 4 billion euro to 12 billion euro to 18 billion euro to 35 billion euro over the last 26 months will know exactly what stock to put in government forecasts." The most serious issue was that, just to finance the debt, the economy would have to grow at a faster rate than the IMF/EU interest rate—which was seemingly impossible.

Most Irish will say, understandably, that they are already taxed to the hilt. This is particularly true because of value-added taxes on consumption (21 percent on most purchases), which bring the overall tax rate, on average, to around 50 percent. Most Irish people do not pay property taxes, however, and the direct income tax is overall quite low. In an *Irish Times* editorial on 25 September 2010, Garret FitzGerald wrote, "Amongst the 30 developed countries in Europe, North America, and East Asia that constitute the [Organization for Economic Cooperation and Development], Ireland has by far the lowest level of taxation on incomes—subject to the single exception of Mexico. This is true at every level of income, although the tax differential is least marked in the case of those on the highest level of incomes." FitzGerald estimated that "if we levied taxes on income at rates similar to other developed countries, revenue from income taxation would have been about one-third, or 4 billion euro, greater than the amount actually raised." He concluded, "If the public are left under the delusion that they are overtaxed, rather than grossly undertaxed, their reaction as taxes inevitably start to rise could be dangerously volatile." While the Irish do indeed have a high tax rate when the value-added tax is taken into account, this tax is common across the European Union, while the income tax rate, FitzGerald points out, is well below average.

A major point of controversy is the corporate tax of 12.5 percent, which was far below that paid across Europe. Many Europeans have seen this as unfair, though the Irish reasonably argue that geography and transport costs justify the lower rate. They also point out that they are providing a service that benefits the rest of Europe's markets as a global gateway. Still, those in Europe to whom Ireland has turned for help see the corporate tax rate as a casualty of Ireland's economic crisis. The European commissioner for economic and monetary affairs, Olli Rehn, reinforced this view on taxes. Rehn was quoted by RTÉ on 1 October 2010 as saying at a meeting of European finance ministers in Brussels, "It is a fact of life" that Ireland will no longer be a low-tax economy "after what has happened." He said, "Ireland in the coming decade will not be a low-tax country, but it will rather become a normal-tax country in the European context." The American Chamber of Commerce responded by informing the Irish government that the Taoiseach had to "send a very clear message" that the corporate tax would remain unchanged. In a statement to the press, Lionel Alexander, president of the American Chamber of Commerce in Ireland, said, "At a time when the economy is in deep recession, nothing which would impact on the continued investment in Ireland by our existing base of multinationals, or would deter new investment in Ireland can be countenanced." Ireland was caught in an unseemly tug-of-war between external forces that had made their own judgments as to what Ireland could, and could not, do. Dublin's freedom of movement—indeed, its very sovereignty—seemed to be slipping away daily. Writing in the *Irish Independent* on 5 October 2010, Eamonn McCann put the problem succinctly: "The people know voting won't do it. Which raises the more fundamental question . . . what, then?"

Ireland could reduce its debt or lighten the pain on its people in a few untouched places—even symbolic actions would have value. Some changes would require commitments of sacrifice from people like U2 and its publishing business, which had fled the country to avoid paying taxes. Others who have been reported on in the Irish media include Denis O'Brien, an Irish telecom mogul, who is worth about €2.2 billion but has moved to Malta to avoid being taxed at home. Michael Smurfit, worth over €300 million, resides in Monaco, again to avoid paying taxes. Overall, nearly six thousand Irish are careful enough to "reside" outside of Ireland for the legally approved 183 days, which allows them to avoid Irish taxes. Even inside Ireland, tax loopholes have allowed very rich people to claim exemptions. While preventing these kinds of tax-avoidance schemes alone will not fix the Irish economy, many Irish see this practice of people not supporting their countrymen purely in order to protect their own wealth as uniquely un-Irish. This sentiment rang particularly true at a time when many parents are going broke to pay for their children's lost mortgages, which come from the property bubble that made many wealthy Irish people rich in the first place.

More complicated is the issue of money that is actually lost in Ireland due to the behavior of multinational corporations. The low corporate tax rate created important incentives for companies like Google to locate their European headquarters in Dublin. By doing so (as well as in the Netherlands and Bermuda), Google manages to save $3.1 billion in taxes annually. *Bloomberg News* reported on 21 October 2010, "Google's income shifting—involving strategies known to lawyers as the 'Double Irish' . . . helped reduce its overseas tax rate to 2.4 percent, the lowest of the top five U.S. technology companies by market capitalization." A tax economist formerly with the U.S. Treasury Department was quoted saying, "It's remarkable that Google's effective rate is that low. . . . We know this company operates throughout the world mostly in high-tax countries where the average corporate rate is well over 20 percent."

According to *Bloomberg News*, the "double Irish" method "takes advantage of Irish tax law to legally shuttle profits into and out of subsidiaries there, largely escaping the country's 12.5 percent income tax." Facebook, also with headquarters in Dublin, was preparing a structure similar to Google's, using Ireland and the Cayman Islands. As to these corporations, Irving H. Plotkin, a senior managing director at PricewaterhouseCoopers LLP, told *Bloomberg News*, "A company's obligation to its shareholders is to try to minimize its taxes and all costs, but to do so legally." Google says that the Dublin subsidiary "was credited by Google with 88 percent of its $12.5 billion in non-U.S. sales in 2009." However, the profits do not go to the Dublin subsidiary, which "reported pretax income of less than 1 percent of sales in 2008 . . . because it paid $5.4 billion in royalties to Google Ireland Holdings," which has its "effective centre of management" in Bermuda. The Irish side of the tax revenue is reduced because Google set up two separate companies. One pays royalties for intellectual property, but this is a reduced tax area in Ireland. The other collects the royalties in a tax haven like Bermuda. By transiting that money through the Netherlands, the company avoids an Irish withholding tax because "Irish tax law exempts certain royalties to companies in other EU-member nations." So, these fees go to Google Netherlands Holdings B.V., which then "pays out about 99.8 percent of what it collects to the Bermuda entity, company filings show." *Bloomberg News* quoted business professor Jim Stewart of Trinity College as saying, "You accumulate profits within Ireland, but then you get them out of the country relatively easily. . . . And you do it by using Bermuda."

Meanwhile, much discussion in Ireland revolved around a sense that major governmental reforms would free up some revenue and that the economic pain could thus be more equally distributed. Talk among reformers focuses on reducing the number of TDs, getting rid of or reforming the Seanad (the largely ceremonial upper house of parliament), cutting judge's and senior civil servants' salaries, cutting public sector wages across the board, and abolishing pensions for former presidents and ministers. Amazingly, the Irish president, who serves in a mainly ceremonial position, actually earned more in 2010 ($433,000 a year) than the president of the United States. The Irish foreign minister earned more than the American secretary of state. Top civil servants in Ireland earned about $400,000 a year compared to $150,000 for their U.S. counterparts. And yet, many Irish people noted that while Dáil members were cutting welfare in the 2011 budget, they themselves were not taking a pay cut. Even if such savings would be modest in the overall budget, this kind of broader approach would make a dent. Furthermore, knowing that some who had contributed to the disaster were helping pay to fix it might at least make the economic pain more palatable to the broader Irish public. The really bad news, which few in Ireland were talking about, is that the Irish Professional Insurance Brokers association estimates that, eventually, the cost of public pensions will grow larger than the costs of the bank bailouts. Over the next sixty years, these pension costs will likely total €116 billion. In effect, an even bigger fiscal crisis for Ireland lurks around the corner.

TEAR DOWN THE WALLS

A critical question is whether Ireland has completely broken with its age-old tradition of "we don't talk about that" to the point where its leadership and people will confront these long-term economic realities. One of the most difficult pills to swallow is that during the height of the Celtic Tiger, many of the new wealthy class in Ireland did something uniquely un-Irish: they got boastful. Irish leaders—from politicians, to bankers and businessmen, to a new generation of young people who became deeply materialistic and irresponsible in their spending priorities—began lecturing people elsewhere about how great the Irish model was. The *Irish Times* wrote on 6 November 2010, "When the Tiger was in full-throated roar, we also told ourselves we were unique. Back then, we were uniquely gifted—a dynamic, creative, and instinctively entrepreneurial people who had little to learn from the more advanced economies of continental Europe. For a while, as our property bubble grew and public finances spun out of control, we persuaded ourselves that the fundamental laws of economics—or even of book-keeping—did not apply." Writing the next day, 8 November 2010, in the *Irish Times*, Morgan Kelly returned with a severe warning for the people of Ireland: "During September, the Irish Republic quietly ceased to exist as an autonomous fiscal entity, and became a ward of the European Central Bank." Ireland had to repay bonds to cover the costs of the bank bailouts, which it funded with quiet borrowing from the European Union. Kelly warned that Ireland would likely face an additional €30 billion in bank costs from Allied Irish Bank and the Bank of Ireland—leading to a €70 billion bill.

In this context, Morgan Kelly wrote, the €15 billion budget cuts for 2011 were an exercise in futility: "What is the point of rearranging the spending deckchairs, when the iceberg of bank losses is going to sink us anyway?" "The Irish state," Kelly wrote, "is insolvent: its liabilities far exceed any realistic means of repaying them." He warned Ireland was only entering its second act, which would focus on the thousands of families with mortgages they could not pay or that were underwater. Here Morgan Kelly hit on a serious ill that continues to afflict Irish society: "People are going to extraordinary lengths—not paying other bills and borrowing heavily from their parents—to meet mortgage repayments, both out of fear of losing their homes and to avoid the stigma of admitting that they are broke. . . . In a society like ours, where a person's moral worth is judged—by themselves as much as by others—by the car they drive and the house they own, the idea of admitting that you cannot afford your mortgage is unspeakably shameful." This, Kelly argued, "will change" because "if one family defaults on its mortgage, they are pariahs: if 200,000 default they are a powerful political constituency. There is no shame in admitting that you too were mauled by the Celtic Tiger after being conned into taking out an unaffordable mortgage, when everyone around you is admitting the same." He added that "the looming Mortgage War will pit recent house buyers against the majority of families who feel they worked hard and made sacrifices to pay off their mortgages, or else decided not to buy [houses] during the bubble, and who think those with mortgages should be made to pay them off."

"By [2011] Ireland will have run out of cash, and the terms of a formal bailout will have to be agreed. Our bill will be totted up and presented to us, along with terms for repayment. On these terms hangs our future as a nation," wrote Kelly. He noted that Europeans in Brussels did not see Ireland as a major economic problem for them and were not in an altruistic mood. Kelly concluded that an interest rate for a bailout that went beyond 2 percent would be "likely to sink us" but pointed out that when Greece was bailed out, its rate was 5 percent. More likely, the European Union would use Ireland to send a strong warning to bigger economies like Spain and Italy to get their budgets in order. Kelly hit on the key barrier that shows how dangerous the carry-on effects of not grappling with serious problems can be. He wrote, "We lacked the tact and common sense to keep our grubby dealings to ourselves. Europeans had to endure a decade of Irish politicians strutting around and telling them how they needed to emulate our crony capitalism if they wanted to be as rich as we are. As far as other Europeans are concerned, the Irish Government is aiming to add injury to insult by getting their taxpayers to help the 'Richest Nation in Europe' continue to enjoy its lavish lifestyle." Kelly concluded by saying, "Unfortunately, this is where I have to hold up my hands and confess that I have no solutions, simple or otherwise." He added, with a deep sense of tragedy, "Sovereign nations get to make policy choices, and we are no longer a sovereign nation in any meaningful sense of the term. . . . From here on, for better or worse, we can only rely on the kindness of strangers." Nobel Prize–winning economist Joseph Stiglitz also voiced these concerns, saying on 12 November 2010, "The austerity measures are weakening the economy, their approach to bank resolution is disappointing. . . . The prospect of success is very, very bleak."

The bailout came not much later, in early December, with an interest rate of 5.83 percent. The ability to pay it down would require a level of economic growth directly opposite to the direction in which the Irish economy was headed. In early 2011, Irish leaders asserted flexibility on renegotiating the rate with the European Union. Ireland's dilemma was, however, quickly laid bare by French president Nicolas Sarkozy, who said on 13 January 2011, "I deeply respect the independence of our Irish friends and we have done everything to help them. But they cannot continue to ask us to come and help them while keeping a tax on company profits that is half what other countries have." Sympathy for Ireland among those who would help it ran very shallow. Ireland would have to fight to preserve a competitive corporate tax rate. At the same time, the country was also inflicting damage on itself by holding rigidly to its 12.5 percent rate. As the United States began to emphasize its own competitiveness priorities in 2011, it became likely that some American companies in Ireland and possible future investors could find incentives to relocate home or elsewhere, no matter what the Irish tax rate. Furthermore, Dell did not leave Limerick because the corporate tax rate was too high. Other factors might put off companies looking at Ireland, such as the total devastation of its banks and economy and a near decade of political disaster. Ireland had to find other things to sell besides being a place where rich corporations could exploit the country and give little back. The fact that talented Irish workers can now be employed at cut-rate wages is as likely to lure investors as the tax rate. Much more importantly, however, Ireland has to sell itself, as a nation, emphasizing why it is special and unique and why it offers comparative advantages beyond the tax rate. Otherwise, Ireland sells itself short.

In terms of politics, Fianna Fáil politicians often seemed more interested in trying to stay in power by reassuring people instead of leveling with them. Hard economic facts are stubborn things, however, and as one friend in Dublin tells me, "The Irish have built-in bullshit meters." As to Labour, they were very good at critiquing the problems, but it was unclear what policy levers they could pull if they led the country. Fine Gael had serious policies and experienced leadership, but to many Irish voters the party had become part of the institutional gridlock of contemporary politics. During our interview in summer 2010, Father Ciarán O'Carroll asked me rhetorically, "Who leads Ireland?" Certainly, one could come up with a technical answer, but Brian Cowen did not seem to fit the bill. Brian Cowen stood down as the leader of Fianna Fáil on 22 January 2011, ushering in a new era in Irish politics. But the election of a Fine Gael–Labour coalition was merely one of the many million small steps that Ireland had to take. The key question was less who would manage Ireland than who would inspire a nation back off its heels. As Sheila Nunan of the Irish National Teachers Organization said to me, "With Obama, you all had a sense of purpose and hope—we in Ireland are floundering in the dark." Worse, said Andrew Madden, "no one has responsibility for anything—the government is pitting people against people now and yet they are the ones who failed." Ned Costello, of the Irish Universities Association, worried in particular that "a generation of young people are at risk—there is a huge level of questioning of institutions, serious questioning of the political system." In a tragic irony, the primary victims of government cuts to come in 2011 would be Ireland's poorest. A generation of rich people had blown a fortune, and now the poorest would suffer the most—this too was inconsistent with Irish traditions. Meanwhile, in January 2011, a number of TDs and cabinet ministers announced that they would quit politics rather than be held accountable to the voters or fight to implement the policies that had brought such pain to the Irish people.

Most Irish now felt that their national leadership had become a liability and cheered the departure from their daily lives of people like Conor Lenihan, Mary Harney, and Brian Cowen. An *Irish Times* public-opinion poll conducted on 2 October 2010 showed that 70 percent of Irish believed the worst was yet to come for the economy. Only 39 percent felt that a change in political leadership would alter the economic situation. A total of 69 percent said that Ireland's bank liabilities were not manageable for the country. On 5 November 2010, Taoiseach Brian Cowen gave what ironically might have been his best public statement on Ireland's future. Speaking to the Small Firms Association, he said, we must be "prepared to let the world know that Ireland *is* going to make our way through, that Ireland does not accept—does not accept—that it is going to fall by the wayside, that we're not going to throw away all the gains that we've made. . . . We did this in the 80s from a far weaker base, from a far higher level of unemployment unfortunately, a far higher level of interest rates, a far weaker economy, a less diversified economy." At this point, however, few Irish seemed to be listening. As Felicity Fox, a leading Dublin real estate agent, told the *Wall*

Street Journal on 12 October 2010 as she reflected on the 80 percent drop in her business since 2008, "Our major problem at the moment is lack of confidence. We just don't know what's ahead of us. We're not getting that much leadership from the government, I'm afraid." The editor of Trinity College Dublin's student newspaper, Tom Lowe, said in the same report, "For a lot of people, a lot of my friends, there's almost excitement that they might be able to leave. . . . For people who are my age, who are 21–22—just starting out in their careers—you don't want to be stuck in a country that is going to be economically damaged for the next 10 years of your life, you know."

So then, what kind of Ireland do we want to be? What kind of United States? What kind of world? The first step toward renewing Ireland will build on recognizing the realities that confront the nation—and although we must accept that right now most are negative, many positive elements exist as well. The dramatic events of the last thirty years in the country have forced a social change so profound that Ireland's citizenry has had no choice but to see things as they are. Ireland has mostly shed the "we don't talk about that" culture—the blinders are coming off, and many walls have already come down. Watch the television, listen to the radio, sit and chat with people in the pubs or their homes, and you will quickly find that little remains taboo. This is, in a sense, the best thing to come from the "Americanization" of Ireland during the Celtic Tiger. Americans are straight to the point and tend to talk openly—often too much so, to the point of causing unnecessary pain or appearing arrogant. Between their boasting and frankness, however, Americans have a tradition of seeing obstacles for what they are and confronting them directly. That does not mean their actions always work out well, but such openness is an essential American trait, and its roots are firmly planted in the new Ireland.

In many respects, Ireland has adopted and applied this trait better than the United States. I often tell Irish friends, "Look, at least you aren't fighting an endless and unwinnable war in Afghanistan and spending yourselves into a $14 trillion debt, both financed by China." For all of its challenges, Ireland was addressing them now as it could. The United States, however, seemed increasingly unable to enact major change. Washington had clear policy options to address its debt—reform entitlements, cut defense spending, and raise taxes—but it seemed that none of these actions were politically possible. While Ireland was taking a hard look at its deficit priorities, the United States was giving tax breaks to the wealthiest 1 percent of its citizens and restoring banks to their precrash role. Many Irish interviewed for this book were dismayed that Barack Obama experienced so much difficulty getting a health-care plan passed by Congress. Obama's was a moderate, market-driven health-care initiative based on models previously proposed by Republicans; yet, when Obama pushed this plan to address the crisis in the American health-care system, his Republican opponents labeled him a socialist. Many in Ireland find the idea that a rich society would leave its defenseless without basic health care inhumane. It took the ultimate in depravity—the attempted assassination of an American congresswoman from Arizona, which left six dead and eighteen wounded—for the United States to reconsider some of the deeply uncivil rhetoric that had come to debase its politics. Yet, thirty thousand Americans were being killed each year by guns, and their culture was dominated with violent images, whereas in Ireland, despite the rise in crime recently, the police do not even carry guns. America, it seemed, had much to learn from its Irish friends, especially as the Irish had learned so painfully the deep damage that can be done by the American-style approach to inadequate bank regulation. Both countries will do well to note together that those nations that succeed in this new century will be those with comparative advantages in human capital, research, infrastructure, and education and a commitment to sustainable environmental policies. Thus, while cuts in spending are necessary, so are investments that unleash the capacity of people to lead and innovate in key sectors of the economy. Indeed, they might even seek innovative ways to collaborate across the Atlantic.

As for observers like Thomas Friedman, he really owes Ireland and his readers a correction. *The World Is Flat* was widely praised on publication as being a definitive account of globalization—but the account was wrong, at least regarding Ireland. Ireland did put together economic improvements in the 1990s, but Friedman failed to account for either finance or greed in his writing. Though his conclusions about Ireland as a model were deeply flawed, the Irish government embraced and celebrated them. Friedman even inspired Senator John McCain, who nearly became the U.S. president, to tout the Irish model as one for the United States to follow. If other countries had followed the Irish path Thomas Friedman and John McCain sought, they might well have left us with a global economic wasteland even worse than that experienced beginning in 2008. By 2011, the "leaping leprechauns" were not leading the path toward economic renewal; rather it was the tired old Germans that Friedman had criticized. Being wrong as an analyst of globalization is fine—that is part of the learning process—but for having promulgated a major theory of globalization that reinforced a doubling down on deeply damaging economic and political actions in a small and vulnerable country, Friedman might at least rethink his "no apologies" sentiment.

CELTIC REVIVAL

Increasingly, the Irish people are standing up for themselves in the face of the strongest of headwinds, and this is the most important source of the nation's renewal. The generation of Irish under twenty-five is key to Ireland's future. These people had nothing to do with the crash and yet are being forced to emigrate or are left footing the bill. They must learn well from the mistakes of the previous generation and also look positively toward the future. Ireland—and the world—must invest in this generation for the long-term. Ireland's young people are beginning to assert their rights, and they must both speak and be heard as the foundation of progress in the twenty-first century. On 3 November 2010, an estimated twenty-five thousand university students took to the streets of Dublin, protesting inevitable increases in registration fees of up to €2,500 or more. While building a smart economy, Ireland was simultaneously making it harder for people to attend university. As one student marcher told RTÉ, "I'm here because I don't qualify for a grant and—I'm struggling through college. . . . It's so hard to get through college—I just got sacked, so I have no money at all!" Another said, "We are the future of this country, like, people are going to drop out of college now. They're going to end up in unemployment lines. That's nearly 200 euro per week." Yet another student said, "We don't have money. We're all here with part-time jobs or no jobs at all, and we can't depend on our parents to pay for us." Ireland risked creating a deeply stratified society with the rich able to afford higher education and the rest left out. This was certainly no way to build a smart economy; nor was it an investment in the future. Yet, while this new generation was showing that it would engage and stand up for itself, at the same time, its members also had the option of once again emigrating to foreign shores and investing their talents abroad.

The Irish are still innovating—doing what they can to move forward in creative and productive ways. Politically, Elaine Byrne of Trinity College led the charge toward major reform of Ireland's governance. Drawing on her thesis work on corruption and her engagement with the public as a columnist for the *Irish Times*, she called for a new definition of "republic" to be enshrined in the Constitution and the invocation of a citizens' assembly. Following Byrne's lead, in November 2010 *Irish Times* journalist Fintan O'Toole launched a major online petition for political reform in Ireland. He asked people to sign on to agree to a range of initiatives, including, among other ideas, limiting public service pay to €100,000, focusing on local civic democracy and local taxes, ending clientelism, cutting the Dáil to one hundred members and either reforming or eliminating the Seanad, advancing women's role in politics, and reforming laws to bring white-collar criminals to justice. Prominent critics of the existing government and noncareer politicians also stood for election to public office as Independent candidates—as banking expert and commentator Shane Ross and others did in 2011.

Economically, Ireland is tapping into wind- and wave-power production. In July 2009, the country set a national record for energy output from wind generating 999 megawatts—enough to power over 650,000 houses or about 39 percent of Ireland's demand for electricity. These records fell on St. Stephen's Day 2010, the windiest on record in Ireland, which produced 1,228 megawatts of wind-generated power, enough to power eight hundred thousand homes, according to the *Irish Times*. The *New York Times* quoted Irish economist John FitzGerald in August 2009 as saying that the key now for Ireland was to cooperate with Britain on wind-energy production and usage: "If we don't build [such interconnection], wind could prove very expensive for consumers as we could end up with too much wind energy at times, meaning that we may be forced to temporarily shut down conventional plants at great expense, to avoid waste." Ireland has a unique problem in its potential oversupply of wind energy. It is thus moving forward to build a five-hundred-megawatt interconnector linking the national electric grids in Ireland and Wales with a capacity to supply three hundred thousand homes with electricity. Ireland is also exploring how to exploit geothermal energy with plans to build the country's first geothermal electricity-generation plant in south Dublin. This would power up to eight thousand homes. Still, Ireland remained in 2010, according to Sustainable Energy Ireland, over 90 percent dependent on imported fossil fuels—making energy independence all the more important for Ireland. These kinds of initiatives have the potential, according to Ciara Byrne writing in the *New York Times* on 30 November 2010, to create up to one hundred thousand jobs in Ireland and to account for as much as 20 percent of future GDP.

Ciara Byrne highlights the role of universities cooperating across disciplines, among not just scientists but also economists and social scientists, to assess technological and consumer change in this kind of major energy transformation. Likewise, wave power has the potential, reported Byrne, to make Ireland "the Saudi Arabia of wave power, since it has access to the best wave resource on the planet." An Irish company, Wavebob, she noted, recently received a $2.4 million grant from the U.S. Department of Energy to assess and prepare commercial-scale wave-energy demonstration projects in the United States for 2013. The ultimate challenge, though, remains the immediate future as these investments require capital. As Byrne wrote, "The problem with unlocking Ireland's renewable 'pot of gold' is that it requires major upfront capital investment, and cash is exactly what the Irish government doesn't have right now." In my view, it would be innovative for the Irish government to engage in a public-private approach to invest heavily in new energy technology, funded specifically by an increase in the corporate tax rate. If businesses knew this additional tax would, over the long term, lead to lower expenses for them, then a modest increase might be sellable to foreign companies operating in Ireland. This approach would thus benefit employment, business, and the environment—a win for everyone. Reinforcing these assumed benefits, the *Irish Times* reported on 6

January 2011 that a study by a British consultancy firm showed that a fully developed wave and tidal energy sector in Ireland would be worth about €9 billion and create fifty-two thousand jobs in wave energy and seventeen thousand in tidal energy.

At a more microlevel, on 19 August 2010, the *Irish Independent* reported that an Irish scientist, Martin Tangney of Cork, had successfully made biofuel out of whiskey by-products. "Whisky in the Car" said the paper: "Whether it's single malt, single grain, blended, smoke or peat flavoured Scotch, the end result is the same: a clean, carbon neutral fuel that can be blended with regular petrol to run an engine." The *Independent* added, "While whisky purists may gasp at the thought of . . . Glenkinchie, Tullibardine or Benromach going down someone's petrol tank, Prof. Tangney can assure them that not one drop of the liquid gold will ever be wasted making his biobutanol." Rather than growing crops especially for biofuels, using excess materials such as whisky by-products is, according to Tangney, "a more environmentally sustainable option and potentially offers new revenue on the back of one of Scotland and Ireland's biggest industries. We've worked with some of the leading whisky producers to develop the process."

Meanwhile, a group of architects has created the Fumbally Exchange, a cooperative in Dublin of leading design specialists who are banding together to generate progress in their decimated profession. The Fumbally Exchange aims "to cultivate an atmosphere for creative and regenerative growth in a time of great challenges and volatility in our industry . . . to simply be under this creative envelope connecting across many disciplines and with strong bonds across the design world." By pooling their resources, working together, and combining their creative energy, some of Ireland's most skilled people are creating their own futures. Another innovative effort, called Rendez Vu, uses high-technology software to develop study methods for foreign students learning English. *Bloomberg News* quoted Linda Richardson of Rendez Vu on 29 October 2010 as saying, "Well, if you turn on the news at any stage in Ireland, at the moment it's full of doom and gloom and cutbacks and recession. But it's also, a number of people they're saying, 'Look, we're not all going to give up and just go down. We still have lots of ideas. We still have lots of good people working in Ireland, and we have to work our way out of this.'" These sorts of "million small steps" will make the difference for Ireland. I was especially moved in summer 2010 while talking to a taxi driver in Dublin. He got to asking what I was up to in Ireland, and I told him about this book. He proudly pulled out a prototype of a children's educational activity that he and his wife had designed. It was very good. And he dreamed big: "We are going to market this to China!"

Socially, the Irish have already made the most difficult and crucial step toward a Celtic revival—developing the ability to grapple directly and with brutal honesty with once taboo issues. Even those subjects that are almost too difficult to talk about, like the abuse of children in the church, are being confronted. The criminal instances of child abuse in Ireland have shaken people's faith in a core institution of their culture—the Catholic Church. This, however, does not mean that the essence of the nation's faith and values is permanently tarnished. People might find other places to engage in spiritual activity outside the Catholic Mass, but the deep Irish tradition of spiritual thinking persists. Father Ciarán O'Carroll speaks of many good elements of past models of the church. The earliest was one of creativity, learning, and coexistence with nature. The second focused on routine and healthy lifestyles. The third showed how faith and culture intertwine to form long-lasting identities and national pride. The fourth showed an appreciation for education. Now, these are extracts from what were models that also culminated in a crisis of deep, structural abuse of children, of power, and of trust. Yet, the essence of faith and an inherent commitment to the idea that "peace be with you," which ends the Catholic Mass, can still be built upon and renewed. At the foundation of all such relationships— family, friends, society—is love. "People have to love unconditionally," Sinéad O'Connor told me.

When I interviewed Andrew Madden, I sensed a continued deep upset and frustration. Yet, people like him have revolutionized a country and are carrying on a long and proud Irish tradition of the powerless taking on those who abuse authority and trust. This quintessentially Irish trait is at the forefront of rebuilding a society. Sinéad O'Connor struck a key chord when she sang "The Times They Are Changin'." She would keep pressing, as all Irish must, in building on a positive future. O'Connor asked me in October 2010 about the abuse of children, "Why are the politicians, health services, church hierarchy not crying when they're on TV talking about it? Not one of them has been moved to tears. That's very frightening." For all societies, looking in the mirror can be a difficult thing in times of crisis. By 2011 the anger toward the government, bankers, and life in general did mask a degree of collective responsibility—for the economy, the church, and other long-term built-up challenges to Ireland. No doubt, the society as a whole did not create Ireland's fate—but something lurking about did, and it was identified in a 5 December 2010 interview given by former president Mary Robinson to the *Sunday Times*: "Greed was the main problem." She added, "It's our own mistake as Irish people, collectively."

In the depths of hard times, the seeds of renewal are nonetheless germinating. For those who have the skills, talent, and support, this is a time to take major risks, to step forward, to lead. As Ned Costello said to me, the challenge is to see "if we can take what is good in traditions of Irish culture and values, and couple it with what was good in the Celtic Tiger." There was important truth in what Éamon Gilmore said to me: "We will recover, and it will be on a different platform and in a different world." Yet, some Irish still cling to a world devoid of the reality of their new situation. Just as Ireland was cascading into the bailouts and budget cuts, a story by April Drew on the IrishCentral website on 27 November 2010 was headlined, "Irish Still Flocking for Shopping in New York." She described men and their wives laden down with suitcases and shopping bags amid Ralph Lauren shirts and trousers in Macy's on West Thirty-fourth Street in New York City. Just when the government was cutting welfare services to the blind and disabled, one shopper complained about having "skipped a friend's wedding in Spain in September so we could pay for this trip." He said of his and his friend's wives, "All I know is they keep saying, 'This is such a bargain, I can't leave it behind,' so when I hear those words I just switch off, hand over the wallet and keep the head down." Two sisters planned to "shop till they dropped." One man, an electrician who said he worked, on average, three days a week, was more modest: "We'll get a few presents and bits and pieces, but we won't be going too mad." His wife smiled, though, when asked if there was a budget for limiting the shopping and said, "We'll see." By 2011 too many Irish, along with too many Americans, were still looking for a quick fix and fast return to a day that will never return—but still they spent, often on credit, incurring yet more debt.

Back home, the good Ireland was still chugging along as best it could. As I was completing this manuscript, I got an e-mail from Kieran Rose with a note saying, "A different perspective of Ireland." Rose linked to a video (called "Ireland by the Numbers" and produced by the Irish Business and Employers Confederation) that serves as a reminder of this new world in which Ireland commences its revival. Ireland has 960 foreign companies employing 138,000 top-skilled workers doing cutting-edge research in high technology. Of the top ten pharmaceutical companies in the world, eight are located in Ireland, and fifteen of the top twenty-five medical devices are made there. Ten of the world's top-selling prescription drugs are made in Ireland. Over twenty-four thousand people are employed in 160 medical-technology companies, 80 of which are indigenous. For every one hundred jobs created in the life sciences, another one hundred are created in supporting services. Ireland exports €6.9 billion a year in medical devices—the second-biggest producer in Europe. More than 50 percent of the world's leading financial firms and eight of the top ten technology companies are represented in Ireland. Intel, which had been cutting its Irish workforce, was coming back by 2011, announcing a planned $500 million expansion of its Irish operations, which entailed an increase of 1,000 jobs, including 850 construction jobs, in a two-year building enhancement at its County Kildare facility.

American investment in Ireland as a percentage is bigger than that in Brazil, Russia, India, and China combined. Ireland also produces enough beef each year to feed thirty million people, and it is the largest exporter of beef in Europe and the fourth largest in the world. One in five McDonald's burgers served in Europe is made from Irish beef. Ireland exports 80 percent of its dairy production and makes 15 percent of the world's infant formula. Half of the world's fleet of leased aircraft is managed from Ireland. Ireland is the largest provider of cross-border life insurance in the European Union—worth €16.4 billion in premiums in 2009. Ireland is the number one country in Europe for availability of skilled labor. Still, perspective is required in that Ireland's structural unemployment was not going to be solved by these investments alone; nor were they going to fix the problem of economic growth from within the Irish economy.

In November 2010, the UN Development Program released a global quality-of-life index. The United Nations ranked Ireland the fifth-best place to live in the world, after Norway, Australia, New Zealand, and the United States. Ireland, according to the United Nations, has a "very high human development" ranking based on indicators such as life expectancy (80.3 years), per capita income ($33,078), and average schooling (11.6 years). Ireland ranked ahead of Canada, Germany, and the United Kingdom. Indeed, not everyone is leaving who can. On 28 October 2010, the *Irish Times* ran an editorial by Michael Moriarty titled "The Reasons Why I'm Choosing to Stay in Ireland." A twenty-nine-year-old chartered accountant with no children, no mortgage, and an American passport, he said, "My career prospects would surely be better in the U.S. than they would here." But aside from his friends, family, and job, he was staying because "Ireland is changing rapidly. It feels like the country is on a rollercoaster track. And the more I think about, the more I realize that the most compelling reason is that those of us who stay here are the ones that will decide what happens next for Ireland. . . . We, the Irish people, can and will determine the future of the nation. I'm staying because I want to be part of the generation that shapes this new Ireland." He added, "It's not just for those who stand for political office, those who lead protests or those who make the headlines. It is the cumulative weight of the thousands of decisions made by each of us ordinary citizens that is the tide that drives the direction of this country."

The dramatic and progressive social changes that have occurred over the last thirty years in Ireland provide a foundation for a new national identity that is a model for the rest of the world. These changes, such as those related to the church, gay rights, and multiculturalism, serve as a foundation for twenty-first-century human capital set to compete in a global marketplace. Ireland already has a competitive multicultural edge within the European Union. On 17 October 2010, German chancellor Angela Merkel told a youth conference of the Christian Democratic Union, "At the beginning of the 60s our country called the foreign workers to come to Germany and now they live in our country. We kidded ourselves a while, we said: 'They won't stay, sometime they will be gone,' but this isn't reality." She added, "And of course, the approach to build a multicultural society and to live side by side and to enjoy each other . . . has failed, utterly failed." Ireland's National Competiveness Council stated in 2009, "Globalization has created new opportunities for cities." The Dublin Corporation (which in January 2011 appointed Kieran Rose as the head of its International Affairs Division) has noted that "Ireland/Dublin is the third most globalized country/city in the world after Singapore and Hong Kong." The question for Ireland is whether it will not only embrace these changes but invest in and build on them. This holds true regarding not only newcomers to the country and their further integration into society but also Irish people getting the skills they need to compete globally. In this regard, compulsory Gaelic-language study probably does not serve the nation's interests if it comes at the expense of other language skills. Embracing global language studies as a national requirement is a vital and urgent national need. For both immediate budget reasons and for long-term national competitiveness, it is likely time to rethink the Gaelic requirement for young Irish. That is not to say it should be abandoned, but Ireland needs also to require its students to learn non-Irish and non-English languages if the nation is to remain competitive. More broadly, Ireland stands to make advances by embracing its new multicultural identity and seeing the "newcomers" as a major national asset—a group from which much can be learned to help in traversing the seas of globalization.

Ireland is also paving the way in showing the world how peace can be made. Northern Ireland is doing well at the high-end of peacemaking. There is, however, reason for concern that peace building is not occurring at a sufficient pace or depth. The most essential pieces of the puzzle of peace were only just being put into place by 2010. Peace building required sustained engagement by the United States; yet, this "essential ingredient" was missing where needed most—on the streets of the Ardoyne and beyond. So long as eighty-eight "peace walls" stand and over 90 percent of public housing and public schools reflect a "benign apartheid," then Northern Ireland has not peace but only the absence of conflict. Each year that Orange Order marchers insist on unnecessarily provocative parades through Catholic neighborhoods brings Northern Ireland closer to the edge. Each year that wayward Catholic youths are further manipulated by organized crime and dissident Republican nationalists brings Northern Ireland closer to the edge. Each year that the common economic plight suffered by both Catholics and Protestants left behind by the peace process brings Northern Ireland closer to the edge. Each year that the new government fails to address these issues and leaves untouched the question of public housing and education is a step closer to the edge. In 2010, the British government in London once again saw the rise of the Real IRA and other dissident Republican movements as a major security threat. Meanwhile, in November 2010, for the first time since disarmament, the Independent Monitoring Commission reported that members of the Ulster Volunteer Force had been discussing buying weapons and had increased its gathering of intelligence on dissident Republican groups. It would not take much of a spark to reignite the violence that so ravaged the people of Northern Ireland in the past.

Fiona MacMillan of *Sesame Tree* told me that when watching the events around the Bloody Sunday report in June 2010 in Derry, she saw a "photo of a wee girl, six years old—her grandfather had been killed." MacMillan asked, "How do we pass on her attitudes and understand what she sees and thinks? How do we get to her and yet understand that what she thinks and has been told is part of what she is too." Symbols still matter in the North. On 30 October 2010, American rock star Lady Gaga performed in Belfast and surprised her audience by carrying the Irish tricolor flag onstage. Reporting about this on 2 November, the *Belfast Telegraph* quoted a number of people who were at the concert and said it had soured the mood. One attendee said, "A lot of people were not impressed and there was a bit of unease among the crowd. . . . Some people were making comments, and others challenging them." Another said, "I just felt it was inappropriate, but maybe she didn't realize that Northern Ireland was separate from the Republic." The former lord mayor of Belfast was quoted as saying, "You tend to find people at such shows from both religions and those with none, and this won't go down well at all." While there are challenges, the future of Northern Ireland continues to send a message of peace to the world—and truth be told, most folks got a laugh and some enjoyment from Lady Gaga.

Ireland is setting an example for all countries of how to combine national interest with moral principles in foreign and defense policy. Ireland has been "punching way above its weight" in terms of UN leadership, human rights, and peacekeeping for over half a century. As the Irish people move outward again into the world, they can once more show their unique capacity for creativity, innovation, hard work, and productivity. The key for Ireland is, as Brian Caulfield said to me, that the Irish "need to recognize that we are a rock bobbing on an ocean in a globalized world." It would be a "big mistake to try to answer these questions without taking into account the globalized nature of the world today." Ireland will also have to look beyond the United States—as it too struggles with employment, recession, and change. Set for 2012, the most substantial initiative toward Ireland to come from Washington was a project with Fáilte Ireland called The Gathering, a yearlong "call home" to the global Irish with sporting and cultural events in Ireland and around the world drawing together Irishness. Having an American football match, as some planners suggested, in Dublin is not the way to renew spirits or unite a global Irish community. That is a gimmick spurred on by Irish American elites who care much, but really know little, about what is happening across the Atlantic. In fact, Washington was very silent in the midst of the Irish crisis, seemingly ceding handling of the issue to the Germans and their European friends, while the Irish fended for themselves. The Irish are going to have to look to the Middle East, to Latin America, and to Asia—and that means they have to invest heavily in the study of the world, particularly in learning languages from these areas— while at the same time building on the deep ties that do still unite Irish and Americans across the Atlantic.

IRELAND'S MESSAGE TO THE WORLD

On 4 December 2010, the *Irish Times* reported that the "sundering of [a] long-standing cedar tree may be a portent for our times." The 270-year-old tree in County Meath, located on the lands of the "Spiritans," was split in two when hit by lightning. When the bolt hit, some thought it was a meteorite. A monk at a retreat nearby, Brother Cloneth Tryell, described what "looked like a ball of fire and the sky turning red before he heard a large crash." Reportedly, this tree was located near the assumed site of Bile Tortain, one of five sacred trees in Celtic Ireland, which fell over one thousand years ago. When a sacred tree falls, the paper noted, according to legend, it will be followed by a "catastrophic change in the world order." According to Martin Dier of the Meath Archaeological and Historical Society, "How strange then that this magnificent cedar, which is a modern day contender for the role of Bile Tortain, would have seen the birth of sovereignty in 1900s Ireland [and] has seen the end of our economic sovereignty less than a century later." Ireland, like the world around it, has witnessed dramatic changes over the last several decades. From the end of the Cold War through the trauma of September 11, 2001, the Irish people have stood watch over these global changes—and seen many of their own, for good and ill. The Irish have always adjusted, persisted, and renewed. There is every reason to think that once again, the Irish will both persevere and again thrive—albeit in different ways.

My own experience leads me to the basic conclusion that Ireland's message to the United States, Europe, and the world is best described as, "It's time to get back to basics—but in a global context." The late chief of staff of the Irish Defence Forces, Lt. Gen. Dermot Earley carried with him through his life and career a basic five-point plan that spoke to the heart of his Irish traditionalism. At his June 2010 funeral in Roscommon, these five points were distributed on more than twenty thousand cards for the attendees. They were

Enjoy time with my family.
Give the best to my work.
Give back to my community.
Spend my leisure time well.
Make time for God in my life.

These were simple and basic rules, and yet people too busy equating money with happiness would miss out on these vital ingredients of a good life. Rather than pause to consider that slower but steady growth might benefit more people over a longer term, Ireland's leaders—like those in Washington and on Wall Street—doubled down on a bad bet. Too many in Ireland and the United States long for the quick fix; they want to get back to growth, back to wealth, back to easy street. That is neither realistic nor, as the Irish lesson tells us, wise. Sometimes slowing down to reflect on the good things in life is the best path to progress. Taking time for family, enjoyable work, community, leisure time, nature, health, and values is also a measure of progress—more so than the size of one's house, what kind of flat-screen TV or mobile phone one owns, or the make of the car one drives.

Rethinking priorities is no easy feat when so many face hard and painful choices. On 28 October 2010, the BBC ran an extended radio feature titled "Irish Anger." One person, Declan Murphy, summed up the immediate challenge as he and the BBC reporter walked through his hometown in County Limerick. He was selling off the last of his stock in a menswear shop that had been in his family for four generations. He was preparing to emigrate. Murphy said, "It's . . . gut-wrenching. . . . It's soul-destroying. You feel like you've let your family and 121 years of history down. . . . This shop was started by my great-grandfather in 1889." He said that he was lucky that at the end of November he and his family would be leaving for Australia. When asked, "Are you angry?" Murphy said, "I'm angry because I'm leaving a country that I love. I'm Irish through and through. I've been born in this town. . . . I don't want to leave it. But I feel that decision has been taken away from me by somebody else." The politicians, he said "have let everyone down. They've let the whole country down. I don't think anybody's saying enough about it."

Another person featured by the BBC, Seamus Sherlock, described being self-employed in the fuel business, supplying firewood and coal, for twenty-one years. He said that starting in November 2009, "I really noticed things dramatically changing. People just couldn't afford to buy what I was selling. . . . One lady came over one morning. She had one euro fifty. She had a liter of milk in the fridge and enough food for the kids for three days, and she said, 'Listen, I really need coal,' and I told her I'd give her a bag, and she could keep the one-fifty." He said his business folded—he could not sustain that generosity. He found that he owed €2,261 for his electricity bill. "I said, there's no way I can pay this." When he offered 25 percent of what he was earning, he was told that if he did not pay the entire sum in three days, he would be disconnected. He feared he would lose his four children. "I talked to a friend of mine, and he came over one night and sat down with me, and I said . . . 'I don't know that the people running this country realize what we're suffering.' So, I decided I'd do a protest in Dublin. . . . I drove to Dublin, and I chained myself to the main building of the electricity company," said Sherlock. As the day went on, people came up; taxi drivers offered him tea and food. He said, "And really I was so proud to be an Irishman. . . . I actually thought that day there was actually hope for this country." Rather than the community seeing him as an embarrassment and shame to pull the blinders down on, Sherlock's children were applauded at school; the teachers said their father was the "man who stood up for the people of Ireland." Sherlock concluded, "I have a young fella of twelve, and he said, 'Dad, you're a hero,' and I said, 'No, son, I'm just an ordinary Irish fella who stood up for the people of Ireland.'" He then said, "There's kind of a thing in Ireland; you don't really talk about your problems—certainly you don't talk about being in debt." His call to the Irish people was to get "a small bit more vocal—I'm not into this roaring' and shoutin' . . . not into it, screaming down streets . . . just get a small bit more vocal. Maybe stand up and say, 'You know what, people died for us years ago' . . . and I'm fierce proud of those people . . . and I think in a way we kind of lost track of that, and we lost our identity for a small while there."

Rebuilding priorities takes work and steady cultivation. As an Irish friend who recently emigrated to the United States reminded me, "One swallow never made a summer. . . . We need to push our Saints and Scholars angle and become teachers of the world again." He continued, "Anyway, as you well know, Ireland is full of Blarney. Who knows, maybe these massive crises will create a new Joycean moment or drag a Wilde from a closet and get us back to what we are most comfortable with, and that is being Saints and Scholars, not to mention damn good storytellers. We will just have to wait and see, but we also need to seize our future." He told me that his father reminds him often that his great-grandfather heard Daniel O'Connell speak. Daniel O'Connell was an early 1800s leader for Irish rights, and when speaking in public, he often drew crowds in the hundreds of thousands. My friend's father says, "As a result, I have met with people who lived with people before the famine and even back into the eighteenth century." My friend concluded with a reflection about his heritage and that of Ireland: "Finally I feel that blame is in the past. Let's get on with making our future, but never forget that we knew people who heard O'Connell speak."

Father Ciarán O'Carroll said to me, as we departed his house, going into the church at St. Stephen's Green, "The most fundamental question is, What does it mean to be Irish today?" A second and deeply related issue is a variation on Éamon Gilmore's "Are you happy": what is the source of happiness? Irish-born actor Gabriel Byrne, now cultural ambassador of Ireland, gave an interview on 26 October 2010 to the *Wall Street Journal*. Discussing practicing acting techniques in front of a mirror, Byrne said, "Any time I feel, 'Oh, that was a good bit,' you can be sure it's a bad bit because it's just like the mirror that lies to us." The reporter then said, "That sounds very Irish, like the Yeats quote 'Being Irish, he had an abiding sense of tragedy which sustained him through temporary periods of joy.'" Byrne responded, "It's also a Jewish thing. It's also a Russian thing. It's not about 'Oh, a good thing happened, so a bad thing has to happen'; it's about the fact that, hope this doesn't sound too pretentious, the quest as an artist is for perfection, and perfection cannot actually be obtained." In another interview with the *Los Angeles Times* on 25 October 2010, Byrne added, "There's too much pressure to be happy in this culture. . . . We're constantly told that happiness is so accessible, but life isn't like that. Life is a gradual process of acceptance. Once you understand that, you can find some measure of contentment." Byrne, more than most, has insight into how hard this happiness can be to attain: while a child at the Christian Brothers school in Ireland, he was abused by a priest. Now, decades later, like so many Irish people, famous and not famous, Gabriel Byrne is able to spread pleasure, joy, and perspective with his craft and his personality. Of course, happiness exists, but it exists in the balance, not at the extremes; in the balance lie contentment and fun.

The Irish have a capacity to spread a good time wherever they go and under whatever conditions, and this trait brightens even the darkest of days. Placed in the perspective of Ireland's long arch of history, the clear lesson of this story is that the Irish people have taken a major hit with the collapse of the Celtic Tiger and what came after, but the trends over the long run are positive. Ireland is embarking on a renewal, and the quality of the Irish people will stead it well as this country embarks on its million small steps into the future. If we are lucky, what emerges in the years to come from this Celtic revival will be Ireland's most lasting export to the world in the twenty-first century.

WHERE IRISH EYES ARE SMILING

As a final word, I turn the reader's attention back to the effort to find a good title for this book. Mixed in with all the understandably upset-sounding possibilities, one suggestion touched on the Irish soul. It was not the title we used, but it provides the right ending for this story. The suggestion came from a ten-year-old girl called Anna Lyons in County Clare, my wife's god-daughter. She and her brother, Gerry; our own children, Cria, Siobhan, and Alana; and all of their cousins across Ireland—their generation in Ireland, the United States, and the world—they are the key to the future. When their Irish eyes are smiling, they open up the eyes of the world. When her parents asked her to think of a good title for this book, young Anna said clearly, with a truth that a child knows so well, "The Great Country Known As Ireland."

Index

Italicized page numbers locate illustrations

About the Author

Sean Kay is professor of politics and government at Ohio Wesleyan University, where he is chair of the international studies program. He specializes in international security, globalization, international organization, and American foreign policy. Kay is a Mershon Associate at the Mershon Center for International Security Studies at Ohio State University and also a non-resident fellow in foreign and defense policy at the Eisenhower Institute in Washington, DC. He was previously a visiting assistant professor in the government department at Dartmouth College.

Kay received his PhD in international relations from the University of Massachusetts, Amherst. Before joining academe, he was a visiting research fellow at the U.S. Department of Defense's Institute for National Strategic Studies, where he also served as an adviser to the U.S. Department of State on NATO enlargement. He worked previously for the NATO Parliamentary Assembly in Brussels, Belgium.

Kay lectures frequently in the United States and Europe on global security trends and their strategic implications. He has authored numerous articles, book chapters, and opinion pieces in major newspapers on international issues. His previous books include *NATO and the Future of European Security* and *Global Security in the Twenty-first Century: The Quest for Power and the Search for Peace* and the coedited volumes *NATO after Fifty Years* and *Limiting Institutions? The Challenge of Eurasian Security Governance*. One of the United States' leading experts on European and transatlantic relations, Kay has been a regular visitor to Ireland since 1987; in 2007 and 2008, he served as a member of the team that advised Barack Obama's presidential campaign on European policy—including contributions on Irish policy issues. He undertook research for this book while working as a visiting scholar at the Institute for British and Irish Studies at University College Dublin in 2010.